P9-CRS-089

EMILY BRONTE
AND BEETHOVEN

EMILY BRONTE AND BEETHOVEN

Romantic Equilibrium in Fiction and Music

Robert K. Wallace

The University of Georgia Press
Athens and London

© 1986 by the University of Georgia Press
Athens, Georgia 30602

Designed by Kathi L. Dailey
Set in 10 on 13 Linotron 202 Bodoni Book
The paper in this book meets the guidelines for
permanence and durability of the Committee on
Production Guidelines for Book Longevity of the
Council on Library Resources.

Printed in the United States of America

90 89 88 87 86   5 4 3 2 1

Library of Congress Cataloging in Publication Data

Wallace, Robert K., 1944–
    Emily Brontë and Beethoven.

    Includes index.
    1. Brontë, Emily, 1818–1848—Criticism and
interpretation.   2. Beethoven, Ludwig van, 1770–
1827.   3. Romanticism.   4. Music and literature.
I. Title.
PR4173.W34   1986   823′.8   85-8620
ISBN 0-8203-0813-7 (alk. paper)

The illustration on the title spread and part title
pages is an etching entitled "Deepham, Near
Hingham" by John Crome. Reproduced by courtesy
of the Trustees of the British Museum.

To Barbara and Walt Wallace

Contents

Acknowledgments

For this book, as for its predecessor, I wish to thank the students at Northern Kentucky University who have shared with me the pleasure of studying music and literature together. I also wish to thank the Faculty Benefits Committee for timely assistance that aided the research and writing. For reading the manuscript and making helpful suggestions about the text, I am grateful to Calvin S. Brown, Pat Pinson, Peter Rabinowitz, and Jeffrey Siegel.

The Brontë Society kindly provided access to Emily Brontë's music books at the Haworth Parsonage—as well as permission to report my findings both here and in the *Brontë Society Transactions*. Charles Lemon, Sally Stonehouse, Juliet Barker, Winifred Gérin, Philip Barford, and Ian Dewhirst answered specific queries about Emily Brontë's musical studies. P. Raspe of the Conservatoire Royal in Brussels provided valuable information, as well as suggestions for further research. For access to newspaper files for 1842 I am grateful to the periodical department of the Royal Albert Library in Brussels. Staff members at the Cincinnati Public Library, the British Museum, the Library of Congress, the Manchester City Library, and Northern Kentucky University also provided useful assistance.

For the care with which they have designed and produced this book, I wish to thank the staff at the University of Georgia Press. I am also grateful to Hilde Robinson, for her fine work as copy editor, and to Ellen Curtin, for preparing the index.

Finally I wish to thank my parents, to whom this book is dedicated, as well as my wife Joan, for patience, support, and love.

Introduction

Emily Brontë, Beethoven, and Romantic Equilibrium

Themeaning of literature," Jacques Barzun wrote in 1980, "resides in the same motions of the spirit as those aroused by music; only the means differ."[1] Beethoven and Emily Brontë merit comparison to the extent that the "meaning" of their art is comparable. That meaning is comparable to the extent that "the motions of the spirit" are comparable. The motions of the spirit that make these two artists unique within their separate artistic traditions are those that make them most similar to each other. This study is devoted to characterizing—in emotional, spiritual, and stylistic terms—the extent to which the meaning of their art, the human experience it expresses and induces, is comparable.

Although some critics would argue that music and literature cannot successfully be compared, much can be gained by carefully exploring comparable "meaning" and "motions of the spirit" in these two arts.[2] To Beethoven himself it was obvious that music and literature could inhabit the same emotional, spiritual, and stylistic realms. In 1823 he declared that his musical ideas "are roused by moods which in the poet's case are transmuted into words, and in mine into tones, that sound, roar, and storm until at last they take shape for me as notes." Such impulses came to Beethoven "uninvited"; he could not specify their exact source "with any degree of certainty."[3] Part 2 of this study proposes new sources (some of them musical) for Emily Brontë's artistic impulses. But the primary emphasis of this book is on the art itself. Our direct access to the spirit of Brontë and of Beethoven is through the motion of the notes and words whose storm and roar they shaped into art.

The words and notes of each are powerfully emotional. David Cecil points out that Emily Brontë's "attitude to human emotion" is "different from that of her contemporaries. Her characters have extremely intense emotions, the most intense in English fiction."[4] Beethoven's emotions, equally different from those of his contemporaries, are often felt to be the most intense in Viennese music. The "two currents" in the composer's emotional nature are aptly identified by Romain Rolland as "vast love and vast scorn."[5] Equally vast currents clash in *Wuthering Heights*—and in the emotional nature of Heathcliff.

Cecil goes on to say that Brontë's characters are "implacable and irresistible as the elemental forces they resemble; unchanging as the hills, fierce as the lightning." Beethoven's themes and rhythms are equally permeated by the elemental forces of nature. "I could almost grasp them in my hands," he said, "out in Nature's open, in the woods, during my promenades, in the silence of the night, at the earliest dawn."[6] Emily Brontë communed with the materials of her art in the solitude of the Yorkshire moors. She shaped her words, as he shaped his notes, into an "organic form" capable of expressing nature's most vehement—and passive—forces.

In the realm of the spirit, Beethoven and Brontë express comparable visions of mystical union and peace. Philip Barford, searching for an equivalent to the ethereal spiritual realms explored by Beethoven in the late piano sonatas, turned to Emily Brontë's poem "The Prisoner."[7] Philip Henderson, searching for an equivalent to Emily Brontë's "peculiarly personal type of religion," turned to the "yearning and crucifixion and unearthly blessedness of Beethoven's late quartets."[8]

Barford and Henderson are the only critics I have encountered who have compared Beethoven and Brontë directly. But again and again one encounters analysis of the one artist that applies verbatim to the other. For Rolland, the key to Beethoven's genius is twofold: "the direct expression of the personal soul" combined with "the constructive intelligence" (p. 90). One could hardly find a better formulation of the key to Emily Brontë's genius. Granted, most artists express some combination of soul and intelligence. But the intensity of the mix and the directness of expression are special in Beethoven and Brontë, and these qualities take on added significance given the history of styles in their separate arts. Each artist was Romantic in vehement soulful expression, classical in constructive intelligence. This strongly fused combination of emotion and spirit allowed each to create a style that can best be characterized as Romantic equilibrium, a phrase that distinguishes their style from the classical equilibrium of such predecessors as Jane Austen and Mozart.

Jane Austen and Mozart, to which this book is a sequel, presented a working definition of *classical equilibrium* as a framework in which to compare three Austen novels with three Mozart piano concertos.[9] Part 1 of that book is directly applicable to this book: it presents a working definition not only of the classical equilibrium achieved by Austen and Mozart but of the Romantic equilibrium achieved by Emily Brontë and Beethoven. Those working definitions are designed to be expansive, not restrictive. Their goal is to articulate parallel stylistic developments in English fiction and Viennese music, giving precision to the kinds of comparisons that are often found in parallel time charts of the arts but are seldom spelled out in any concrete way. A premise of both books is that Emily Brontë's stylistic achievement is to Jane Austen's as Beethoven's is to Mozart's. The terms *Romantic equilibrium* and *classical equilibrium* express that relationship.

More than any other artists in their separate traditions, Emily Brontë in English fiction and Beethoven in Viennese music shattered the classical equilibrium of their predecessors with the full force of Romantic vehemence, subjectivity, and fragmentation. Yet, while they compare for the infusion of vehement and openly harsh emotion into the earlier, more "classical" forms, so do they compare in the extraordinary control with which they ultimately expressed such emotion. In this sense, the Romantic *equilibrium* they achieved may be said to contrast with the Romantic *transformation* more typical of such Romantics as Berlioz, Liszt, Chopin, and Schumann in music, or Poe, Dickens, Melville, and Charlotte Brontë in fiction.

Part 1 of the earlier work not only established the stylistic position of Beethoven and Brontë relative to Mozart and Austen; in doing so it also explored a variety of categories by which works of prose fiction and instrumental music can legitimately be compared. Those categories, central to an understanding of both Beethoven's and Brontë's art, include the following:

Comparable Terms in Fiction and Music

Equilibrium and balance	vs.	Imbalance
Symmetry and proportion	vs.	Irregularity of form
Restraint	vs.	Vehemence of expression
Clarity	vs.	Ambiguity
Ambiguity as a means	vs.	Ambiguity as an end
Wit	vs.	Sentiment or scorn
Conventional language	vs.	The unconventional

Comparable Themes in Fiction and Music

Individuality within society	vs.	Individuality apart from society
Indoors	vs.	Outdoors
Home	vs.	Away
Sanity	vs.	Madness
Growth	vs.	Transformation
Life	vs.	Death
Happy ending	vs.	Unhappy ending

3

Introduction

The earlier discussion emphasized the degree to which Austen and Mozart, masters of classical equilibrium, tended toward the first component of each successive polarity, whereas representatives of Romantic transformation tended toward the second. One strong measure of the Romantic equilibrium of Emily Brontë and of Beethoven is their shared tendency to straddle each successive "versus" sign. The general similarity of Brontë's and Beethoven's styles, presented in general terms in Part 1 of *Jane Austen and Mozart*, will in this book be illustrated through detailed comparison of individual works.

Although there is no need to re-create that earlier discussion here, the concluding passages from several sections will help to indicate the stylistic context in which the term *Romantic equilibrium* is used in this study.

Equilibrium:

> In works by Austen or Mozart, the disruptive forces that threaten the equilibrium tend finally to be subordinated to the "truth" of an all-encompassing order. In works by Poe, Berlioz, Chopin, Schumann, and Liszt, the disruptive forces often tend to be elevated to the status of truth itself. Here, as in other ways, Beethoven and Emily Brontë might be said to straddle both tendencies. *Wuthering Heights*, like the *Appassionata*, violates its own symmetry while preserving it.

Restraint vs. vehemence of expression:

> Brontë, like Beethoven, offends when necessary. Yet these two artists, so vehement relative to Austen and Mozart, are in some ways models of restraint when compared with certain Romantic artists. Compared to Poe's morbid necrophilia, Brontë's presentations of Heathcliff's visits to Catherine's grave are exceedingly restrained. Compared to the relatively unrestrained chromaticism often found in Chopin or Schumann, Beethoven's wrenching modulations are contained within a strict tonal framework. Ultimately, the overt vehemence of Beethoven and Emily Brontë tends to be powerful because of the underlying restraint with which it is expressed.

Indoors vs. outdoors:

> The out of doors tends to exist in the works of Mozart and Austen for the sake of the human beings who have tamed it and who wish occasionally to occupy it. In Beethoven and Brontë it is a force larger than human lives to which humans must link themselves with feeling and spirit if they are to transcend a human society

that is by definition belittling and stifling. With such high Romantics as Poe, Chopin, and Schumann, the indoor-outdoor distinction sometimes disappears altogether, leaving us in a psychological dreamworld devoid of spatial moorings.

Sanity vs. madness:

"Madness" in Austen and Mozart tends to take the form of temporary deviations from the "sanity" by which it is measured and into which it finally becomes incorporated. In Brontë and Beethoven the deviations are more massive and threatening. While the disturbances are often contained by the "sanity" of a large structural form, they at the same time call into question the adequacy of such forms as vehicles for the expression of that which is truly irrational and subjective. In certain works by Poe, Berlioz, and Schumann, madness can be said to triumph over sanity as it has conventionally been understood. Such madness expresses itself in forms which by previous standards are ambiguous and unresolved—while at the same time achieving a unity of effect and execution that is, paradoxically, the unity of the unresolved or the unreliable.

Happy vs. unhappy endings:

Mozart and Austen generally wrote in a classical (or neoclassical) style in which the comic or happy ending was conventional. Poe and Chopin both wrote in Romantic styles in which the unhappy ending was itself becoming a convention. In this way, as in others, the works of Emily Brontë and Beethoven might be said to straddle both tendencies.

The Romantic equilibrium that Brontë expressed in words and Beethoven expressed in notes derives in each case from a powerful ability to combine equilibrium with tension, vehemence with restraint, clarity with ambiguity, sanity with madness, the classical with the Romantic. That powerful ability is what most distinguishes the contribution of each to the history of style in their separate arts.

One measure of the unique positions Beethoven and Brontë occupy in the history of styles is Barzun's formulation of the kind of equilibrium attained by the "true" Romanticist. "The perfection of Romanticism," he writes in *Berlioz and the Romantic Century,* "is to bring into a tense equilibrium many radical diversities. It consequently produces work that shows rough texture, discontinuities, distortions—antitheses of structure as well as of substance. From the classical point of view these are flaws; but they are consented to by the Romanticist—indeed sought after—for the sake of drama; they are not oversights on the artist's part but planned concessions to the medium and the aim it subserves—as in engineering one finds gaps, vents, or holes to balance the effects of expansion by heat or stress of vibration."[10] The dynamics specified here

5

apply to musical works as various as Berlioz's *Symphonie fantastique*, Schumann's *Carnaval*, Chopin's "Funeral March" Sonata, and Liszt's B-minor Sonata—and to fictional works as various as Balzac's *Père Goriot*, Dickens's *Great Expectations*, Poe's *Narrative of Arthur Gordon Pym*, and Melville's *Moby-Dick*. Yet, for reasons already suggested above, they do not apply quite so closely to Beethoven's *Appassionata* or Brontë's *Wuthering Heights*.

As Barzun goes on to say, the true Romanticist "abandons the ready-made formula" of his classical predecessor(s) "because its excessive generality gives it too loose a fit." But Beethoven and Brontë, instead of abandoning the ready-made form, tend to transform it through intensification. Beethoven's *Pathétique* Sonata, Opus 13, does not so much abandon the sonata form of Haydn and Mozart as animate it with radically intense materials. The *Appassionata* Sonata, Opus 57, further intensifies the form. Even Beethoven's last sonata, Opus 111, transcends the classical form without entirely abandoning it. Similarly, *Wuthering Heights* does not so much abandon the "domestic novel" perfected by Jane Austen as animate its form with radically intense materials. It does so, as we shall see, in ways that correspond to the varied achievements of the three aforementioned Beethoven sonatas.

For all of the overt Romantic transformation Beethoven brought to the classical forms perfected by Haydn and Mozart, he preserved not only their outward proportions but also the sense of stable tonality by which to measure departures from equilibrium and returns to it. This is one reason why Charles Rosen considers Beethoven an exponent more of the classical style of his predecessors than of the Romantic style of his successors.[11] Similarly, Emily Brontë, for all of the intensification she brings to the world of Jane Austen's novels, remains surprisingly within the confines of that world. Whereas Austen wrote that "3 or 4 Families in a Country Village is the very thing to work on," Emily Brontë limits herself to two families in a country village. Austen's novels are often criticized for their narrow geographical range, but *Wuthering Heights* is narrower still: its action encompasses a four-mile radius, compared with fifty miles in *Pride and Prejudice*. Yet Brontë's novel is never accused of being restricted in range, because of the cosmic energies that are unleashed within its limited spatial frame. Like Beethoven she intensified, heightened, and ultimately transcended the forms of her most classical predecessors, yet without abandoning them.

That the emotion, the spirit, and the style—in short, the meaning—of these two artists would be close enough to merit a sustained comparison of their art is, in some ways, improbable. Beethoven appeared at the vanguard of the Romantic movement in music, making his first stylistic impact in the late 1790s, the decade of Mozart's death and of Haydn's peak productivity. From the last years of the eighteenth century through the first quarter of the nineteenth, Beethoven's works poured and stammered forth. His spiritual and musical growth throughout his celebrated three "periods" is perhaps best reflected in the nine symphonies, the sixteen string quartets, and the thirty-two piano sonatas. Each of these groups represents the stylistic turning point in the history of its genre. In Beethoven's output is found not only the destination of the classical symphony, quartet, and sonata but the point of departure for the Romantic symphony, quartet, and sonata.

Emily Brontë's art appeared at the end of the Romantic age, at least in England. Born in 1818, a year after the death of Jane Austen, she died in 1848, the year after *Wuthering Heights*, her one and only novel, was published. As she did not long survive its publication, and as the greatness of *Wuthering Heights* itself was not properly recognized until the twentieth century, neither her life nor her art entered into the great tradition of English fiction immediately, in the way that Beethoven's life and art entered the mainstream of Viennese music, even when seeming to push against the current. Even so, this one novel is one of the great documents of English (and European) Romanticism. This is so even though it was conceived and written well out of the geographical, as well as the temporal, mainstream of the Romantic movement.

Beethoven's creative life, unlike that of Emily Brontë, has been heavily documented: an extraordinary amount of material is available concerning the sources and stages of his artistic development. There are, of course, the works themselves, in the three celebrated stages, or periods. To supplement the works we have the composer's letters, his notebooks, his conversation books, the testimony of innumerable acquaintances, and so forth. This wealth of material— including his own musical manuscripts, the Heiligenstadt Testament, the letter to the "Immortal Beloved," the court records of his battle for the custody of his nephew Carl—surrounds his music and achievement in a sometimes luminous haze, but it does not in itself explain how or why he was able to transform the human torment and ecstasy it represents into enduring music.

By contrast, material relating to Emily Brontë's creative life is almost nonexistent. What we know of her artistic and spiritual development we know essentially from *Wuthering Heights* and from the poems and juvenilia. The manuscript of the novel does not survive, nor do we have any detailed information concerning her negotiations with its publisher. From her personal correspondence, little beyond a few "birthday notes" survives in her own hand. What we

7

know about her life from her sister Charlotte and an occasional friend such as Ellen Nussey does not account for the burning power of the fiction she wrote, nor probably could we account for it if we knew much more. In her life, as in previous English fiction, there seems to be no obvious source for her vision or her style.

In fact, what little we do know about the conditions of Emily Brontë's life tends to make her creation of *Wuthering Heights* even more mysterious. All of the influences of family, locale, nationality, and chronology that produced Emily Brontë produced Charlotte Brontë as well; the difference in range and intensity of expression between these two sisters is one measure of how little studies of environment and even heredity can contribute to resolving the question of *why* a given artist is able to create. Cecil's tribute to the uniqueness of emotion in Emily's fictional world used Charlotte's *Jane Eyre* as a foil: beside the passions of Heathcliff, "even Mr. Rochester's passions seem tame and tea-party affairs."

One biographical difference between the two sisters is that Emily was musical whereas Charlotte was not. Curiously, more information is available about the music Emily played than about the literature she read. But that information has never been studied systematically. Part 2 of this study describes her experience at the keyboard: from her first lessons as a teenager in the 1830s, to her advanced studies in Brussels in 1842, to her acquisition of a new piano and of the eight-volume *Musical Library* during the years in which she wrote *Wuthering Heights*.[12] Analysis of that experience establishes the prominence of Beethoven in her musical life. It also suggests that her knowledge of Beethoven's music contributed to the creative process that resulted in *Wuthering Heights*—as did what she would have known about Beethoven's life from reading about it.

Readers for whom source studies take precedence over the art itself may prefer to read Part 2 of this study before Part 1. For me, however, the extent to which Emily Brontë may actually have been influenced by her knowledge of Beethoven and his music is subordinate to the comparable value that inheres in the art they both created. I will therefore address the degree to which his artistic expression may have influenced hers only after exploring the extent to which her fiction and his music have comparable meaning.

Emily Brontë's foremost biographer, Winifred Gérin, has argued that Emily's imagination remained fired not by the "Victorian age of her maturity, but the Romantic age of her adolescence; the era of Byron, Beethoven, and Blake. The influences of that era were lasting, and made her the rebel and visionary she remained to the end."[13] Part 2 of this study demonstrates that the "Victorian age of her maturity" was in many ways an age of Beethoven. Her assimilation of his music and his legend in the 1840s sets in a new light the time lag between the

Romantic equilibrium he achieved at the beginning of the Romantic age in music and she achieved near the end of the Romantic age in literature.

Individuals who are first exposed to *Wuthering Heights* or to Beethoven's most powerful works tend to be struck more by the vehemence of the emotion than by the beauty of the form which contains it. Once one has assimilated the brute emotion it becomes possible to perceive the ultimate "equilibrium" that "grounds" the radical tensions (the phrasing is Charles Rosen's). Historically, successive generations of critics and reviewers have responded similarly to these two artists, registering a sequence moving from emotional shock to aesthetic awe.

Initial reviews of *Wuthering Heights* read much like the initial reviews of Beethoven's music. In December of 1848 the *Quarterly Review* accused the novel of "repulsive vulgarity." The *American Review* in the same year allowed that "the book is original. It is powerful; full of suggestiveness. But still it is coarse."[14] Words such as *repulsive, vulgar, original, powerful, suggestive,* and *coarse* run like a litany through the initial reviews of Beethoven's works—beginning even with the First and Second symphonies, which sound comparatively lame to twentieth-century ears. One early critic denounced the First Symphony as "a caricature of Haydn pushed to absurdity," whereas another found the finale of the Second to be "a gross enormity, an immense wounded snake, unwilling to die, but writhing in its last agonies, and bleeding to death."[15] Such vitriolic comments were extreme among the reactions to Beethoven's earliest works, but they established themes that would become more and more persistent throughout his career.

Britannia's 1848 review of *Wuthering Heights* finds it "in parts very unskillfully constructed: many passages in it display neither the grace of art nor the truth of nature, but only the vigor of one positive idea—that of passionate ferocity." This novel portrays a world which "knows nothing of those breakwaters to the fury of the tempest which civilized training establishes to subdue the harsher workings of the soul." Even so, there is a fascination in its "primeval rudeness" and "some forms are the more picturesque from their distorted growth amid so many obstacles."[16]

On 13 February 1805 the *Allegemeine musikalische Zeitung* reviewed Beethoven's *Eroica* Symphony with a similar mixture of wonder, admiration, confusion, and doubt. The symphony was found to be "a daring, wild, fantasia, of inordinate length and extreme difficulty of execution. There is no lack of striking and beautiful passages in which the force and talent of the author are obvious; but, on the other hand, the work seems often to lose itself in utter confusion." The reviewer, though counting himself one of "Beethoven's warmest admirers," finds "in the present work much that is odd and harsh, enormously increasing the difficulty of comprehending the music, and obscuring its unity almost entirely."[17]

When contemporary reviewers of either artist weren't trying to cope with the harsh emotion or to penetrate the seeming obscurities of form, they tended to invoke nature images to convey the quality of the work under review. *Britannia*'s reviewer, finding "savage grandeur" rather than "sylvan beauty" in *Wuthering Heights*, complained that the book left "an unpleasant effect on the mind. There are no green spots on which the mind can linger with satisfaction. The story rushes onward with impetuous force, but it is the force of a dark and sullen torrent, flowing between high and rugged rocks." Such words were often used to describe Beethoven's music: Rolland's image of the *Appassionata* is that of a "thunderous sea of blood . . . closed with the pillars of Hercules" (p. 172).

Contemporary reviewers also tended to accuse Beethoven and Brontë of being utterly immoral. The spokesman for the *North American Review* (1848) felt that *Wuthering Heights* was "an attempt to corrupt the virtue of the sturdy descendants of the Puritans." Forty-five years earlier, Dionys Weber, a music master in Prague, forbade young Ignace Moscheles to corrupt himself with such "eccentric stuff" as Beethoven's Sonata *Pathétique*—a charge that was extended at the Prague Conservatory to the *Eroica* Symphony ("a dangerously immoral composition").[18]

If certain contemporary writers and pedagogues thought Beethoven's art was immoral, many of his Romantic followers were to see it as representing the highest morality: that of the unfettered artist. Composers as varied as Berlioz, Liszt, Schumann, Wagner, and Tchaikovsky saw him as the composer who shattered the complacency of the Old Regime, who burst the bounds of convention, and who thereby freed the artist to express his SOUL in whatever way his genius allowed. This perception of Beethoven as Romantic Savior and Redeemer, as we shall see in Part 2, pervaded the musical life of Brussels during Emily Brontë's study there in 1842. Its first extended exposition in English-language prose had occurred a year earlier, in Moscheles's 1841 translation (with supplements) of Schindler's *Life of Beethoven*.

By the end of the nineteenth century the image of Beethoven the Redeemer had been fortified by George Grove's *Beethoven and His Nine Symphonies* (1896). Discussing the Second Symphony, Grove asserts that Beethoven's "changes of key and tone were too abrupt" for such "older composers" as Haydn and Mozart. For Grove, Beethoven's predecessors were inhibited because, as "domestic servants," they "wore powder, and pigtails, and swords, and court dresses, and gold lace. . . . Being thus forced to regulate their conduct by etiquette, and habitually to keep down their emotions under decorous rules and forms, they could not suddenly change all their habits when they came to make their music." Beethoven, however, "had set such social rules and restrictions at nought. It was his nature, one of the most characteristic things in him, to be free and unrestrained."[19]

Paul Henry Lang's summary of the nineteenth-century response to Beethoven probably speaks for Emily Brontë, the music student, as much as it does for such writers as Moscheles and Grove. Those who heard Beethoven's "agitated and yearning themes, who were struck by the irresistible propulsive force of the allegros, the majesty of the adagios, the menacing humor of the scherzos, and the wild rhythms of the finales, recognized that this music, compared to that of his predecessors, is somewhat raw, gnarled, even unfinished. There were some who were repelled . . . but many more, despite or perhaps even because of these qualities, found Beethoven's music to be warmer, more intense, and more fulfilling than any other they had known." For such listeners, Lang goes on to say, Mozart was "a sun that warmed without leaving its lawful orbit," whereas "Beethoven was a comet that followed uncharted paths without submitting to a systematic world order, giving rise by its very appearance to unsanctioned ideas."[20] *Wuthering Heights* made a comparable impression on many nineteenth-century readers accustomed to Austen.

Twentieth-century critics, having assimilated the shock of Beethoven's unsanctioned orbit, have tended to investigate the classical order that he imposed upon the uncharted paths he so dramatically explored. Rosen's *Classical Style* is the most persuasive effort of twentieth-century criticism to view Beethoven as more classical than Romantic—a concept that would have been incomprehensible in the nineteenth century. Rosen allows that "the equilibrium between harmonic and thematic development so characteristic of Haydn and Mozart is often lost in early Beethoven, where thematic contrast and transformation seem to outweigh all other interests." With the *Appassionata*, however, Beethoven "returned decisively to the closed, concise, and dramatic forms of Haydn and Mozart, expanding these forms and heightening their power without betraying their proportions."[21] As Lang puts it, Beethoven stretched those forms to "their maximal tensile strength"—at the same time that he "condensed and concentrated the texture. . . . It was the very fact that Beethoven's particular genius could admit so many romantic elements into an essentially classical concept that gave him his unique and revered position."[22] That position, in the words of Donald Grout, is that of "a colossus astride the two centuries."[23]

Emily Brontë is seldom described as a colossus. But the qualities that Lang finds unique in Beethoven's "solution" in Western music are the very qualities unique to her "solution" in English fiction. These include the large-scale equilibrium stretched to its maximal tensile strength, the condensed and concentrated texture, the overwhelming coercive power needed to maintain such a tense equilibrium, and the ability to allow Romantic elements to "pour into" an essentially classical concept, thereby being "salvaged from destruction."

Although no literary critic has actually labeled *Wuthering Heights* neoclassical rather than Romantic, the twentieth century has witnessed a successful effort to map out the system and order in the novel, to discover the powerfully symmetrical structure that carries—and to some degree resolves—its raw Romantic energies. Early in the century Charles Percy Sanger gave his lecture, "The Structure of *Wuthering Heights*," complete with a chronological summary of the book's happenings and a perfectly symmetrical ancestral chart of the novel's two families, the Earnshaws and Lintons. Sanger's study revealed for the first time the care with which Emily Brontë laid out the legal, ancestral, and temporal layers of the seemingly formless book.[24] Later such critics as Dorothy van Ghent (1953) demonstrated the way in which Brontë's employment of recurrent motifs serves to unify seemingly disparate sections of the novel—a process, as we shall see, that is comparable to Beethoven's use of short musical motifs to unify his large-scale structures. Van Ghent and others also showed how the double narration by Lockwood and Nelly helps to keep the larger-than-life actions of the novel in a manageable perspective—and how the love triangle of the second half of the book effectively balances and comments on that of the first half.[25]

In short, twentieth-century criticism has uncovered the equilibrium—the symmetry of form and of internal dynamics—which makes *Wuthering Heights*, in its way, as concise and unified as an Austen novel. To a nineteenth-century reader, such an idea would have been no less bizarre than the idea that Beethoven's works were, in their way, as concise and unified as Mozart's. In 1966, however, Inga-Stina Ewbank could make the following declaration with perfect accuracy and ease: "What is outstanding about *Wuthering Heights* is the sense of form displayed by Emily Brontë—a sense which, before her, had been shown only by Jane Austen. Like Jane Austen, she achieved a structure which, in every part, is the visible embodiment of the theme, by the exclusion from the novel of anything not necessary, anything that would dissipate concentration." She goes on to say, of course, that "here the similarity stops." What Jane Austen "includes" within that structure "is just what Emily Brontë excludes"—such things as "parties, picnics, and country dances."[26]

Northrop Frye compares the two novelists with a different end in mind, but he makes a similar distinction between what the fiction of each "includes." He finds the plot and dialogue of Austen's fiction to be "closely linked with the conventions of the comedy of manners," whereas those of *Wuthering Heights* are "linked rather with the tale and the ballad," which "seem to have more affinity with tragedy." Because of this, "the tragic emotions of passion and fury, which would shatter the balance of tone in Jane Austen, can safely be accommodated" in Emily Brontë.[27] In a like vein Beethoven accommodates the passion and fury that would shatter the balance of tone in Mozart. He does so by transforming the "comedy of manners" in music into a vehicle capable of carrying tragic emotion. This he achieves (in the words of Maynard Solomon) by "the incorporation into musical form of death, destructiveness, anxiety, and aggression, as terrors to be transcended within the work of art itself."[28] Such are the psychic energies Emily Brontë incorporated into the world of Jane Austen.

As suggested above, Beethoven's and Brontë's unique kind of perfection of form can generally be experienced only after a reader or listener (or a century of critics) has assimilated the "tragic emotions of passion and fury" those forms have been stretched in order to accommodate. This strong and rugged tension between form and content—this rugged and unsentimental Romantic equilibrium in which the 'equilibrium' is as strong and forceful as the 'Romantic'— is their deepest and most significant affinity.

THE NOVEL
AND THE SONATAS

A stylistic term such as *Romantic equilibrium* must originate on a high level of generality. It can be validated, however, only when applied to the peculiar forms and particular meanings of individual works of art. Before engaging in specific comparisons between Brontë's fiction and Beethoven's music, a word must be given to the process of selecting the works to be compared.

Wuthering Heights, her only novel, is the unchallenged candidate to represent Emily Brontë's fiction. Choosing Beethoven works to compare with it has been both difficult and easy. It has been difficult because any choice will of necessity omit important manifestations of his art. It has been easy because there are such riches from which to draw. From them I have chosen three piano sonatas: Opus 13 (the *Pathétique*), Opus 57 (the *Appassionata*), and Opus 111, the last sonata.

Wuthering Heights has important emotional, spiritual, and stylistic affinities with Beethoven's three major periods, early, middle, and late. In writing one novel and in living barely thirty years, Emily Brontë, of course, did not experience three creative "periods" comparable to those of Beethoven. But she did compress several disparate imaginative worlds into her one protean novel. The Romantic, even Gothic, excesses of passion and vengeance embodied by Heathcliff during much of the novel are framed by material that is much more conventional. One such framing device is the narrative presence of Mr. Lockwood, who could almost be said to belong in the fictional world of Jane Austen. Another is the relatively tame love story of Hareton and Cathy, whose marriage ends the novel on a note not unlike that of Jane Austen's conventional "happy endings." The mixture between the demoniacally passionate and the comparatively placid love stories is further compounded by the presence of the unworldly and sublime visions experienced by Catherine and later by Heathcliff shortly before death. The coexistence of these three imaginative worlds has often made it difficult for those critics who feel intuitively that the work is nevertheless the product of one unified vision to articulate that intuition. The comparison with works from Beethoven's three periods will offer a valuable perspective from which to address this difficulty.

The choice of one piano sonata from each of the three periods was not for lack of alternatives in other musical genres. Each period could have been represented by a symphony (such as numbers 1, 5, and 9) or by a string quartet (selected from the Opus 18, the Opus 59, and the "late" quartets, for example). One might also have chosen a symphony from one period, a sonata from another, a quartet from a third. Yet the choice of three works from the same instrumental medium seemed preferable for efficiency of comparison and ease of understanding. And the piano sonatas seemed to offer the richest possibilities. "More than any other category of Beethoven's music," William S. Newman has written, the piano sonatas "give a rounded view of his styles and forms throughout his creative periods. Furthermore, unlike the keyboard sonatas of Haydn and Mozart, they have generally been ranked among the most important works in the total production of the creator."[1] In addition, the piano sonatas most clearly and most purely illustrate those aspects of Beethoven's "solution" in instrumental music that are most directly comparable to the prose achievement of *Wuthering Heights*.

The piano sonata was for Beethoven what the piano concerto was for Mozart: the instrumental form for a soloist into which he most fervently poured his imagination, his soul, his emotion, and his sense of organic form. Compared to Mozart's twenty-seven piano concertos, more than a dozen of which are masterpieces, Beethoven wrote but five. Compared to Mozart's nineteen piano sonatas, however, Beethoven composed thirty-two; in quality and in scope even more than in quantity they dwarf those of his predecessor.[2] Beethoven's relative proclivity for solo rather than concerted pianism reflects his own temperament, but it also reflects the times: solo expression apart from relations with an orchestra was to become increasingly important in the Romantic age, leading eventually to a work such as Schumann's Sonata in F minor, Opus 14, subtitled "Concerto without an Orchestra."

Given the desirability of choosing a piano sonata from each of Beethoven's three periods, it remained to decide which of the thirty-two to use. I chose those that most closely relate to the "motions of the spirit" in *Wuthering Heights*. Opp. 13, 57, and 111 each relate to an important imaginative plane of the novel: the first to the Lockwood plane, the second to the violent Heathcliff plane, the third to the mystical Catherine and Heathcliff plane. The three sonatas also relate well to each other. Opus 13 and Opus 111, both in the key of C minor, measure as well as any two works the distance from early to late Beethoven. The *Appassionata*, in F minor, is the ideal work from the middle period with which to measure the transition from the imaginative plane of the early period toward that of the late. The choice of three minor-key works does ignore a significant part of Beethoven's sonata output, the numerical majority of which are in a major key.[3] But minor-key works are certainly appropriate for comparison with the emotional climate of *Wuthering Heights*. Besides, Opus 111 turns out to be in C major as much as it is in C minor; this, too, corresponds to important aspects of the novel. A final reason for choosing these three sonatas is that they are well known. Some of the literary readers of this book will already have heard them, just as some of the musical readers will have read *Wuthering Heights*.

When Beethoven began writing piano sonatas at the turn of the century, most sonatas had three or four separate movements. The *Pathétique*, Opus 13, has three movements that are separate. The *Appassionata*, from the middle period, squeezes the conventional three-movement form toward two by fusing the second and third movements (as does its major-key counterpart, the *Waldstein*, Opus 53). The last sonata, Opus 111, is in two movements only. Taken together, these three works illustrate Beethoven's evolution from the conventional separate-movement form, to a fused-movement form, to a form whose two separate movements are wholly sufficient for what is being expressed.[4] This tendency toward "organic" form is one of the qualities that most distinguishes Beethoven's style from that of Mozart, who wrote eighteen of his nineteen piano sonatas in three separate movements.

When *Wuthering Heights* was published in December of 1847, the three-volume novel (by then known as the "triple-decker") was still as much in vogue as it had been in Jane Austen's day. In fact, it was because *Wuthering Heights* filled only two volumes that the publication was "completed" by Anne Brontë's short novel *Agnes Grey*. Curiously, whereas modern reprints of Austen's novels almost always retain the volume indications of the originals, this is almost never done with *Wuthering Heights*. Even in the scrupulously edited Norton Critical Edition one has to search through the scholarly notes in order to learn that the novel was originally published in two volumes, the first of which concluded with chapter 14, before the death of Catherine Earnshaw. Certainly it is one measure of the rushing torrent of this book that even cautious, historical-minded editors have not thought fit to restore its original division into volumes. By not doing so, however, they have deprived the work of some important structural effects, as will be shown.

Whether *Wuthering Heights* is read as one volume or two, it contains three endings. One is the conventional ending that closes the book. A happy marriage is projected for Cathy Linton and Hareton Earnshaw, the surviving descendants of Wuthering Heights and of Thrushcross Grange. They can be expected, more or less, to live "happily ever after" along with the other characters—Nelly, Joseph, and Lockwood—who are still alive.

The second ending of the novel also closes the book, but it is far from conventional. It takes the form of Catherine and Heathcliff's double "marriage" in death: below the ground there is the impending molecular union of two corpses that will decompose at a speed guaranteed to outpace that of Edgar; above the ground there is the spirit-bond of their more ethereal selves, perceived by local residents as ghosts. Whether this ending is intended to be "happy" is perhaps impossible to say; like much of the book it explores realms of experience unsanctioned by conventional morality.

Neither of the two endings specified above, though, seems to be the ending most strongly remembered by most readers of the book. The essential ending of the novel seems to be Catherine's death and Heathcliff's being left alone without her. Long after reading the book, most readers do not remember the courtship of Cathy and Hareton or the change Heathcliff goes through shortly before his death so much as they remember the dramatic end of Catherine's life—and of the passionate, tragic love story.[5] This ending occurs barely halfway through the book.

I specify these three endings in some detail because all of them, taken together, constitute the ending of *Wuthering Heights*. In themselves they demonstrate how this novel operates on several imaginative planes, as opposed to the single plane of Jane Austen's novels, with their conventionally happy endings. More to the point here, these three endings of *Wuthering Heights* correspond to the endings of the three Beethoven sonatas with which the novel will be compared.

Opus 13, the *Pathétique*, has a "conventional" ending that seems as contrived and artificial to some students of the sonata as the happy marriage of Cathy and Hareton seems to some readers of *Wuthering Heights*. After the intense drama of the first movement and the soulful yearning of the second, the conventional rondo structure of the finale strikes many listeners as lacking in force. Just as most readers of *Wuthering Heights* remember the fury and passion of Heathcliff and Catherine more than the love of Cathy and Hareton, so do most hearers of Opus 13 remember the ominous, crashing chords which open the first movement more than they do the musical material of the more conventional finale.

Opus 57, the *Appassionata*, corresponds in its ending to the brutal, fatalistic "ending" most readers seem to take away as their core emotional experience from *Wuthering Heights*. The searing, turbulent, strife-filled world of the first movement is followed by the heavenly calm of the second movement, but before that movement can complete itself it is fused with the "frozen grief" of the third movement, a grief that burns but does not thaw and that is unable to escape the dark realms of F minor in order to achieve a major-key transformation. This work ends with the unvaried "passionate ferocity" that *Britannia*'s reviewer found in *Wuthering Heights*.

Opus 111, the last sonata, ends in a way that parallels the condition achieved by Catherine and Heathcliff's spirits at the end of the novel: escape from the "shattered prison." Transcending the dark, brutal, fatalistic ending at the middle of the novel is the weightless, timeless, unworldly release Catherine achieves at her death and Heathcliff glimpses shortly before he dies. Just as the first movement of Opus 111, in C minor, expresses concentrated passion and conflict, so does the second movement, in C major, express release and unworldly joy. This is not the rather arbitrary last-minute release glimpsed toward the end of the finale of the *Pathétique*, where the minor-key texture is pierced by what Tovey calls the effect of "very high light."[6] This release is complete and profound: developed throughout the *Arietta*, it matches the first movement's expression of conflict both in bulk and in eloquence. The unworldly release achieved and glimpsed by Catherine and by Heathcliff partakes of comparable "motions of the spirit," as we shall see, though it is not rendered in such detail. Emily Brontë's poetry will help us grasp its spirit.

Each of the next three chapters compares one imaginative plane of *Wuthering Heights* with one Beethoven sonata. Such a structure presents certain challenges to both reader and writer, but it is the best way I have been able to devise for exploring the "uncharted paths" of similarity between Brontë and Beethoven. The symmetrical structure of Part 2 of *Jane Austen and Mozart*, in which three novels were compared with three piano concertos, volume by volume and movement by movement, must here give way to a more organic structure, better suited to the artists (and art works) under discussion. Because the Romantic equilibrium expressed by Beethoven in music and by Brontë in fiction derives much of its historical meaning from the classical equilibrium expressed by Mozart in music and by Austen in fiction, I will contrast them with these earlier artists when appropriate.

Chapter One

Mr. Lockwood and the Sonata
Pathétique: Romantic Intensity
in a Classical Frame

The story of *Wuthering Heights* begins and ends with Mr. Lockwood. He is the one character in the novel who might have been found in Jane Austen's fiction. He is educated, polite, and upper class. One measure of his conventionality is that we never learn his first name—just as one measure of Heathcliff's unconventionality is that he does not use a last name. Mr. Lockwood is so sensitive to nuance and decorum that he once carried on a courtship by eyebrows only, a courtship about which he feels guilty even though he never spoke to the girl. His "romance" could have taken place in Jane Austen's Lyme:

> While enjoying a month of fine weather at the sea-coast, I was thrown into the company of a most fascinating creature, a real goddess in my eyes, as long as she took no notice of me. I "never told my love" vocally; still, if looks have language, the merest idiot might have guessed I was over head and ears: she understood me at last, and looked a return—the sweetest of all imaginable looks. And what did I do? I confess it with shame—shrunk icily into myself, like a snail; at every glance retired colder and farther; till, finally, the poor innocent was led to doubt her own senses, and, overwhelmed with confusion at her supposed mistake, persuaded her mamma to decamp.[1]

For jilting the girl, society stamped Mr. Lockwood with "the reputation of deliberate heartlessness," which he felt was undeserved. So he has sought out the solitude of a rented estate in Yorkshire, which is where we find him—not yet knowing of his "amorous" background—on the first page of the novel.

As the opening sentence informs us, the year is 1801, which makes Mr. Lockwood roughly a contemporary of the characters in Austen's fiction. From the very first page this exile from Austen's world is thrust, physically and psychically, into a vehement world of tempestuous passions and social lawlessness. His presence at the end of the story one year later is one measure of the degree

23

to which Brontë, in stretching and intensifying Austen's decorous world, does not entirely break out of its bounds. So is the fact that it is technically through Mr. Lockwood that we hear the whole story. Yet Lockwood does change; what he learns by the end of the novel about himself and others is one measure of the degree to which Brontë, while preserving Austen's world, has transformed it. Intimations of later transformations occur even in the opening chapters, during Lockwood's initiation to the Heights.

Beethoven's Sonata *Pathétique* was published in 1799. It is in the three-movement form favored by Haydn, Mozart, and their classical contemporaries; the movements themselves follow the fast-slow-fast pattern typical of the classical sonata before Beethoven. The first and last movements are in the key of C minor, the second movement in the contrasting key of A-flat major. In size, this sonata retains the classical proportions among the movements while stretching the overall length. It runs to 593 bars, whereas, according to William S. Newman, the average length of Haydn's keyboard sonatas is 255 bars, of Mozart's, 415.[2]

Apart from the Grave introduction (and its later intrusions into the Allegro), the individual movements of Opus 13 are extremely simple, even predictable, in overt structure. The first movement, Allegro molto e con brio, displays what has come to be known as textbook sonata-allegro form. The exposition consists of three clearly distinguished themes and is given an exact repeat. After a relatively short thematic development, the recapitulation restates the three themes in their original order and is followed by a coda. The slow movement, Adagio cantabile, unfolds in a simple a:b:a:c:a:coda form. The third movement, Allegro, is a rondo of the a:b:a:c:a:b:a:coda variety. Not only the overt structure of these movements but much of the melodic material that fills it belongs as much to Mozart's world as Mr. Lockwood does to Austen's. Indeed, Newman has discovered at least five passages in Beethoven's *Pathétique* that seem to be directly related to Mozart's C-minor Piano Sonata, K. 457. Other musical passages in the *Pathétique* have been compared (and sometimes "traced") to compositions by Dussek, Cherubini, J. B. Cramer, and Grétry.[3]

Yet in spite of the ways in which Opus 13 can be seen as a conventional—even in some ways derivative—sonata of the classical era, it is at the same time a harbinger of musical Romanticism, embodying a vehemence of expression that seems to sweep away the old rules of decorum and social ease. As Tovey points out, "its pianoforte style . . . utterly eclipsed anything Mozart could conceive," even though "in actual depth of idea, and even in pathos, this sonata does not surpass, if it equals, Mozart's in the same key."[4] Much that was felt to be new and powerful in the sonata can be traced to the force and imagination of the Grave introduction to the first movement.

The introduction is only ten bars long, but it provides a context in which the conventional first-movement patterns that follow are given a different meaning than they would otherwise have. This bold, mysterious, powerful introduction initiates a new era in the piano sonata—as does, in English fiction, the man named Heathcliff whom Lockwood encounters on the first page of *Wuthering Heights*. A detailed comparison of the opening bars of the sonata with the opening pages of the novel will help to show the degree to which Beethoven and Brontë, in Lang's words for Beethoven, "condensed and concentrated the texture" of the large-scale forms of their predecessors.

Beginnings

In the social world of Jane Austen, introductions between strangers tend to be formal, predictable affairs. The parties who are meeting greet and acknowledge each other according to accepted rules. In this nicely regulated verbal world every antecedent phrase has a consequent. (For composers such as Haydn and Mozart antecedent phrases also tend to have a consequent; that is, the second phrase answers and perfectly balances the first.) In the verbal world of Emily Brontë, however, as in the musical world of Beethoven, an antecedent phrase is not always so predictably followed by the expected consequent.

On the first page of *Wuthering Heights* Mr. Lockwood tries to initiate a conversation with Heathcliff by "announcing" his own name. He is met with silence. Lockwood then asks, "Mr. Heathcliff?" The only answer is "a nod." Again met with silence, Mr. Lockwood must launch a third initiative. He introduces himself in language that might have been used by Mr. Collins or Mary Bennet in *Pride and Prejudice*; his language, however, approaches even closer to self-parody than theirs, perhaps because Heathcliff's silence has unsettled him.

> "Mr. Lockwood, your new tenant, sir. I do myself the honour of calling as soon as possible after my arrival, to express the hope that I have not inconvenienced you by my perseverance in soliciting the occupation of Thrushcross Grange: I heard, yesterday, you had some thoughts—"
> "Thrushcross Grange is my own, sir," he interrupted, wincing, "I should not allow anyone to inconvenience me, if I could hinder it—walk in!" (p. 13)

The very fact that Heathcliff interrupts Mr. Lockwood in mid-sentence is a violation of social decorum. The first words with which he does so—

"Thrushcross Grange is my own, sir"—are technically inconsequent, for Mr. Lockwood has in no way challenged Heathcliff's ownership of the Grange. But he does pick up on Lockwood's word *inconvenienced*, which he puts to his own use. Heathcliff responds to Lockwood, but in doing so he follows his own instincts and preferences, not the expectations of his interlocutor.

Heathcliff's words are short and forceful. Only "inconvenience," echoed from Lockwood, has more than two syllables. The elaborate sentence that he interrupts, on the other hand, features seven such words: *possible, arrival, inconvenienced, perseverance, soliciting, occupation,* and *yesterday.* Whereas Lockwood's unfinished sentence is highly structured in syntax, marshalling forty-one words in search of one complete idea, Heathcliff's brusque twenty-two-word sentence expresses three separate ideas, all with such force that their meaning is clear in spite of the irregular mode of expression. The force of his phrasing is intensified by the exclamation point with which the sentence concludes.

Heathcliff's short opening speech gains added force from the manner in which it is delivered: "The 'walk in,' was uttered with closed teeth and expressed the sentiment, 'Go to the Deuce!'" Such explicit description of facial expression and of intonation (punctuated with yet another exclamation) is as pervasive in *Wuthering Heights* as it is rare in Austen's fiction. But still we have not quite exhausted the disruptive force of Heathcliff's short opening speech. In addition to his midsentence interruption of Lockwood, the partially inconsequent words with which he interrupts, and the exclamatory force and harsh intonation of those words, his posture remains to be considered. For Heathcliff's physical bearing belies the import of what he has said. He has commanded Mr. Lockwood to "walk in!" But "the gate over which he leant manifested no sympathizing movement to the words."

Short of fisticuffs, an introduction between two individuals could hardly be more intensely resistant. Yet Lockwood, in the face of resistance, pushes ahead. He "accepts the invitation" that has been so ambiguously offered by "pushing [his] horse's breast" against the gate. Heathcliff lets him in, leads him sullenly toward the house, and then calls out: "Joseph, take Mr. Lockwood's horse; and bring up some wine." Upon hearing this compound order, Lockwood retains enough presence of mind—and condescension—to think to himself: "Here we have the whole establishment of domestics, I suppose. . . . No wonder the grass grows up between the flags, and cattle are the only hedgecutters" (p. 13). His introduction to Wuthering Heights will continue indoors.

Here, on the very first page of the novel, is a striking contrast between two worlds. Viewed historically, the contrast juxtaposes a polite, proper, decorous representative of the Old Regime with an impulsive, decisive, incisive Romantic individualist. Yet the opposition, dramatic as it is, is not total. Heathcliff and Mr. Lockwood are able to communicate, though not with ease. The old forms of politeness are not yet entirely obliterated by the new force of imperiousness. On the first page of *Wuthering Heights*, at least, the old and the new coexist side by side, united by the subtlety as well as the strength of Emily Brontë's prose. So will they coexist, though in a different form, at the novel's end. And so will their coexistence take on new dimensions as the novel is read more than once. For the texture of this opening exchange is so "condensed and concentrated" that it is not possible to register all its subtlety, or even all its power, on a first encounter.

Consider, for example, the word *wincing* in the account of Heathcliff's abrupt opening speech. On a first reading of the novel one is not likely to give much attention to the word. On a subsequent rereading, however, when one knows Heathcliff the sufferer as well as Heathcliff the landlord, the word counts. It carries strong, if unspecified, emotional force, suggesting that some unspoken pain has caused him to declare, out of strict sequence, that he is the owner of Thrushcross Grange. The pain may come from remembering how he acquired the property and what he has lost; it may come from remembering the hurt the Grange has brought him ever since he and Catherine first visited it as children; it may come from being exposed to Lockwood's convoluted syntax. Whatever the source of the pain, the word *wincing* "condenses and concentrates the texture" of his opening speech in a way that single words seldom do in Jane Austen.

Even Mr. Lockwood's behavior on the first page of the novel takes on added dimension when reread in the knowledge of all that follows in the book. For all his stiffness, he negotiates a difficult introduction to a most unaccommodating man with some resourcefulness—something we can fully appreciate only after having witnessed Heathcliff's treatment of other strangers, and even kin. Furthermore, Lockwood reports the opening encounter to the reader with admirable dispatch. Emily Brontë's fictional world is more overtly dramatic than Jane Austen's in its verbal, social, and physical contrasts, but it is no less economical, even taut, in its expression of them.

Equally terse, yet forceful and suggestive, are the opening bars of the Grave introduction to the Sonata *Pathétique*. To listeners accustomed to hearing the clear articulation of an antecedent phrase at the beginning of a typical sonata in 1799, the harsh C-minor opening chord provided a powerful shock. The *fp* dynamics of the opening chord (a harsh minor-key *forte* sound being transformed immediately into a soft *piano*) are shocking in themselves. For here we have compressed into the smallest possible compass a sharp contrast in dynamics

27

and mood that Beethoven's classical predecessors tended to express in a more leisurely manner—and after careful preparation. The extension of the opening *fp* chord into a lyrical melodic phrase consisting of soft chords only compounds the effect: the power and brusqueness of the opening *forte* chord contrasts with the relative delicacy and garrulousness of the *piano* continuation as strongly as the speech patterns of Heathcliff contrast with those of Lockwood. In the first bar of the sonata, no less than on the first page of the novel, two conflicting principles are strongly contrasted (Figure 1).

Figure 1

The sense of conflict and resistance within bar 1 is further intensified by the rhythmic irregularities and the melodic motion of the lyrical continuation phrase. The emphatic dotted rhythm creates an abruptness and angularity of motion as marked as that of the opening conversation in the novel. Melodically, a subtle form of tension develops between the right hand in the treble and the left hand in the bass. As the main figure in the treble ascends and then falls, its counterpart in the bass descends and then rises. In music criticism this is called contrary motion. One must listen closely to hear it, but it does add density and tension to the opening bar. The contrary motion of Heathcliff's posture—barring the gate while asking Lockwood to "walk in"—adds comparable density and tension to the opening conversation.

As in the novel, a dramatic use of silence adds to the terse mystery in which the work begins. Following the harsh contrast between *forte* and *piano*, the irregular rhythm, and the contrary motion, the emphatic rest at the end of bar 1 adds to the exclamatory force of the whole. The silence it creates also prepares for the return of the entire opening phrase in ascending sequence in both bars 2 and 3. The shock of a strong *forte* breaking a silence, then, occurs not only at the beginning of bar 1 but also at the beginning of bars 2 and 3. In a manner typical of Beethoven, this twofold repetition intensifies the shock while at the same time making a pattern of it.

Now that the listener expects silence again toward the end of bar 3, the second half of the opening phrase extends itself into bar 4. This extension is the first "consequent" that has been given to the thrice-repeated "antecedent" of the opening phrase, and in this sense it creates a partial sense of equilibrium—as does Heathcliff's grudging invitation in the face of Lockwood's reiterated initiative. As in the novel, however, the sense of equilibrium is far from complete, for this belated response to the opening statement dissolves into passagework rather than resolving into a clear cadence. A descending scale completes the first stage of the introduction and leads to its second stage at the beginning of bar 5.

After Lockwood accepts Heathcliff's gruff invitation to "walk in" and regains his composure by reflecting condescendingly on the number of servants, he is ready to "inspect the penetralium" of the house itself. For a short time he is his garrulous, relaxed, somewhat discriminating self—until he is ferociously attacked by the huge dog he is foolish enough to provoke by making eyes at it. From that point on, he experiences a series of forceful shocks that startle him, that silence him, and that send him away at the end of chapter 3 an altered man on an uncharted path. Some of the shocks are harsh and violent: Heathcliff's language to "Mrs. Heathcliff" and the young boy; the dogs that attack Lockwood in both chapters 1 and 2. Others are more muted: the refusal of "Mrs. Heathcliff" to answer when addressed; Heathcliff's ominous silences; the mysterious relationship among the three principal residents. The shocks multiply when a heavy snow forces Lockwood to stay overnight. His harrowing night in the oak closet, where his blood-soaked dream-encounter with Cathy's ghost is followed by Heathcliff's grief-stricken appeals to the same specter, causes him to awaken a shaken man.

As Lockwood leaves the Heights at the end of chapter 3, he is coherent but severely disoriented. The social landmarks that have guided him all his life offer no clue by which he can understand the violent, strange individuals he has just encountered. Just as his moral landscape has been temporarily obliterated by his harsh introduction to the Heights, so has the very path by which he had arrived been obliterated by a "billowy, white ocean" of snow. "I had remarked on one side of the road, at intervals of six or seven yards, a line of upright stones, continued through the whole length of the barren: these were erected, and daubed with lime, on purpose to serve as guides in the dark, and also, when a fall, like the present, confounded the deep swamps on either hand with the firmer path; but, excepting a dirty dot pointing up here and there, all traces of their existence had vanished." As he traverses this altered landscape toward his refuge at Thrushcross Grange, he is guided by Heathcliff, an unlikely Virgil: "My companion found it necessary to warn me frequently to steer to the right or left, when I imagined I was following, correctly, the windings of the road" (p. 35). Lockwood's treacherous descent through the snow completes his introduction to Wuthering Heights.

Bars 5–10 complete the Grave introduction to the Sonata *Pathétique*. Like the concluding portion of Lockwood's introduction, they move from relative equilibrium to acute disorientation. Bar 5, which had been prepared for by the descending scale at the end of bar 4, introduces the original opening phrase in a new and harmonious key: E-flat major, the relative major of C minor (Figure 2).

Figure 2

Adding to the altered mood is the fact that the entire phrase is *piano* this time, the harsh opening chord having lost its *forte* force. With the opening chord softened, the minor-key dissonance supplanted, and the contrary motion in the bass replaced by stable chords in E-flat major, the feeling is one of flowing ease. Before the bar can end, however, this new mood is completely transformed by sudden *ff* chords anchored in the bass, which, using the dotted rhythmic figure from the opening phrase itself, create a new principle of opposition. This dramatic and new separation between treble and bass, between *p* and *ff*, and between major and minor keys removes the principle of conflict from the phrase itself and redistributes it between these two separate versions of the phrase. This two-phrase conflict is compressed into one bar—rather than the more leisurely two bars, punctuated by rests, in which the opening phrase was heard twice in bars 1 and 2. It is repeated in sequence in bar 6, with new harmonic changes increasing the tension. Here, too, Beethoven intensifies the shock while making a pattern of it.

Having twice been interrupted and smashed by the *ff* chords in the bass, the soft treble version of the phrase is suddenly allowed to expand itself in bars 7 and 8, much as did its earlier counterpart in bars 3 and 4. But it is no more able to find rest than was Mr. Lockwood within the confines of Wuthering Heights. This tentative treble continuation is accompanied in bars 7 and 8 by disturbing key changes, by ominous repeated chords that underline these changes in the bass, and by a rising *crescendo*. In bars 9 and 10 the bass is mostly silent as the treble continues to search, without success, for composure. Finally, the treble plunges into a scale which resembles the one at the end of bar 4 in its downward direction but differs from it in being entirely chromatic and in falling nearly three octaves. Its descending chromatic plunge is, as Eric Blom says, "a ruthless tearing up of this introductory page."[5]

The descending scale that ends the Grave introduction resembles Lockwood's perilous descent from the Heights in being a "transition" passage (in this case to what Blom calls the "fiery Allegro"). But the similarity goes deeper than that. As the new-fallen snow obliterates the stone markers by which Lockwood had earlier charted his course, so the descending chromatic scale blots out, for the moment, any sense of melodic stability in the right hand. The treble is able to keep its harmonic bearings only through the gruff notes sounded in the bass. The transition out of the Grave introduction is as ominous and unsettling as is Lockwood's descent, accompanied by Heathcliff, from Wuthering Heights.

Both the Grave introduction to Opus 13 and Mr. Lockwood's introduction to Heathcliff and the Heights have begun with terse, intense drama which, unfolding in two stages of increasing intensity, has ended in disorientation and radical ambiguity. The very first bar of the Sonata *Pathétique*, like the very first page of *Wuthering Heights*, dramatizes conflicting principles with an intensity, density, compression, and sense of resistance more extreme, more powerful, and more overtly violent than is typical of even the most dramatic works by such earlier artists as Mozart and Austen. The next nine bars of the sonata and the first three chapters of the novel go on to expand and intensify the conflicts between loud and soft, high and low, and major key and minor, on the one hand, and the conflicts between social backgrounds, verbal habits, and physical dispositions, on the other, in such a way that by the end of bar 10 and chapter 3 the polite nineteenth-century listener or reader has been transported into a brusque, violent world that is fraught with peril, that is uncharted by traditional social, psychological, and artistic traditions, and that is intensely exciting.

Each is also a world that for all its vehemence of expression seems to have a severe logic of its own. Each of the first eight bars of the Grave introduction has at least one version of the opening phrase, though none of those versions is the same. Each of those bars also embodies a striking conflict between loud and soft, between high and low, between major and minor, or between sound and silence. The first three chapters of the novel are themselves full of striking repetitions and variations. Just as Heathcliff fails to answer Mr. Lockwood's opening words on the first page of chapter 1, so does "Mrs. Heathcliff" fail to answer his attempted introduction in chapter 2. Just as a whole pack of dogs physically attack Lockwood in chapter 1, so is he again attacked by dogs in chapter 2. Just as the dogs which attack him in chapter 2 extinguish the lantern he is carrying as he attempts to escape from the Heights, so does a gust of wind blow out the candle he holds as he hears Heathcliff sobbing for Catherine's ghost in chapter 3. In both Brontë's and Beethoven's worlds forceful motifs are repeated again and again both for their short-range dramatic intensifying effect and for their long-range unifying structural effect, as we shall see.

One final similarity in these opening bars and opening pages is the emphasis on transformation. Just as the musical phrases and literary motifs cited above give unity to the opening of each work through repetition, so do they give contrast through transformation. Each successive version of the opening musical phrase is transformed by dynamics, register, rhythm, or harmony, making each manifestation different while remaining recognizably the same. The same is true of Lockwood's encounters with resistant people, dogs, and candles, each occurrence differing in its force, locale, level of energy, or element of surprise. These seemingly arbitrary changes in Lockwood's condition are as restless and fitful as those in the music. Such sudden and violent transformations of opening motifs contrast sharply with the opening of most works by Beethoven's and Brontë's classical predecessors, who tend to establish more secure patterns of stability, pace, and articulation from which later departures may be made. The first chapter of Austen's *Pride and Prejudice* and the opening bars of Mozart's Piano Concerto No. 9 (K. 271) illustrate this contrast of styles.

Pride and Prejudice begins with a celebrated opening sentence: "It is a truth universally acknowledged that a single man in possession of a good fortune must be in want of a wife." The rest of chapter 1 is brief, consisting of a conversation between Mr. and Mrs. Bennet in which they, and Mrs. Bennet in particular, apply this proposition to a certain Mr. Bingley, newly arrived at nearby Netherfield Park. As in *Wuthering Heights*, the opening conversation is brimming with tension. Mr. and Mrs. Bennet are not strangers in the sense that Mr. Lockwood and Heathcliff are: they have been married for twenty-three years. Even so, there is plenty of conflict between them. In fact, the concise first chapter, which occupies only three pages, reveals a complete contrast of character simply through their speech patterns. This is so even though the conversation is composed of perfectly balanced antecedents and consequents which on the surface—if only on the surface—indicate perfect harmony.

Mr. Bennet disagrees completely with his wife's approach to the topic under discussion. Yet he neither interrupts her nor cuts her off. Instead he makes a game of his discomfort, ironically avoiding overt confrontation through mental arabesques that allow him to express his individuality and disdain. He does this with technically polite questions ("Is he married or single?"), with devastating commonplaces ("In such cases, a woman has not often much beauty to think of"), and with ironic reassurances ("You mistake me, my dear. I have a high respect for your nerves. They are my old friends").[6] All of the tension and resistance buried in these opening pages is distanced by the conventions of the comedy of manners, the same conventions that Heathcliff so brusquely ignores in his more vehement opening encounter with Mr. Lockwood. The narrator's restrained presentation of the Bennet conversation contains no indication that Mr. Bennet winces, though no doubt he does. Nor is there the slightest indication of the physical posture of the speakers. The tension, while strong, is entirely between the lines, as it were. There are exclamation marks in half of Mrs. Bennet's utterances, but they are so habitual with her that they lose any force. All the force in this exchange is with Mr. Bennet, who never exclaims.[7]

Mozart's Piano Concerto No. 9, like Beethoven's Opus 13, begins with an unusually condensed passage of tension and conflict. But the feeling is paradoxically one of expansion and ease. As soon as the orchestra begins the opening theme in the first bar, the piano interrupts—and completes—that theme in bars 2 and 3. The interruption is shocking because it is unexpected; in no other

Mozart piano concerto does the solo enter until the orchestra has finished its entire exposition. Because the solo answers the orchestra's antecedent phrase with a satisfying consequent phrase, however, its individuality disrupts the surface harmony no more than does Mr. Bennet's on the first page of *Pride and Prejudice*. As Rosen puts it, "the stately" is not only "opposed to the impertinent," but is "balanced perfectly by it."[8] No less than Beethoven and Brontë, Mozart and Austen are capable of compressing a conflict into a small space. When they do so, however, the threshold of overt violence tends to be considerably lower.

We mentioned above that Beethoven intensified the shock of the first bar of the Grave introduction, and made a pattern of it at the same time, by repeating the opening phrase in sequence in bars 2 and 3. Mozart intensifies the shock of the piano's interruption, and makes a pattern of it, when he repeats the first three bars of the concerto in bars 4–6. There is, however, an important difference. Whereas Beethoven's repetitions already begin to transform the theme, Mozart's repeat is exact. And this will be essentially true of the opening theme each time it returns throughout the entire first movement. The "shock" of the piano's interruption of the orchestra's theme recurs at the beginning of the solo exposition, at the beginning of the development, at the beginning of the recapitulation, and at the beginning of the coda, thereby creating a long-range structural pattern as well as a short-range dynamic one. But at each restatement the notes of this opening theme remain the same, the only variation in the pattern coming at the beginning of the recapitulation, where the solo and orchestra briefly steal each other's material—another "shock" that is softened by the comedy of manners in which it occurs. This theme, unlike that of Beethoven's Grave introduction, is not transformed by the experience it undergoes. It changes no more in the course of the first movement than does the stalemate between Mr. and Mrs. Bennet in the course of the first volume, even though the tensions it contains just below the surface, like the tensions between the Bennets, are highly expressive.

The four "beginnings" briefly discussed here illustrate Paul Henry Lang's contention that "Romanticism should not be taken as the antithesis of classicism, nor was it a mere reaction to it, but rather a logical enhancement of certain elements which in classicism were inherent and active, but tamed and kept in equilibrium." Lang claims that the same "subjectivist" tendencies are present in both period styles, the essential difference being in the added "vehemence" with which they tend to be expressed by the more Romantic artist.[9] Heathcliff's opening conversation, in contrast to that of Mr. Bennet, measures just such an increment of vehemence, as do the first three bars of the Sonata

Pathétique in contrast to those of Piano Concerto No. 9. Even so, these more vehement beginnings by Brontë and Beethoven do achieve a kind of equilibrium. It is a Romantic equilibrium resulting from the powerful restraint with which the vehemence is expressed—and from the patterns made by the resultant shocks.

Classical Frames

Having considered some of the short-range ways in which the opening bars and the opening pages of the Sonata *Pathétique* and *Wuthering Heights* have "condensed and concentrated the texture" of their classical predecessors, let us now examine some of the long-range structural patterns which allow these two works to express a Romantic intensity within the confines of a classical frame. In considering the long-range structure of either work we must begin with the sections we have already discussed: the introductions. Dramatic in themselves, the two introductions both play complex and interesting roles in the narratives that follow.

Structurally, the first three chapters of *Wuthering Heights* are an introduction to the narrative per se. Similarly, the last three chapters, in which Lockwood returns to the Heights in 1802 and again interacts with some of the characters, are an appendage to the main story. That story, told by Nelly, begins in chapter 4 and runs nearly thirty chapters, overlapping with the conclusion involving Mr. Lockwood again at the end. It consists of Nelly's history of Wuthering Heights, Thrushcross Grange, and their inhabitants, beginning in the 1770s and running up to the perplexing situation Lockwood encounters when he arrives in 1801. Mr. Lockwood, therefore, is not involved in the bulk of the story, which has occurred long before his first visit to the Heights. That story unfolds in two long narrative arcs. The first, running from chapter 4 through the beginning of chapter 16, features the love story of Heathcliff and Catherine and concludes with Catherine's death. The second, beginning with the second Catherine's birth at the beginning of chapter 16, features Heathcliff's implacable revenge and curious death, linking up at the end with Lockwood's return and with the impending marriage of the second Cathy and Hareton.

At the beginning of this chapter, I suggested that Mr. Lockwood was the one character in *Wuthering Heights* who could have been at home in a novel by Jane Austen. For the sake of argument, let us assume that this *is* an Austen novel and that the first three chapters are not introductory to the main action but in fact central to it. Here is what we would find. Two young people are in love with each other but do not yet realize it because pride and prejudice blind them to each other's sterling qualities. Hareton's pride, affronted by the manner in which Cathy and her erstwhile husband Linton have made fun of his ignorance, prevents him from acknowledging even to himself how much he loves her. And Cathy's prejudice against someone so lowborn and uncouth causes her to be unaware of her own regard for him. In addition, an external obstacle blocks the growth of true love. Heathcliff keeps them at each other's throats, creating an atmosphere inimical to thoughts of love.

Lockwood's own pride and prejudice, in the opening chapters, prevent him from perceiving these dynamics. At first he assumes that the young woman is married to Heathcliff. He then assumes, again wrongly, that she is married to "the clown at my elbow, who is drinking his tea out of a basin and eating his bread with unwashed hands . . . Heathcliff, junior, of course." He further assumes that Cathy, as "the consequence of being buried alive," has "thrown herself away upon that boor, from sheer ignorance that better individuals existed! A sad pity—I must beware how I cause her to regret her choice." Justifying this fantasy that the attractive young woman will be attracted to himself, Lockwood allows that "the last reflection may seem conceited; it was not. My neighbor struck me as bordering on repulsive. I knew, through experience, that I was tolerably attractive" (p. 21).

The three chapters that conclude the novel feature a perfect comic reversal of the deceptions and self-deceptions that Lockwood, Hareton, and Cathy experience in the introduction. Cathy does marry "the clown" at Lockwood's elbow— and with good reason. What is more, Lockwood, so quick to meddle and to make assumptions early in the novel, has learned some tact and restraint. As late as chapter 31, when Nelly had finished her story in January of 1802 and Lockwood was about to leave the Heights, he was still thinking of Cathy as a fantasy object: "Living among clowns and misanthropists, she probably cannot appreciate a better class of people, when she meets them" (p. 240). In the next chapter, however, when he returns in September of 1802 and sees Cathy and Hareton studying together through the window, he acts with more modesty and dignity. Seeing them about to "issue out and have a walk on the moors," he does not intervene, as he might well have done earlier in the novel, but rather swings around to the back kitchen in order to speak with Nelly. He has grown enough to value Cathy and Hareton's love, as they have grown enough to achieve it. In the previous chapter Cathy had openly made fun of Hareton's ignorance, causing him to toss into the fire the precious books he was assiduously studying in order to please her; now, as Mr. Lockwood looks in through the window, the two are lovingly studying together in the light of the fire.

At the Lockwood-Cathy-Hareton level, the last three chapters resolve the mystery and tension of the first three chapters and leave us with a happy ending as conventional as those in Austen's novels. What is more, the process takes about one year, the average time span in an Austen novel.[10] Lockwood first arrives in November of 1801 and returns the following November. Cathy and Hareton are engaged to be married at New Year's.

Within the frame of this comic love story, which features the reversals, the obstacles, and the typical time span of an Austen novel, we find the "real" *Wuthering Heights*—the tragic love story of Catherine and Heathcliff that Nelly begins in chapter 4 and begins to conclude in chapter 30: "Thus ended Mrs. Dean's story" (p. 236). Narrated through a long flashback, this story takes thirty years, not one. It too is a story of pride (Heathcliff's) and prejudice (Catherine's). But it ends in death and separation, not courtship and marriage. This is the story that will be discussed in the next chapter, along with Beethoven's *Appassionata*. It is often said of Beethoven that he expanded the classical forms and filled them with Romantic material. The account I have just given of the "outer" structure of *Wuthering Heights* shows one way in which Emily Brontë expanded Jane Austen's forms to a similar effect. The full force of the tension between the essentially comic outer story and the essentially tragic inner one will not be felt, of course, until we consider Heathcliff and Catherine, as we do in the chapter to come.

In this connection, a word must be said about the original division of the novel into two volumes. Although Lockwood nearly drops out of the novel during Nelly's account of the historical tale, there are times when her narrative is interrupted in order to remind us of the narrative present. One such interruption comes in the last paragraph of chapter 9— "At this point of the housekeeper's story, she chanced to glance towards the time-piece over the chimney" (p. 80)— and continues a few paragraphs into chapter 10. The next major break comes, significantly, at the end of volume 1 in the original edition.

Nelly, running on in chapter 14, has been wondering aloud to Lockwood whether she was right in having given a letter from Heathcliff to the then-married Catherine Earnshaw Linton. She is interrupted by the arrival of Kenneth, the doctor who ministers to Lockwood as well as to most of the characters in the historical tale. Nelly's last words in volume 1 are these: "But here is Kenneth; I'll go down, and tell him how much better you are. My history is dree as we say, and will serve to wile away another morning." The volume ends with Lockwood's commentary, set off by double spacing: "Dree, and dreary! I reflected as the good woman descended to receive the doctor." This shift emphasizes the comic frame in which the tragic narrative is set. It also allows Lockwood to fantasize again about the young woman in the opening chapters: "Let me beware of the fascination that lurks in Catherine Heathcliff's brilliant eyes. I should be in a curious taking if I surrendered my heart to that young person, and the daughter turned out a second edition of the mother!" (p. 130). We must wait until volume 2 to find out what happened when Nelly did deliver Heathcliff's letter, seventeen years before, to the Catherine who was by then Edgar Linton's wife.

Technically, the second volume of the novel begins not with the burning climax to Catherine and Heathcliff's love story, which follows soon enough in chapter 15, but with Mr. Lockwood's convalescence. "Another week over—and I am so many days nearer health, and spring! I have now heard all my neighbour's history, at different sittings, as the housekeeper could spare time from more important occupations" (p. 130). Whether the division into volumes 1 and 2 was made by the publisher or by the author, it functions exceedingly well in maintaining the dual structure—and thus the Romantic equilibrium—of the novel. It does so by sharpening the distinction between Lockwood's story and Nelly's, between the tragic love story and its comic frame. It is a division I feel should be retained in modern reprints.

Having seen now how the structure of *Wuthering Heights* serves to enclose a tragic tale within an essentially comic frame, it will be revealing to take a closer look at the structure of the Sonata *Pathétique* and the material it contains. As stated before, the overt structure of its three movements, apart from the Grave introduction, is perfectly conventional. The fast-slow-fast progression of the movements, the home-away-home key progressions, and the "textbook" shape of the opening Allegro, the slow movement, and the finale closely follow the clearly articulated structures of Beethoven's classical predecessors. Yet this work, especially on early encounters, seems vehemently Romantic. Let us briefly consider why.

We have already discussed the most obvious reason: the ten-bar Grave introduction that establishes a mood of vehement expression, of sharp conflict and contrast, and of mysterious premonition before the opening Allegro even gets under way. Of all of Beethoven's striking introductions, this one was seized upon most eagerly by his Romantic successors as a model for creating a powerful mood before the beginning of the exposition per se. But the function of this introduction does not end there. Twice the Grave introduction, with its ominous silences, its crashing chords, and its soulful melody, invades the Allegro itself. Its first incursion occurs immediately before the development section begins, the second during the coda. Furthermore, part of its opening phrase is actually combined with the first theme of the Allegro during the development section.

Such integration between the introduction and the Allegro intensifies the dramatic short-range emotion of the movement at the same time that it expands the long-range expressive possibilities of the sonata-allegro form. It is one of the earliest examples of the "organic" form that would distinguish Beethoven's contribution to the development of the sonata structure.[11]

Apart from the two incursions from the introduction, the overt form of the Allegro molto e con brio could hardly be more regular. There is an exposition, a development, a recapitulation, and a coda. The exposition consists of an impulsive first theme, a dramatic bridge passage, a contrasting, more lyrical second theme, and an ascending closing theme. After these have all been introduced, the entire exposition is given an exact repeat. This repeat, however, instead of creating a mirrorlike unity, has an asymmetrical effect, for it does not include the most dramatic music we have heard so far—the Grave introduction. In this context, the dramatic intrusion of material from the Grave after the repeat of the exposition at once violates our expectation that the development section will begin immediately after the repeat of the exposition, *and* gratifies our need to hear all of the earlier material before going on to the development. This is a striking example of Beethoven's ability to maintain the classical principles of equilibrium and proportion while at the same time expanding and straining them.

Numerous examples of tension achieved through equilibrium and equilibrium achieved through tension can also be found within the exposition itself. All of the themes, the impetuous first theme (bars 1–24), the bold bridge passage (25–41), the lyrical second theme (42–78), and the ascending closing theme (79–102) consist within themselves of melodic repetition obvious to the ear. (For example, the eight-bar melody of the first theme literally repeats itself.) Yet because of the melodic, rhythmic, and harmonic contrast within and among these themes, the effect is one of impetuous forward thrust. In *The Sonata in the Classic Era* Newman used a series of examples from this movement to illustrate Beethoven's ability to expand and intensify the range of the sonata-allegro form while remaining true, at the same time, to its traditional sequences and proportions.

> Here we may note how, besides motivic cumulation, Beethoven had other means of intensifying if not actually peculiarizing the melodic, rhythmic, and harmonic flow in his sonatas. The metric drive in his quick movements may be heightened by the almost inexorable persistence of simple accompaniment figures, as in Op. 13/i/11–27, where the impelling broken octaves that set up the hot pulse are scarcely recognizable as the erstwhile lowly murky bass. . . . At the same time, tension may be added to the metric drive by unexpected thrusts on the "weak"

beats, as by the right-hand syncopations in the same theme of Op. 13, or by the right-hand *sforzando* octaves (mss. 27–28 and 31–32) in the bridge that follows. And, in turn, these thrusts may be pointed up by stinging harmonic dissonances, as by the double appoggiaturas on the offbeats in the continuation of that bridge (mss. 45–49). Moreover, the increasingly refined articulation may contribute to the headlong rush by further defining the shifts of accents, as in the development section of the same movement, where left-hand, two-note slurs convert adjacent pairs of beats from weak-strong to strong-weak (mss. 149–158). And the dynamic markings may contribute, whether they see a crescendo to its logical climax (mss. 137–139) or "disappoint" it in a "Beethoven *piano*" (mss. 207–211). (p. 129)

The elements of Beethoven's keyboard style summarized here—the inexorable metric drive, the hot pulse of broken octaves, the unexpected thrusts on weak beats, the shifting of accents from weak-strong to strong-weak, and the powerful climaxes achieved or disappointed—are the qualities that, in their vehemence and force, most distinguish his style from that of his classical predecessors. Comparably vehement and forceful qualities distinguish Emily Brontë's style from that of her fictional predecessors. Her methods of intensification have already received some attention in our discussion of the Lockwood introduction. A more systematic treatment of such qualities appears in the chapter to come, where comparison of the central Heathcliff section of the novel with the *Appassionata* makes possible even more forceful juxtapositions.

In the present context it is enough to point out that the elements of Beethoven's style that Newman summarizes here are the qualities Tovey had in mind when he wrote that "the pianoforte style" of the Sonata *Pathétique* "utterly eclipsed anything Mozart could conceive." Yet this style is expressed within a classical structure deriving directly from Mozart's precedent. Such vehement expressiveness within a classical frame is one measure of Beethoven's Romantic equilibrium, as is Brontë's framing of the Heathcliff story within the Lockwood story.

In its harmonic structure, too, the first movement of the Sonata *Pathétique* reveals a Romantic expressiveness within a classical frame. As expected from its key signature and from classical precedent, the movement per se begins in the key of C minor and ends in the key of C minor, with some harmonic contrasts in between. Within this expected home-away-home pattern, however, Beethoven makes certain departures from the traditional key progressions that express harmonic pressures reminiscent of those in the Grave introduction. At the beginning of the Allegro the plunging chromatic scale of the Grave gives way to the first theme in the "home" key of C minor. But the presentation of that theme is harmonically ambiguous; "much of it is strongly F minor."[12] The second theme begins not in the relative major, E-flat major, as expected, but in E-flat minor. The Grave intrusion before the beginning of the development section begins in G minor and quickly, hauntingly modulates to the remote key of E minor, in which the development begins. The recapitulation begins, as expected, in the home key of C minor. But the contrasting lyrical theme, now expected in C minor, returns in F minor before modulating to the home key, which then prevails during the rest of the recapitulation and the coda.

The above departures from expectation add to the mystery and power of the first movement and give its C-minor tonality an even darker flavor than it would otherwise have. Beethoven imbues the traditional home-away-home harmonic boundaries with as much inner tension and surprise as Emily Brontë does the narrow, yet dramatic geographical boundaries of her novel.

As one would expect from the music of Beethoven's classical predecessors, the first movement of the Sonata *Pathétique* is followed by a contrasting second movement. After the fiery Allegro comes a soulful Adagio cantabile. After C minor comes the contrasting key of A-flat major. After a tense sonata-allegro movement preceded and interrupted by a Grave introduction comes a simple structure based on a songlike refrain punctuated by two episodes (a:b:a:c:a form). In place of propulsive rhythms and impetuous thematic material is the measured pulse of an unending melody. Because of the variety of ways in which Beethoven has intensified the norms of classical expression in the first movement of the *Pathétique*, this movement seems even more hymnlike and calm than it would if found in a sonata by his classical predecessors. The contrast between the flowing grace of the Adagio cantabile and the impetuosity of the Allegro is so great that the traditional comparison is that of a calm following a storm—an effect to be achieved with even more force, of course, in the second movement of Opus 57, the *Appassionata*.

The prevailing mood of this movement is immediately established by the glorious opening melody in A-flat major. The melody is intrinsically soothing, even consoling, but its effect is heightened by the fact that there was no comparable moment of grace in the first movement. There the lyrical second theme, though it contrasted with the first, was still propulsive in its motion. That theme had eventually reached the key of E-flat major, but the fact that it was originally introduced in E-flat minor makes this opening theme of the Adagio cantabile the first melody in the entire sonata to have begun in a major key, a fact that greatly heightens its pathos. The most dramatic patch of major-key melody in the first movement had come in the Grave introduction, when the opening theme had been restated softly in E-flat major in bar 5—only to be crushed by the *forte* answer in the same bar. Here the spacious eight-bar melody not only unfolds undisturbed but is answered in full an octave higher, creating in the contrast of registers a principle of dialogue that will be characteristic of much of the movement.

Following the eight-bar opening melody and its eight-bar repetition an octave higher (the "a" section of the movement), the first episode (b) begins in the key of F minor, changing the harmonic mood considerably. This sets up a welcome return of the opening melody (a) in its original key, but without its melodic extension. The second episode (c) enters in the harmonically remote key of A-flat minor. Here the contrast with the soothing melody becomes increasingly intense, being expressed in a dialogue between treble and bass that reaches an impassioned eloquence before subsiding again into the comforting strains of the opening melody (a), again in A-flat major. After the melody is again answered an octave higher, a coda follows whose new theme animates the end of this movement and anticipates the movement to come.

This soulful Adagio cantabile has prompted much speculation as to its biographical (and literary) meaning for Beethoven, much of it fueled by an 1823 entry in his Conversation Books. The composer, responding to Schindler's observation that "two principles" are operating in the movement, not only agreed with him but allegedly suggested that the music represents an extended dialogue between a man and a woman that is finally resolved at the end of his next two sonatas, Opus 14. From this thin biographical thread hang whole theories connecting the Sonata *Pathétique* to Beethoven's own love life or to such legendary unfortunates as Romeo and Juliet or Hero and Leander.[13] But even critics who eschew such one-to-one reductionism have found the entry in the Conversation Book highly suggestive. Mathis Lussy wrote an entire book on Opus 13 which interprets the sonata as "a contest between an unhappy man and fate."[14] The musical urgency and drama of the *Pathétique* do suggest such a contest, whether or not one is moved to relate it to the particulars of Beethoven's daily life or possible literary inspiration. As "a contest between an unhappy man and fate," this work anticipates the even more passionate *Appassionata*.

Arnold Schmitz expanded the Schindler-Beethoven conversation about the "two principles" in the second movement of the Sonata *Pathétique* into a book in which the "zwei Prinzipe" are seen as the key to Beethoven's character and his style throughout his musical career.[15] Ernest Newman, in a famous essay on the later Beethoven, advanced the same argument, also with reference to the 1823 Conversation Book.

A certain principle of polarity can be seen to underlie all his thinking, a tendency to conceive and manipulate things in antitheses. We can trace this tendency from its cell form to its full organic growth. It reveals itself first of all in a bias towards an antithesis within the narrow limits of a phrase, then in an antithesis within the sentence, then in the dramatic antithesis of leading themes indicative of a conflict of psychological "principles"—and so on to the total work as a purposeful antithesis of movements. . . . The whole of his more significant work has been one attempt after another, in the most protean of forms, to balance forces in the world of ideas and emotions which he felt to be locked in an inveterate struggle.[16]

From the vantage point of the later Beethoven, Opus 13 is an early attempt at expressing the kind of contrasting principles that will find even more protean expression in such works as the *Appassionata* and Opus 111. The context provided by the later works helps to measure the degree to which the Sonata *Pathétique*, while strongly expressive of Beethoven's powerful psyche, still contains its vehemence within a classical frame.

Even so, one would not want to underestimate either the fateful mood or the expression of polarity within Opus 13 itself. Whatever Beethoven's actual program, if any, for the second movement, he created striking contrasts between the refrain and the episodes, between major and minor, and between the voices that embody dialogue from low to high and from high to low. More striking, of course, is the principle of contrast as it operates between the second movement and the first. Had the first movement not been so obsessively impetuous or so relentlessly minor-key in its harmonic gestures, the Adagio cantabile might have been felt simply as a contrasting movement, rather than also as a *principle* in contrast to that of the first. The entire impetus to experience the sonata as expressive of contrasting principles and not simply contrasting materials, began, of course, in the first bar of the Grave introduction, in the strong polarity between the *fp* chord and its *piano* successors in the opening phrase.

The principle of polarity established in the opening bars of the Grave introduction returned when material from the Grave twice invaded the Allegro itself. Its first return established a period of calm between the exposition and the development sections—but only after the harshness of its opening *fp* chord. The second return, in the coda, more purely represented the principle of calm, for the opening *forte* chord was this time omitted. This majestic passage began *p*, built slowly to a *sf*, and then returned to a hushed *pp* chord—only to be crushed by eleven bars of the stormy first theme of the Allegro, which returned with a vengeance and built to a full crescendo on *ff* chords.

As was noted above, these dramatic returns of the Grave introduction within the Allegro contribute both to its short-range dynamic contrasts and its long-range structural balance. They also insinuate the principle of calm into the world of storm, anticipating and foreshadowing the soothing world of the second movement. This effect of the Grave introduction in bridging from the Allegro to the Adagio contributes, both structurally and emotionally, to the organic relationship between the two movements and to the transformation of their contrasting materials into contrasting principles as well.

Comparable principles of polarity and transformation operate in *Wuthering Heights*, even in the Lockwood portion of the novel we have been analyzing in connection with Opus 13. In the first three chapters Wuthering Heights itself comes to embody the principle of human and psychological storm. This symbolic function arises from the tempestuous human situations Mr. Lockwood encounters there, both in his waking life and in his dreams. It also arises from the name of the dwelling and from its physical location. Mr. Lockwood's description is justly famous.

> Wuthering Heights is the name of Mr. Heathcliff's dwelling. "Wuthering" being a significant provincial adjective, descriptive of the atmospheric tumult to which its station is exposed in stormy weather. Pure, bracing ventilation they must have up there, at all times, indeed: one may guess the power of the north wind, blowing over the edge, by the excessive slant of a few stunted firs at the end of the house; and by a range of gaunt thorns all stretching their limbs one way, as if craving alms of the sun. (p. 14)

Thrushcross Grange, by contrast, is situated calmly in a valley, surrounded by fruit trees. Because of this, and also because it soon becomes for Lockwood a strongly wished-for refuge from the tumult he experiences at the Heights, it comes to embody the principle of calm. If Thrushcross Grange were in a Jane Austen novel, we might say that it *is* calm but not that it represents a *principle* of calm. Being juxtaposed with Wuthering Heights, however, it acquires a symbolically dualistic meaning it might not have in another context—as does the "calm" Adagio cantabile of Opus 13 when juxtaposed with the "stormy" Grave and the "fiery" Allegro. This symbolic polarity expressed by the Grange and the Heights, of course, becomes even more evident in the Heathcliff part of the story that will be compared with the *Appassionata*.

The dichotomy between storm and calm that is symbolically established in the Lockwood section of *Wuthering Heights* is quite literally present as well. We have already mentioned the actual snowstorm that transforms the surrounding landscape into a "billowy, white ocean" in chapter 3, forcing Mr. Lockwood to spend an unwelcome night at the Heights. When Lockwood returns to the

Heights at the end of the novel in 1802 he experiences "sweet, warm weather—too warm for travelling; . . . In winter, nothing more dreary, in summer, nothing more divine, than those glens shut in by hills, and those bluff, bold swells of heath" (p. 241). The principle of calm has quite literally transformed the house and its inhabitants as well. The gate, when Lockwood approaches it, is no longer shut. Heathcliff is dead. Hareton and Cathy are happy and harmonious. The last paragraph of the novel is as calm as its opening pages were stormy: "I lingered round [the graves], under that benign sky; watched the moths fluttering among the heath and hare-bells; listened to the soft wind breathing through the grass; and wondered how any one could ever imagine unquiet slumbers for the sleepers in that quiet earth" (p. 266).

As striking as these contrasts between storm and calm may be, those in the Heathcliff part of the novel are much stronger, with the "storm" principle embodied so inexorably that the reader who reaches the last page can well imagine "unquiet slumbers" under that "quiet earth," whereas the "calm" principle is embodied so ethereally that the same reader can also imagine, above that earth, unearthly animation.

The third movement of the Sonata *Pathétique* is often felt to be a disappointing anticlimax following the impetuous, brute force of the first movement and the wonderful calm of the second. Indeed, the problem of ending a vehement minor-key work with sufficient force was to occupy Beethoven throughout his career. The rondo form bequeathed to him by his classical predecessors was wonderfully adapted to the conventional "happy ending" expected in the major-key works that predominate in the output not only of Haydn and Mozart but of Beethoven himself. But the loose, episodic structure of the rondo did not lend itself so well to the few but powerful minor-key works by these composers. Mozart's best solutions to the problem are found in the theme-and-variations finale to his C-minor Piano Concerto (K. 491) and in the sonata-allegro finale to his late G-minor Symphony (K. 550).

Beethoven's solutions were to take three forms: powerful major-key transformations (the last movements of the Fifth and the Ninth symphonies); relentless minor-key fury (the last movement of the *Appassionata*); and ethereal major-key transformation (the Arietta of Opus 111). These varying solutions had not only their technical but also a spiritual side. Before Beethoven wrote the finale to the *Appassionata* or to the Fifth Symphony he was to undergo the struggle against deafness so movingly attested to by the Heiligenstadt Testament of 1802. Before he wrote the finale of the Ninth Symphony or the Arietta of his last sonata he was to live another twenty years without the normal use of his precious ears. When he composed the *Pathétique* in 1798, he was twenty-eight years old (the age at which Emily Brontë finished *Wuthering Heights*). He poured his finale into the conventional rondo form, leaving his most probing resolutions of the storm-calm dichotomy for the future—and contrasting—solutions of the *Appassionata* and Opus 111. In 1801 a major step toward an adequate third-movement expression of the vehement side of his character was to come in the finale to the *Moonlight* Sonata, where he employed, instead of the rondo, the more serious sonata-allegro form. This advance was to be consolidated in the *Appassionata*.

Just as many listeners feel that the concluding rondo of Beethoven's Sonata *Pathétique* does not do justice to the turbulent passion of the first movement, so many readers feel that the relatively conventional Lockwood-Cathy-Hareton conclusion to *Wuthering Heights* does not do justice to the turbulent world it encloses. Even classical artists such as Mozart and Austen, of course, are occasionally criticized for endings that are felt to be too conventional. (The third volume of *Pride and Prejudice* and the third movement of Mozart's Piano Concerto No. 21, K. 467, and often so criticized.) Such objections to the endings of the Sonata *Pathétique* and *Wuthering Heights*, however, seem to be much more strongly felt, for the vehemence of these works sets up expectations which the loose-knit rondo, however appropriate its material, and the novelistic "happy ending," however carefully prepared, have great difficulty satisfying. Yet the fact that Beethoven and Brontë did pour their passion into conventional forms which they made strong and capacious enough to hold it does give their Romantic art a different kind of meaning from that of those artists who abandoned those forms altogether. In this sense their Romantic equilibrium contrasts with the Romantic transformation typical of such artists as Poe or Chopin.

At the end of Poe's "Fall of the House of Usher" the Lockwood-like narrator flees from the total dissolution of the house he had approached on the first page of the story. At the end of Chopin's "Funeral March" Sonata, an ambiguous one-minute Presto brings a four-movement structure to a radically abrupt end. Chopin's concluding Presto "tears up" the sonata even more than the plunging scale that disrupts the end of the Grave introduction of the *Pathétique*. But its radical ambiguities are allowed to end the entire work, not just the introduction to an opening movement. Similarly, Poe's *Narrative of Arthur Gordon Pym* concludes with the narrator plunging into a "billowy, white ocean" near the South Pole from which he, unlike Mr. Lockwood in chapter 3, does not return home. Beethoven and Brontë resemble Chopin and Poe in the radical ambiguities and discontinuities they characteristically evoke; they differ in the ways in which they tend to resolve—or transcend—them by the end of the work.

Humor

Finally, a word must be said about the humor in Beethoven and Brontë, for this will be the only place to say it. The Lockwood section of *Wuthering Heights* contains considerable humor, especially in the three opening chapters. Humor is not a strong characteristic of the Heathcliff part of the novel, which moves rather in the realm of sarcasm and scorn. Nor is humor a strong characteristic of Opus 13, Opus 57, or Opus 111. Much of Beethoven's music, however, does express the kind of humor that is found in the early pages of *Wuthering Heights*.

The social comedy implicit in the contrast between Mr. Lockwood's and Heathcliff's diction on the opening page continues throughout the first three chapters. Lockwood is awkwardly juxtaposed not only with Heathcliff and Joseph, not only with "Mrs. Heathcliff" and "the clown," but with a variety of animals, dead and alive. In every case, the difference in language, background, disposition, and situation is so strong that Lockwood hardly knows how to behave. Instead of the fine gradations of juxtaposition that make for wit based on common assumptions in the socially homogeneous world of Jane Austen, we have here the gross juxtapositions of the heterogeneous that make for humor, much of it physical and some of it verging on the slapstick.

A prime example of such broad-scale humor comes when Mr. Lockwood, still in chapter 1, decides to insult three of Heathcliff's dogs by making eyes at them—a scene that echoes his eyes-only seaside flirtation, described a page earlier.

> Not anxious to come into contact with their fangs, I sat still; but, imagining they would scarcely understand tacit insults, I unfortunately indulged in winking and making faces at the trio, and some turn of my physiognomy so irritated madam, that she suddenly broke into a fury and leapt on my knees. I flung her back, and hastened to interpose the table between us. This proceeding roused the whole hive. Half-a-dozen four-footed fiends, of various sizes and ages, issued from hidden dens to the common centre. I felt my heels and coat-laps peculiar objects of assault; and, parrying off the larger combatants as effectually as I could with the poker, I was constrained to demand, aloud, assistance from some of the household in re-establishing peace. (p. 16)

Mr. Lockwood's refined language, ill-equipped for descriptions of physical activity, contributes mightily to the humorous effect. So does his acute physical discomfort. The awkward movement of his body matches that of his syntax, resulting in humor more rustic than genteel. A few pages later, he assumes that

"Mrs. Heathcliff," with whom he is trying to ingratiate himself, is favorably disposed to the "dogs" on the couch; they turn out to be dead rabbits.

Beethoven, too, delights in rustic juxtapositions. These often take the form of unexpected harmonies and unprepared accents which break through the classical forms seemingly designed to contain them. Such breakthroughs, when not tragically disorienting, tend to be ponderously humorous. Examples abound in the early sonatas and symphonies. Among the piano sonatas the finale of Opus 10, No. 3, which precedes the *Pathétique*, is a fine example. The miniature rondo can hardly carry the powerful material given to it in the episodes. An even more ponderous example is the trio of the Fifth Symphony, memorably compared by Berlioz to the "gambols of a frolicsome elephant." Reportedly, Beethoven played the last movement of the *Pathétique*, the rondo in C minor, with gruff humor. Czerny reports that Beethoven would improvise at the keyboard with such expression and originality that his listeners would be moved not only to tears but to "loud sobs"—after which he "would burst into loud laughter and banter his hearers on the emotion he had caused them."[17]

Mozart, of course, "very rarely allowed his music to express that degree of incongruity indulged in" by Beethoven.[18] Austen likewise eschewed the kind of rustic abruptness to which Brontë subjected Lockwood. But in Brontë and Beethoven, the humor, no less than the pain, can assault the beholder with physical force.

Chapter Two

Heathcliff and the *Appassionata*: Elemental Strife, Organic Form

The strongest link between the Heathcliff story of *Wuthering Heights* and Beethoven's *Appassionata* is the quality of emotion that each expresses. When Cecil writes that Emily Brontë's characters have "extremely intense emotions, the most intense in English fiction," he is writing about Heathcliff and Catherine, not Mr. Lockwood. As intense as are the emotions of the Sonata *Pathétique* (1799), they are dwarfed by those of the *Appassionata* (1804–5). The "two currents" that Rolland finds in Beethoven's character—"vast love, vast scorn"—nowhere clash more violently than in Opus 57; nor in English fiction do such currents clash more violently than in the love of Heathcliff and Catherine. The "passionate ferocity" that the *Britannia* reviewer found to dominate *Wuthering Heights* dominates the *Appassionata* too; in each case the ferocity of the psychic strife seems inextricably related to the elemental strife of nature.

David Cecil's famous analysis of the storm/calm dichotomy in *Wuthering Heights* applies even more obviously to the *Appassionata*. Cecil argues that the novel's "whole created cosmos, animate and inanimate, mental and physical alike, is the expression of certain living spiritual principles—on the one hand what might be called the principle of storm — of the harsh, the ruthless, the wild, the dynamic; and on the other the principle of calm—of the gentle, the merciful, the passive, and the tame."[1] In the history of the piano sonata before 1805 it would be difficult to find music more "harsh, ruthless, wild, and dynamic" than the outer movements of Beethoven's *Appassionata*—or music more "gentle, merciful, passive, and tame" than its inner movement. Nor could one easily find a musical work of such scale whose "whole created cosmos" consists of such a stark contrast between two such principles.[2] The contrast between the principles of storm and calm pervades all components of the work: melodic, harmonic, rhythmic, structural.

Likewise, it would be difficult to find a British novel whose "whole created cosmos" compares to the one Cecil so admirably summarizes for *Wuthering Heights*. The contrast between the principles of storm and calm is easily as pervasive as in the sonata: it is geographical, familial, psychological, social, even meteorological. This principle of contrast extends to nearly every detail of fact, feeling, and mood in the novel; it would be difficult to find a single element of character, setting, action, or structure that does not have its place in the storm/calm dichotomy.

Structurally, Heathcliff's tempestuous story of love and revenge runs from chapter 4, where at the age of six he is brought to Wuthering Heights as an orphan, through chapter 33, where at the age of thirty-eight he gives over a life of revenge because he feels "a change" approaching. His love for the living Catherine is terminated by her death in chapter 16, an event that gives temporary pause to the emotional storm in which Heathcliff has been enveloped; that storm, however, becomes all the more relentless and unyielding in the brutal chapters after her death. In the *Appassionata* the emotional storm of the first movement is punctuated by the temporary calm of the second, only to be invaded by the even more relentless and unyielding storm of the finale. Before comparing the psychic contents and the structure of the sonata with those of the Heathcliff section of *Wuthering Heights*, it will be well to locate the sonata within the context of Beethoven's "middle" period.

In 1802, at the time of the onset of deafness and the outcry of the Heiligenstadt Testament, Beethoven declared, according to Czerny, "I am not satisfied with my previous works; from here on I shall follow a new path."[3] That path led directly into his "middle" period, and the *Appassionata*, as much as any single work, consolidates and intensifies the features of Beethoven's evolving middle-period style. His twenty-third piano sonata, it stands to the *Pathétique*, his eighth, much as the *Eroica* Symphony stands to the First and Second symphonies.

The first movement of the *Eroica*, Opus 55, does not merely expand the classical sonata-allegro form perfected by Haydn and Mozart. Rather it forges an organic transformation of that form, muscularizing it so that it can carry Beethoven's grand utterances of heart and mind, not without strain, but in such a way that the strain emphasizes the strength of the structure. The unprecedented length of the first movement transforms the feel of sonata-allegro form while maintaining its overall proportions; the tremendous tension Beethoven introduces in the development section is balanced by the breadth and strength of the coda. In this sense the *Appassionata*, Opus 57, is a worthy pianistic counterpart to the *Eroica*. Its first movement is more muscular and intense than that of the Sonata *Pathétique*, especially in the development and coda. Its third movement, in sonata-allegro form, is fully the equal of its first movement in length, in the intensity of its development section, and in the fury and power of its coda.

Other formal features of the *Appassionata* look ahead to those of the Fifth Symphony, Opus 67 (1808). The celebrated "fate" motif that opens the symphony and pervades its first movement is anticipated by the four-note "fate" motif that follows the first theme of the *Appassionata* and plays an important structural role later in the first movement. The celebrated fusing of the third and fourth movements of the Fifth Symphony is anticipated, with even more drama, by the fusing of the second and third movements of the *Appassionata*. Even the obsessive rhythms of the Fifth Symphony are anticipated in the *Appassionata*, especially in the first and last movements. All of these features "condense and concentrate the texture" even more intensely in these works than in Beethoven's early-period works; at the same time they contribute to their long-range structural unity. One important difference between the *Appassionata*, in F minor, and the Fifth Symphony, in C minor, is that the sonata does not end with a major-key transformation. Its relentless F-minor finale, matching the first movement not only in its sonata-allegro structure and its psychic intensity but also in its nearly unrelieved minor-key harmony, gives the *Appassionata* a kind of concentration and unity which not even the Fifth Symphony achieves.

Finally, the *Appassionata* can be briefly related to the two even-numbered symphonies that follow the Third and the Fifth—the gracious Fourth and the expansive Sixth, the *Pastoral*. In these two works the principle of "calm" tends to prevail as much as does the principle of "storm" in their odd-numbered companions. The second movement of the *Appassionata*, even though it gives way to the passionate ferocity of the third movement, does have "motions of the spirit" in common with these two symphonies. In addition, the *Appassionata* has its own calmer counterpart among the piano sonatas: its grand middle-period neighbor, the *Waldstein* Sonata, Opus 53 (1803–4). In the words of Romain Rolland, "This white sonata in C, that flows like clear water, is the most intoxicating ecstasy in nature—an ecstasy controlled by the mind."[4] Rolland calls the second movement of the *Appassionata*, by contrast, "a zone of anti-cyclone between two typhoons" (p. 161).

Rolland is not the only writer who has used the dichotomy of storm and calm to indicate the character of the *Appassionata*, whose outer movements are nearly always described as "tempestuous." After comparing the storm/calm dichotomy of the *Appassionata* with that of the Heathcliff story of *Wuthering Heights*, we will explore the degree to which the "organic form" of each work reflects its creator's passionate response to the spirit of nature. We shall discover that Rolland's assertion about the *Waldstein* Sonata—that the most intoxicating ecstasy in nature is an ecstasy controlled by the mind—is not so paradoxical as it seems.

According to Schindler, Beethoven regretted later in life that he had attached the name *Pathétique* to Opus 13. He felt that the French title had made the work popular with some who did not understand it, and had drawn attention away from other sonatas Beethoven felt were equally deserving. Schindler argues that the term *pathétique* in fact "summarizes the fundamental character of all of Beethoven's music." He is speaking of the general meaning of the word: "That which is truly pathetic expresses a strong emotion earnestly and with dignity."[5]

The title *Appassionata* was given to Opus 57 by the publisher, not the composer, but there is no evidence that Beethoven objected. (He applied the term to several of his own works, including the first movement of Opus 111, to be discussed in Chapter 3.) The *Appassionata* was Beethoven's personal favorite among the sonatas for over a decade, until he composed the *Hammerklavier*, Opus 106. Tovey suggests that its title "is justified by the eminently tragic tone of the whole work. No other work by Beethoven maintains a tragic solemnity throughout all its movements." He goes on to specify the motions of the spirit that give the *Appassionata* its essential unity. "The first movement of a sonata tells a complete story which no later movement can falsify: hence Beethoven is under no compulsion to follow up even the most tragic first movement by a tragic finale." But he does exactly that. "The very beginning of the finale is itself a final stroke of fate, after which there is not a moment's doubt that the tragic passion is rushing deathwards."[6] The kind of fateful action Tovey perceives differs sharply from the general earnestness and dignity that Schindler, speaking of the "truly pathetic," finds in all of Beethoven's music.

Chapters 4–15 of *Wuthering Heights*, no less than the first movement of the *Appassionata*, tell a "complete story" in themselves. It is the story of Heathcliff's ill-fated love for Catherine until her death. This story contains enough tragic passion for an entire book, but it is followed by Heathcliff's relentless revenge on others after Catherine is dead (chapters 17–31). Chapter 16, the transitional period of calm, contains its equivalent of "a final stroke of fate, after which there is not a moment's doubt that the tragic passion is rushing deathwards." Heathcliff's story, like the *Appassionata*, embraces not merely the true pathos of emotions that are earnest and dignified, as are the emotions of Mr. Lockwood, for example, but the more powerful emotions of pity and terror—the emotions of tragedy.

New Beginnings

Throughout the Lockwood introduction to *Wuthering Heights*, the adult Heathcliff contributed considerably to Lockwood's experience of the principle of storm. In his harsh interruption of Lockwood's opening speech, in his ruthless oppression of "Mrs. Heathcliff" and "the clown," in his wild sobbing to the ghost of Cathy, and in the mood of incipient violence he inculcates, Heathcliff seems personally to embody the principle of storm that is made literal in the "billowy, white ocean" of snow that envelops the Heights in chapter 3. During his own introduction to Wuthering Heights, however, Heathcliff is more the recipient than the generator of storm.

Heathcliff's arrival at the Heights, thirty years before that of Mr. Lockwood, is narrated in chapter 4 by Nelly Dean, who was present as a teenage friend of the Earnshaw family. The family has been anxiously awaiting the return of Mr. Earnshaw, who had traveled by foot to far-off Liverpool. On the third day, late at night, "the door-latch was raised quietly and in stept the master." Surrounded by his family, he offers his wife a bundle wrapped in his great coat, saying, "You must e'en take it as a gift of God, though it's as dark almost as if it came from the devil" (p. 38). The gift is six-year-old Heathcliff, not yet named. His reception by the family establishes a pattern of rejection, acceptance, and rejection—of storm, calm, and storm—that will characterize the rest of his life.

As the children crowded near the "dirty, ragged, black-haired child," he only "stared round, and repeated over and over again some gibberish that nobody could understand." The first rejection comes from Mrs. Earnshaw, who "was ready to fling it out of doors; she did fly up—asking how he could fashion to bring that gipsy brat into the house." Some semblance of order is restored by Mr. Earnshaw's explanation of how he found the boy "starving, and houseless, and as good as dumb in the streets of Liverpool." Mrs. Earnshaw "grumbled herself calm." But then Hindley and Cathy begin "searching their father's pockets for the presents he had promised them. The former was a boy of four-teen, but when he drew out what had been a fiddle, crushed to morsels in the great coat, he blubbered aloud, and Cathy, when she learnt the master had lost her whip in attending on the stranger, showed her humor by grinning and spit-ting at the stupid little thing. . . . They entirely refused to have it in bed with them, or even in their room, and I had no more sense, so I put it on the landing of the stairs, hoping it might be gone on the morrow. . . . This was Heathcliff's first introduction to the family" (pp. 38–39).

This brutal introduction makes Mr. Lockwood's encounter with the adult Heathcliff in chapter 1 look civilized by comparison. The young boy has no name with which to announce himself (a few days later Nelly "found they had christened him 'Heathcliff'; it was the name of a son who died in childhood, and it has served him ever since, both for Christian and surname"). The language barrier between him and his interlocutors is total; there is not even the grudging communication that takes place between the adult Heathcliff and Mr. Lockwood in chapter 1. Instead, the boy's antecedent phrases of "gibberish" are answered by Mrs. Earnshaw's calling him a "gipsy brat" and, after the period of calm, by Cathy's spit. The subsequent triple rejection by Cathy, Hindley, and Nelly anticipates the blow that Cathy will unknowingly deliver nine years (and five chapters) later, when she says to Nelly in a conversation Heathcliff will overhear, "It would degrade me to marry Heathcliff" (p. 72). The dynamics of rejection, acceptance, and rejection are harsh enough in themselves; they are rendered the more painful—for young Heathcliff as well as for the well-intentioned Mr. Earnshaw—by the context of "homecoming" in which they ironically occur.

The *Appassionata,* unlike the Sonata *Pathétique,* begins quietly. The mysterious, brooding first theme, in F minor, spans three and a half bars and nearly two octaves. The first part of the theme, plunging low and rising high, covers the two octaves in barely two bars; the rest of the theme is nearly immobile, centering on a trill (Figure 3). After the theme is repeated in ascending sequence (bars 4–8), its trill section detaches itself from the whole and is itself repeated in sequence, these two versions of the trill figure being separated, still *pp,* by the four-note "fate" motif that will play a vital intensifying function throughout the first movement (Figure 4). First heard in the bass (bar 10), this motif alternates between bass and treble until its strong assertion, *forte,* at the end of bar 13 initiates a plunging set of arpeggios that "tears up" this opening passage as much as did the chromatic descent at the end of the Grave introduction of Opus 13.

Figure 3

Figure 4

This dramatic descent leads to a counterstatement of the opening theme. Traditionally, the counterstatement is a moment of clarification and stability in the classical sonata-allegro form; the main theme is restated so as to more firmly fix its character before the rest of the movement unfolds. *This* counterstatement, however, is an assault on the character of the theme; pounding chords dismember rather than reinforce its shape (Figure 5). In only a few bars, the principle of storm has obliterated the uneasy calm in which the movement has opened.

Nothing could be harsher than the manner in which the chords in bar 17 interrupt the *pp* restatement of the opening theme after it reaches F, its fourth

Figure 5

and lowest note. The harshness is expressed by the extreme contrast of loud and soft, by the disruption of a statement that is only just getting underway, by the mass of the chords that dwarf the single-note melody, and by syncopation. Although the *ff* dynamics begin on the single notes that open bar 17, the piled-up chords follow on the off-beat, this "unexpected thrusting on a weak beat" interrupting what in the opening melody was a dotted half-note tied to a dotted quarter. After the massive chords march up exactly two octaves and cross the bar line, they allow the melody to resume where it had left off, *p* this time, rather than *pp*. But before the melody can move from F to C for its concluding trill figure, the *ff* chords invade again. With this second interruption the harsh has become ruthless. After a bar of ascending chords, the melody resumes with the trill figure. But it too is smashed by *ff* chords.

In itself, the counterstatement is harsh and ruthless. But our perception of these qualities is heightened by the way the theme itself had been introduced. The original *pp* dynamics of the theme created an uneasy sense of calm which could then be violated. The double presentation of the complete shape of the theme in bars 1–8 allows us to perceive its mutilation in the counterstatement. The storm unleashed in the counterstatement will again erupt in the theme that closes the exposition, in the development, in the recapitulation, and in the coda, but before doing so it must wait out the relative calm of the second theme and the suspense of the extended repeated-note bridge that leads to it.

In spite of their harshness, the chords that dismember the theme in bars 17, 20, and 22 are, on paper, mirror images. The combination of violence and symmetry could hardly be more concentrated than it is in bars 20–21 and bars 22–23, where a two-bar pattern of storm/calm is repeated note for note—until slight changes in bar 23 prepare for the transition to the repeated-note figure. In their relentless ascending motion, the chords somehow complement the wild downward motion of the arpeggios in bar 14, though they seem to be satisfying only themselves. Even more intensely than in the Grave introduction of the Sonata *Pathétique*, these chords give us the unexpected thrusts on a weak beat, the unmediated contrast between strong and weak, and the powerful climaxes achieved or frustrated that are characteristic of Beethoven's style at its most vehement.

This transformation of a classical sonata-allegro counterstatement into an episode of Romantic vehemence and fragmentation is as shocking as is the transformation of the conventional homecoming scene when Mr. Earnshaw returns to Wuthering Heights with the young Heathcliff. The psychic and verbal abuse the young boy receives, the number of attackers, their violence of expression, their superiority of age and status—all these factors combine as a threat to his personality and person as severe as the threat of the *ff* chords that batter the first theme in the counterstatement of the *Appassionata*.

Emotional Storm

In their combined symmetry and violence, bars 20–21 and 22–23 of the counterstatement express in microcosm the ruling principles of the entire first movement. As Rosen points out, the Allegro assai of the *Appassionata* is "almost rigidly symmetrical in spite of its violence, as if only the simplest and most unyielding of frames could contain such power." Its sonata-allegro structure could hardly be more clearly delineated in its structural units or in its succession of themes. The movement

> falls into four clear sections: all of them (exposition, development, recapitulation, and coda) begin with the main theme; the recapitulation follows the thematic pattern of the exposition with the minimum of alternation necessary to return to the second group in the tonic; both the development and the coda conform to this pattern by playing the thematic material they select in the order set forth in the exposition; in addition, the development and the coda have very similar structures, except for the final Più allegro at the end.

Within this rigid frame, even more symmetrical than that of the first movement of the *Pathétique*, the violence, as Rosen puts it, "is achieved simply and efficiently."[7] Every detail of melody, harmony, and rhythm contributes to the emotional storm that rages within this classical frame. But perhaps the strongest measure of the tragic power of the "complete story" told in this movement is the fate of the main theme, from beginning to end. That fate, as we shall see, is similar to that of the main character of the novel.

We have already seen the simple, efficient violence with which the quiet first theme has been dismembered in the counterstatement, turning a normally reassuring moment in the sonata-allegro structure into one of brutality. At the beginning of the development section (bar 65), the complete theme is reintroduced, calmly, in a remote key. But its opening notes must repeat themselves before the theme can get underway, and the trill phrase, after the entire theme is heard, repeats and extends itself several times in new keys, as if searching for harmony and rest. This searching results in a new, vehement transformation of the first part of the theme, which strides in ascending surges until a return of the repeated-note figure from the exposition finally leads on to the second theme. This muscular striding is accompanied by vehement passagework both high and low.

Structurally, it replaces the counterstatement of the exposition. Emotionally, it represents the first time that the main theme has incorporated the storm principle into itself, rather than being violated by it.

The most dramatic transformation of the main theme comes at the beginning of the recapitulation (bar 135), the point of the sonata-allegro structure when the first theme is expected to return to its home key, and in its original shape. This theme does return, and its shape is as it originally was, but the simple violence of a dominant pedal now throbbing in the bass turns "an important moment of resolution into a long-sustained, menacing dissonance" (Rosen, p. 400). This menace continues throughout the recapitulation of the main theme, throbbing beneath the trill passage, the fate motif, and even the arpeggios that lead to the counterstatement. All of the dramatic rests that had punctuated the uneasy calm of the opening bars of the exposition are obliterated by the throbbing dissonance in the bass. And now, during the counterstatement, the brutal chords violate the theme five times rather than three, the trill figure this time being smashed three times rather than once. In response to the final blow, however, the trill figure does something new: it moves higher than before, and answers *forte* rather than *piano*, returning to *piano* only for its last note, which introduces the repeated-note bridge to the second theme. The trill figure too has reluctantly incorporated the principle of storm. We never hear it again.

When the main theme returns, quietly, to begin the coda (bar 203), it has lost its trill figure altogether. It begins low in the bass and seems to search for its complete self, finding, instead, the second theme, without transition. At the very end of the coda, the "ghost" of this theme (Tovey, p. 182) returns one last time, again without its trill figure. It sinks from *p* to *pp* to a final close, *ppp*, falling four octaves as it does so.

Such violent dismemberment and transformation of a theme throughout an entire movement is unprecedented in the music of Beethoven's classical predecessors. Nor does it occur in Beethoven's first-period works. Even in the fiery Allegro of the Sonata *Pathétique* the main theme had remained recognizable and intact throughout, the pressure it underwent in the development section being offset by its repeat in the exposition, by the repeat of the exposition itself, and by its robust return in the recapitulation and again in the coda. Here, however, the principle of transformation spans the entire first movement with the process of dynamic change, affecting even the second theme. The force of the thematic attack and ultimate denudation is intensified by another break with tradition: Beethoven omits the repeat of the exposition. In a repeat, the first theme, after being dismembered in the counterstatement, would have been heard again complete before undergoing the rigors of the development section. By not repeating the exposition, Beethoven plunges into transformations not only more drastic but more immediate than could have been expected.

An early compensation for the trials endured by the first theme of the *Appassionata* is the consolation provided by the second theme. After the pressures induced by the fate motif, the wild descending arpeggios, and the harsh ascending chords, and after the sustained suspense of the repeated-note bridge passage, the warm second theme brings a welcome sense of relief. After the emotional storm of the counterstatement, it brings a genuine sense of calm. It resembles the first theme in its *pp* dynamics and in its rhythm, clearly derived from the first part of the earlier theme. But its calm is less uneasy. Its A-flat major tonality—the relative major of F minor—contrasts agreeably with the minor-key first theme, and its sweet *dolce* character creates a relatively peaceful effect. So does the fact that its two-bar antecedent phrase is answered directly by a two-bar consequent (Figure 6), giving the theme itself a balanced, rounded-off quality lacking in the first theme, which melodically as well as harmonically ended with a question rather than an answer.

Figure 6

As soon as this theme is restated in a higher octave, however, its balanced melody breaks down, the consequent phrase disintegrating into an "enormously expanded minor cadence filling the next 8 bars themelessly" (Tovey, p. 179). This crisis leads, through a deliberate plunging scale, deep into the bass. There a brutal closing theme, again in the minor key, reintroduces the principle of storm with a vengeance. "This harsh and turbulent closing theme," as Rosen puts it, "is not in the relative major but decisively in the minor of the relative major. Almost all of Mozart's and Haydn's works in minor color the relative major of the second group with this minor mode, but neither of them had gone so far as to close an exposition with it: once again, in this work, Beethoven extended classical harmonic language without violating its spirit" (p. 400).

In the development section the second theme answers the new pressures expressed by the first theme with a calm appearance in D-flat major. Beginning in its fourth bar, however, a rising bass pushes the theme higher and higher, taking it to new keys and compressing it eventually into its last two melodic notes. As the bass rises, the dynamics become *sempre più f*, thereby incorporating the principle of storm into this theme too. The pressure is so intense that one hardly notices that here the restatement of the theme comes to a melodic cadence for the first (and only) time. This compressed cadence, however, brings no relief. Cascades of themeless arpeggios now carry the "passion," in Tovey's words, "beyond articulate utterance" (p. 181).

In the recapitulation the second theme acts much as it did in the exposition, except that now it is announced in F major and transposed into F minor before giving way to the fateful closing theme. This time, however, its disintegration in the higher octave seems more inevitable than before—after the pressure it had endured in the development.

In the coda, the trill-less version of the first theme passes directly on to the second theme, now heard higher than ever before. But again the theme cannot sustain itself: in a crescendo stunted with *sf* accents, it disintegrates into themeless confusion. After a tremendous climax on the "fate" motif introduces the Più allegro, the second theme is now announced in the "home" key of F minor. But here it has, in Tovey's words, "lost all calm" (p. 182). A strong crescendo leads to its fragmentation and final disintegration.

Like the first theme, this consoling, contrasting theme in A-flat major has endured a series of transformations that have taken it far from its original home and have fragmented its original shape until it too has internalized the spirit of storm. Such transformation of a second theme throughout a movement violates the custom of Beethoven's classical predecessors as much as does that of the first theme. Curiously, for such a tempestuous movement, both main themes are originally calm, *pp*. The storm of the movement is not in the themes themselves but in what happens *to* them, until each finally incorporates the tempest within itself.

Tovey points out that Beethoven's original sketches for this movement did not include a contrasting theme in the major mode. The melodic material for the entire movement was to have been in the minor. "The glorious afterthought" of the A-flat-major second theme "converted the whole movement from the gloom of a storm to the active passions of a tragedy" (p. 178). Heathcliff's sullen youth is likewise converted by the love of Catherine. Her friendship is, originally, as consoling as the second theme of the *Appassionata*.

The violence with which the leading themes are treated in the first movement of the *Appassionata* is easily measured against the symmetrical outlines of the movement's four-part structure, each new section beginning with the main theme. The living love story of Heathcliff and Catherine is not quite so schematic in its narrative structure, but it too has four largely symmetrical sections which serve to frame its simple, efficient violence. Just as the orderly progression of themes and dramatic shifts of harmonic setting clearly divide the four structural sections of the "complete story" told in the first movement, so do the orderly progression of characters and the dramatic shifts of physical locale clearly divide the four structural sections of the "complete story" told in chapters 4–15 of *Wuthering Heights*.

Chapters 4–6 introduce the main characters, the contrasting locales, and the initial action of the emotional storm that will conclude only with Catherine's death. These chapters begin with Heathcliff's arrival at Wuthering Heights as an orphan; they end with his and Cathy's nighttime excursion to Thrushcross Grange, from which he returns and she does not. Chapters 7–9 retain the same characters and the same locales but increase the tensions among them. These chapters begin with Cathy's dramatic return from Thrushcross Grange after five weeks with the Lintons; they end with Heathcliff's dramatic departure from the Heights after hearing Cathy say it would degrade her to marry him, followed by Cathy's delirium at his loss. Chapters 10–12 again feature the same characters and locales, but unleash even stronger emotional storms than before. This section begins with Heathcliff's dramatic return after three years' absence; it concludes with his dramatic elopement with Isabella Linton. Chapters 13–15, again remaining with the same characters and locales, push the emotional storm through to its tragic, exhausted end. This section begins with Isabella's brutal reception at Wuthering Heights as Heathcliff's wife; it ends with Catherine's final delirium, following a "last reunion" with Heathcliff. She dies that night, as we learn immediately in chapter 16.

This largely symmetrical structure, like that of the first movement of the *Appassionata*, consists of four sections whose psychic contents are ever more intense. Its internal dynamics serve only to heighten, not to resolve, the tensions implicit in the material. This structure frames brutal violence and harsh transformations comparable to those in the sonata movement. Much of the tragedy of the Allegro assai is expressed in the fate of its two main themes. Much of the tragedy of chapters 4–15 is expressed in the fate of its two main characters.

We have already seen the brutality with which young Heathcliff was attacked by Mrs. Earnshaw, Hindley, Cathy, and even Nelly during his introduction to Wuthering Heights. Without a transition, Nelly continues the exposition of his early days: "Miss Cathy and he were now very thick; but Hindley hated him, and to say the truth I did the same; and we plagued and went on with him shamefully." At first Heathcliff accepts such treatment passively: "He seemed a sullen, patient child, hardened, perhaps, to ill-treatment: he would stand Hindley's blows without winking or shedding a tear." Even when he is driven by Hindley to physical retaliation, Nelly thinks him "not vindictive" (pp. 39–41).

Heathcliff's poise and self-control elevate his position in the eyes of Mr. Earnshaw, who in chapter 5 becomes so enraged by Hindley's persecution of the boy that he sends his son away to college. Later in the chapter, however, as a storm rages outside, Mr. Earnshaw dies, leaving Heathcliff with only the friendship of Cathy to protect him from the domestic violence sure to come. Both Cathy and Heathcliff "set up a heart-breaking cry" when they see that Mr. Earnshaw is dead. But later that night Nelly witnesses the consolation that Heathcliff has found in Cathy's friendship. Now "they were calmer, and did not need me to console them. The little souls were comforting each other with better thoughts than I could have hit on; no parson in the world ever pictured heaven so beautifully as they did, in their innocent talk; and, while I sobbed and listened, I could not help wishing we were all there safe together" (p. 44).

This island of calm is dispelled soon enough in chapter 6. When Hindley returns to become master of the Heights, he and his wife Frances convert Heathcliff into a servant. "Heathcliff bore his degradation pretty well at first, because Cathy taught him what she learnt, and worked or played with him in the fields. . . . It was one of their chief amusements to run away to the moors in the morning and remain there all day, and the afterpunishment grew a mere thing to laugh at" (p. 46). At the end of chapter 6 they make their first excursion to Thrushcross Grange. As they look in through the window at the "splendid place carpeted with crimson," they see Edgar and Isabella Linton "shrieking" and "weeping" over a little dog which "they had nearly pulled in two between them" (p. 47). Heathcliff and Cathy are at this moment as close as they will ever be. Their vast love for each other is matched by the scorn they feel for their harsh persecutors at home and for the young Lintons beyond the great glass window. When they "laugh outright at the petted things," however, Cathy is caught by one of the Lintons' dogs. The two of them are dragged indoors for what turns out to be a variation upon Heathcliff's original introduction to Wuthering Heights.

The Lintons, like Mrs. Earnshaw, reject Heathcliff for his gipsylike appearance. But they pamper Cathy. Cast outdoors, Heathcliff peers back in through the window and sees her treated as a fairy-tale princess. Had Cathy wished to escape, Heathcliff tells Nelly, "I intended shattering their great glass panes to a million fragments, unless they let her out" (p. 49). But she seems content inside. For the moment, however, Heathcliff is not jealous. As he looks in at Catherine he sees only that the Lintons "were full of stupid admiration; she is so immeasurably superior to them—to everybody on earth, is she not, Nelly?" (p. 50). Chapters 4–6 are the fictional exposition of the conditions of Heathcliff's childhood; chapters 7–9 are the fictional development section.

Heathcliff's sullen, defensive, confusing behavior in chapter 7 when a "wonderfully whitened" Catherine returns from five weeks with the Lintons reveals the psychic stress he has suffered in her absence. Their meeting recalls Heathcliff's first arrival at the Heights; despite the fact that it is Cathy who is returning, he is the one who is being inspected, or who most feels himself so. Seeing her transformed features, he hides from sight. "Cathy, catching a glimpse of her friend in his concealment, flew to embrace him; she bestowed seven or eight kisses on his cheek within the second, and then stopped, and drawing back, burst into a laugh, exclaiming—'Why, how very black and cross you look! and how—how funny and grim!'" This comment—and its aftermath—causes him to "dash head foremost out of the room," exclaiming, "I shall be as dirty as I please" (pp. 51–52).

As Christmas approaches, Nelly tells Heathcliff that he has nothing to fear from Edgar Linton's blond hair and blue eyes if he will only imagine a glorious heritage for himself and wash his face. He does everything he can to clean up and make himself presentable, but when Hindley banishes him to his room he vows lifelong revenge. When Nelly rebukes him, saying, "It is for God to punish wicked people," Heathcliff asserts that "God won't have the satisfaction that I shall" (p. 57). Here, for the first time, at age thirteen, Heathcliff has incorporated the principle of emotional storm deeply within himself. His ungodly vow, as well as Hindley's action that provoked it, have occurred, ironically, on Christmas Day.

Although Cathy comforts Heathcliff on Christmas night, she thereby initiates the pattern by which she encourages both Edgar and Heathcliff without wishing to choose between them: she "adopted a double character without exactly intending to deceive anyone" (p. 62). As Heathcliff "recoils with angry suspicion from her girlish caresses," Cathy grows closer to Edgar. In chapter 9 her "double character" articulates itself in the extraordinary confession to Nelly that she has accepted Edgar's proposal of marriage even though she loves Heathcliff vastly more. Heathcliff runs away without hearing her contrast her transitory love for Linton ("foliage in the woods") with her enduring love for him ("the eternal rocks beneath"). After Cathy searches for him all night in the storm, "she bursts into uncontrollable grief. . . . The remainder of her words were inarticulate" (pp. 74, 78). In chapters 7–9, she and Heathcliff have both undergone pressures similar to those in the development section of the *Appassionata*. He, like the first theme, has incorporated the principle of storm for the first time. She, like the second theme when pushed by the relentless bass, has paradoxically lost her coherence during her most complete self-statement ("Nelly, I *am* Heathcliff"), breaking finally into "passion beyond articulate utterance."

The mature Heathcliff's return at the beginning of chapter 10 is as ominous as the recapitulation of the first theme of the *Appassionata*. Although physically a changed man, inwardly he remains sharply divided between his vast love for Catherine and his vast scorn for the Lintons. It can be only a matter of time until emotional storms break out even more violently than before. His presence at the Grange is encouraged by Cathy, who can see no more than before why she should have to choose between the company of the two men she loves. The brutal, inevitable confrontation between Edgar and Heathcliff in chapter 11 drives Cathy into another delirium ("I'll try to break their hearts by breaking my own") from which she awakens in chapter 12, dreaming to Nelly of her early days at Wuthering Heights, when she was "half savage, and hardy, and free" (p. 107). In the meantime, Heathcliff has eloped with Isabella, of whom he has recently said, "You'd hear of odd things, if I lived alone with that mawkish, waxen face; the most ordinary would be painting on its white the colours of the rainbow, and turning the blue eyes black, every day or two; they detestably resemble Linton's" (p. 93). His elopement at the end of chapter 12 turns upon the Lintons (and Catherine) the emotional storm they had visited upon him at the end of chapter 6, when he was thrust out of the Grange while Cathy stayed inside.

Whereas chapters 10–12 are in many ways an adult recapitulation of the fictional exposition in chapters 4–6, chapters 13–15 are a fictional coda, a further intensification of the heightened development in chapters 7–9. At the beginning of chapter 7, Heathcliff had shown his vulnerability by the confused aggression with which he had welcomed the "wonderfully whitened" Catherine to the Heights. At the beginning of chapter 13 the extent to which he has internalized the principle of storm (and lost his "trill," so to speak) is shown by the implacable hate with which he "welcomes" Isabella to the Heights as his wife. He speaks scathingly of her "marvellous effort of perspicacity to discover that I did not love her" (p. 127). Yet despite his hatred of his own spouse, it is inconceivable to him that Edgar would forbid the still-delirious Catherine to see him. His love for Cathy is so great, he tells Nelly, that if he were married to her and she wished for Edgar's society, he would see that she had it, despite his hatred of Edgar. "I would have died by inches before I touched a single hair of his head!" (p. 125). Heathcliff has totally internalized the principle of emotional storm, of vast scorn, but he nevertheless remains capable of vast love, of a vision beyond the storm.

Nelly's reluctant decision to allow the two lovers to meet one last time brings the living love story to a conclusion as violent and abrupt as the Più allegro in the first movement of the *Appassionata*. Catherine accuses Heathcliff of having ruined her married life with Edgar by returning; he accuses her of having ruined her own life and his too by marrying someone she does not love. She momentarily escapes the intense pressure by speaking of "this shattered prison." But before she escapes into the "glorious world beyond," she and Heathcliff find themselves "locked in an embrace from which I thought my mistress would never be released alive" (p. 134). A brutal but tear-washed colloquy ensues, after which Edgar's inevitable return from church precipitates Catherine's last loss of consciousness, from which she does not recover.

The emotional storm, the passionate ferocity that surges through the violent symmetry of this tragic love story has transformed Heathcliff and Catherine as much as the storm of the first movement has transformed the main themes of the *Appassionata*. No less than the main theme in the counterstatement, Heathcliff has been assaulted by implacable forces beyond his control before being able to define his character in an indelible way. At first passive in the face of the assaults, he eventually learns to incorporate the principle of storm within himself. The inward vehemence and vengeance he generates alter his character as much as the main theme is altered when it incorporates the principle of storm into itself in the development section and returns with its new-found menace in the recapitulation. By the beginning of the coda the main theme has been stripped entirely of its trill figure, which itself had finally incorporated the principle of storm during the counterstatement of the recapitulation. Heathcliff, in the words of John Hagan, has been "stripped of his humanity through intolerable suffering and loss."[8] This shows in his perversion of the love-principle when he scornfully brings Isabella to Wuthering Heights as his bride. Although a glimpse of his residual humanity does show through in his impassioned last meeting with Catherine, it is difficult to imagine how that quality would ever be able to express itself after her death.

Catherine too has undergone transformations that have altered her entirely from the young girl who grew up at Wuthering Heights. These changes are brilliantly condensed in chapter 12, in the dream which she tells Nelly "kept recurring and recurring till I feared for my reason." In it, she "was enclosed in the oak-panelled bed at home; and my heart ached with some great grief which, just waking, I could not recollect" (p. 107). Violently juxtaposed in this dream are Catherine Earnshaw, her father's daughter; Catherine Heathcliff, half-savage, and hardy, and free; and Catherine Linton, the lady of Thrushcross Grange. Catherine is all of these women, and their conditions differ as distinctly as do the successive versions of the once consoling theme in the first movement of the *Appassionata*.

Significantly, Heathcliff and Catherine resemble the two main themes of the Allegro assai movement not only in being transformed throughout their narrative but in being closely related to, even derived from, each other. Catherine says to Nelly in chapter 9, "I *am* Heathcliff." Here the spiritual bond that is *felt* between them, even when they are in opposition, is made literally explicit. This deep spiritual bond is evident both in their calm moments (as when they console each other after the loss of Mr. Earnshaw) and in their more extreme moments, when either or both are "pushed beyond articulate utterance" by forces internal or external. Examples of such extreme moments include their joint "heart-breaking cry" when they see Mr. Earnshaw is dead, their joint howls of laughter at the despised Linton children, and Cathy's "uncontrollable, inarticulate grief" when Heathcliff leaves Wuthering Heights.

The two main themes of the Allegro assai are related to, even derived from, each other to a comparable degree. We have already pointed to the rhythmic and melodic similarities between the first theme and the second. These are obvious enough that one does not require the analysis of a Schenker or a Réti to drive the point home.[9] As with Cathy and Heathcliff, these intrinsic similarities are evident both in their calm moments (the first, *pp* statement of each, for example) and in their moments of extreme stress (the first theme in the counterstatement, the second when pushed by the bass in the development). Each theme also reveals a self-weakness, a tendency to be violated. The main theme, as Rolland points out, "is constituted of two elements so closely joined to each other that at first sight they seem to be only one." They begin to separate, however, as early as bar 9, when the self-separation of the trill figure first reveals the "duality" that will become evident in the counterstatement. Rolland describes this duality as "two in one: two Selfs in opposition; a wild Self-force, a trembling Self-weakness" (pp. 152–53). A different kind of weakness is expressed by the second theme, which at first "is humanized, touched with tenderness, by affectionate inflexions." Yet even on its first appearance, this theme "lacks the strength to maintain its affirmation to the end," disintegrating into the fateful closing theme, itself intrinsically violent. Increasingly throughout the movement it becomes a reservoir of "broken energy" (pp. 154–55).

Heathcliff and Catherine also show an initial self-weakness, a tendency to be violated. Heathcliff, like the first theme, embodies a duality between "a trembling Self-weakness" and a "wild Self-force." The former shows in the passivity with which he originally responds to his traumatic initiation to the Heights and to the brutal attacks that follow. Only later does he incorporate the "wild Self-force" into himself in order to give some anchor to his personality. Catherine's self-weakness, like that of the second theme, seems to come from within. She too is "touched by tenderness, by affectionate inflexions." But she too lacks "the strength to maintain her affirmation to the end." The early vacillation she shows in her treatment of Heathcliff (first spitting on him, then becoming "very thick") later deepens into her "double character," her psychic split, and her terminal madness.

These transformations in the main themes and main characters are a clear departure from Beethoven's and Brontë's classical predecessors. Themes and characters in Mozart and Austen tend to be more stable, autonomous, and inviolate. Many Romantics, on the other hand, pressed the transformation of theme and character to even further extremes (see "Growth and Transformation" in *Jane Austen and Mozart*). In major works by Chopin and Poe, for example, the leading themes or characters become so thoroughly transformed and violated that the distinction between their separate identities becomes entirely eroded. This does not happen in the *Appassionata* or *Wuthering Heights*. Heathcliff and Catherine, like the F-minor and A-flat-major themes, do undergo brutal transformations. The two characters, like the two themes, are related to, even derived from, each other. Yet each pair remains two and not one. Each member of the pair has a separate fate which strongly sets into relief that of the other. The shared fate of these characters and themes stops short of the solipsistic stage of Romanticism, in which only one individual exists whose inward realities, endlessly multiplying, are the only realities. The art of Beethoven and Brontë, for all its inwardness, remains dramatic and dialectic.

Our discussion of the large four-part structures of the first movement of the *Appassionata* and of chapters 4–15 of *Wuthering Heights* has emphasized the symmetrical violence with which the two main themes and the two main characters have been transformed. Now we may look at several smaller motifs within each structure that serve not only to intensify the emotional storm but to make a pattern out of it. For even the small-scale disruptions in these works tend to contribute to large-scale patterns in the distribution of violence.

The clearest example in the first movement is the four-note "fate" motif that appears but four times: in the exposition, at the end of the development, in the recapitulation, and at the climax within the coda. "The entrance of this motif," Rosen points out, "invariably marks an explosion." We have already seen its dramatic function in the exposition, leading from the trill figure of the opening theme to the plunging arpeggios that introduce the brutal counterstatement. What we have not yet noted is its harmonic function there. The opening theme itself is announced in F minor. But the two subsequent statements of its trill figure are in C major, the dominant, and in D-flat major, its minor second. As Rosen points out, the first sounding of the "fate" motif on the notes of D-flat and C (Figure 4) reflects these two key areas and compresses the harmonic ambiguity of the entire opening statement into one four-note motif. It also anticipates the harmonic question marks and Neapolitan harmonies that are to play a dramatic role later in the movement.

Rosen calls the second appearance of the "fate" motif, at the end of the development section, "a stupendous [climax], unequalled in earlier piano music." It not only brings to an ominous halt the inarticulate close of the development section but again refuses to resolve into the tonic for the start of the recapitulation, setting up the prolonged tension of the menacing ⁶⁄₄ chord that covers even the return of the "fate" motif itself in the recapitulation. Therefore the brutal *ff* statement of the motif that begins the Più allegro section of the coda is "the first time that this motif is resolved" harmonically (Figure 7). "This motif, in short, articulates every important climax and, with extraordinary brevity and concentration, the final resolution. It is a monad of the universe in which

Figure 7

it exists, serving as a tiny mirror; its tension and resolution are those of the entire structure."[10]

Literary critics have already given considerable attention to the motifs of windows, imprisonment, and violence that mirror the tensions and resolutions of the structure of *Wuthering Heights*. Windows, in chapters 4–15, like the "fate" motif in the first movement, "invariably mark an explosion." At Thrushcross Grange in chapter 6 Heathcliff plans on "shattering the great glass panes into a million fragments" if Cathy wishes to escape. Inside the Grange in chapter 12, Cathy, telling Nelly of her dream, thinks of being outdoors with Heathcliff and demands, "Open the window again wide, fasten it open!" In chapter 15, this same window represents spiritual escape from "this shattered prison." This explosive pattern of window motifs began in chapter 3, with Mr. Lockwood's dream in the oak-panelled bed. "I discerned, obscurely, a child's face looking through the window. Terror made me cruel; and finding it useless to attempt shaking the creature off, I pulled its wrist on to the broken pane, and rubbed it to and fro till the blood ran down and soaked the bed-clothes" (p. 30).

Another motif in chapters 4–15, which I shall call the inspection motif, also had its beginning in the Lockwood introduction (when Mr. Lockwood and the inhabitants of the Heights mutually inspected each other). Its first manifestation in the historical tale is young Heathcliff's being inspected—and rejected—by the bulk of the Earnshaw family in chapter 4. This scene of initiation is balanced by his and Catherine's being inspected—and his being rejected—at Thrushcross Grange at the end of chapter 6. Then follows Heathcliff's and Catherine's painful mutual inspection of each other at her return from the Grange at the beginning of chapter 7. Then there is Nelly's inspection of an overtly changed Heathcliff when he returns after three years at the beginning of chapter 10. This is followed by the inspections Isabella Linton endures in chapters 11 and 13. In chapter 11 Heathcliff stares at her "as one might do at a strange, repulsive animal, a centipede from the Indies, for instance, which curiosity leads one to examine in spite of the aversion it raises" (p. 92). In chapter 13, when she arrives at the Heights as Heathcliff's wife, she is inspected by Joseph, whose "first act was to elevate his torch to a level with my face, squint malignantly, project his under-lip, and turn away" (p. 116).

The window and inspection motifs in the novel, no less than the "fate" motif in the sonata, allow us to measure the successive intensities of the prevailing emotional storm. They, too, serve as "tiny mirrors," reflecting "the tension and resolution of the entire structure." The last living confrontation between Catherine and Heathcliff merits comparison with the last, dramatic intensification in the coda, when the "fate" motif is announced *pp* in a calm bar of *adagio* before being violated *ff* by the same motif in the Più allegro in the next bar (Figure 7). The deathbed setting of that final meeting causes one to expect a comforting moment of forgiveness and peace. Instead we find a harsh confrontation complete with mutual accusations of murder. In the context of *Wuthering Heights* as a whole, this sudden outburst of the principle of storm is not unusual. But in the context of a "last reunion," of a deathbed scene, it becomes no less dramatic than the last *ff* manifestation of the "fate" motif in the context of the *adagio* bar that precedes it. The coda of the first movement, no less than the last hours of Catherine's life, is marked by a new and "organic" outbreak of the principle of storm which has violated the conventional expectations of the listener and reader throughout.

Just as the final appearance of the "fate" motif in the coda brings its first resolution into the "home" key of F minor, so is the "last reunion" of Catherine and Heathcliff a final resolution of the inspection motif as it has operated throughout chapters 4–15. Here for the last time Heathcliff enters Thrushcross Grange in order to "inspect" Catherine's condition inside. Their mutual accusations and sobbing embrace resolve, on the living level, the volcanic tensions they have repressed all their lives. The "fate" motif on the one hand and the inspection motif on the other have come to be as important as the main themes and main characters themselves in giving structure and meaning to the "complete stories" so tragically concluded at the end of chapter 15 and at the end of the Allegro assai.

Calm/Storm

David Cecil defined the principle of calm in *Wuthering Heights* as "the gentle, the merciful, the passive, and the tame." Such a principle governs the second movement, Andante con moto, of the *Appassionata*. Occasionally, the principle of calm had operated in the first movement: the *pp* statement of the first theme, the "consoling" second theme, the *adagio* version of the "fate" motif in the coda. But each episode of calm in that movement served to set up the crushing power of the principle of storm. Structurally, the same may be said of the more extended and more perfect calm of the Andante con moto: that its main function is to dramatize the harrowing return of the principle of storm in the third movement, a storm that interrupts the second-movement calm even before the movement can end. Structurally the movement *is*, as Rolland says, a "zone of anti-cyclone between two typhoons." But spiritually it is, in Tovey's words, an expression of "the ultimate faith underlying the tragic emotion" of the outer movements (p. 178).

The second movement is a theme and variations in the simple pattern of *air et doubles*. The theme consists of two phrases of eight bars each, with each given an immediate repeat. (Figure 8 shows the first half of the theme, entirely in the bass clef). Variations 1 and 2 follow the same pattern, each being increasingly animated while at the same time remaining close to the structure of the theme itself. Variation 3 unfolds more freely, quickening in pace, moving higher in register, and breaking out of the confines of the repeat signs. Even so, it leads directly back to the theme itself, again low in the bass, but without repeats. Rather than ending peacefully, however, the theme disintegrates (one measure *pp*) and crashes (one measure *ff*) into the fury of the finale.

Figure 8

On one level, the Andante con moto expresses utter immobility and repose. "The simplicity of the design is beyond belief. The theme is almost immobile, the periods are of absolute equivalence. The first eight bars express a divine repose of the soul. In the eight bars that follow, the soul, in its tender religious aspiration, thrice lifts its hands but hardly stirs from its place. The variations of this inward hymn bring no breath of trouble to the paradisiac calm" (Rolland, p. 160). Rosen follows Rolland in calling this movement a hymn, writing of the "complete stillness of the hymn which is its theme." But that same stillness "makes the slightest increase of motion deeply telling." One such increase is the "successive rise step by step" in the register of each variation. This deliberate ascent makes the return of the theme in the bass following the heights reached in variation 3 seem like "a true sonata recapitulation," bringing with it an "extraordinary" sense of release (p. 438). Such a feeling of release is all the more moving for having been denied during the exacerbated recapitulation of the first movement.

Throughout this theme and variations, the tonality remains anchored in D-flat major, a soothing contrast to the stinging F-minor of the Allegro assai. But the harmonic stasis creates, in Tovey's words, "a dream that must be shattered at the first hint of action" (p. 177). That hint arrives in the form of the broken diminished-seventh chord, *pp*, that replaces the cadence in the tonic when the original theme returns. The *ff* answer an octave higher shatters the calm of the Andante con moto and begins the storm of the third movement, Allegro ma non troppo. Once the principle of storm breaks through the "paradisiac calm," there is no respite.

In the emotional storm that raged throughout chapters 4–15 of *Wuthering Heights* there had been occasional moments of calm: the short-lived peace during Heathcliff's introduction to the Heights, the mutual consolation he and Catherine found during the night of Mr. Earnshaw's death, the outdoor calm that followed the storm in which Cathy searched for Heathcliff in chapter 9, the calm that bathed the Grange early in chapter 15, before Catherine's last reunion with Heathcliff. None of these calms, however, endured long enough to make a lasting impression before being swept up into the impending return of storm, whether psychic or meteorological. The calm that follows upon the death of Catherine at the beginning of chapter 16, memorably rendered by Nelly, is somewhat more enduring.

> Next morning—bright and cheerful out of doors—stole softened in through the blinds of the silent room, and suffused the couch and its occupant with a mellow, tender glow.
>
> Edgar Linton had his head laid on the pillow, and his eyes shut. His young and fair features were almost as death-like as those of the form beside him, and almost as fixed; but *his* was the hush of exhausted anguish, and *hers* of perfect peace. Her brow smooth, her lids closed, her lips wearing the expression of a smile. No angel in heaven could be more beautiful than she appeared; and I partook of the infinite calm in which she lay. My mind was never in a holier frame than while I gazed on that untroubled image of Divine rest. I instinctively echoed the words she had uttered, a few hours before. "Incomparably beyond, and above us all! Whether still on earth or now in heaven, her spirit is at home with God!"

Nelly imagines "a repose that neither earth nor hell can break"; she feels assured of an "Eternity . . . where life is boundless in its duration, and love in its sympathy, and joy in its fulness" (p. 137).

Structurally, Nelly's inspired articulation of Catherine's condition of peace is obliterated by the vehemence of Heathcliff before the chapter can end. In duration, it is more evanescent than the Andante con moto of the *Appassionata*. But its motions of the spirit do correspond to those Tovey finds in the Andante: "the ultimate faith underlying the tragic emotion." For the moment, we can leave Catherine's calm spirit at home in Nelly's earthbound vision of divine rest. In Chapter 3 we shall follow it into unworldly realms of ethereal calm that have their counterpart not in Opus 57 but in Opus 111.

The third-movement storm of the *Appassionata* breaks out in the form of thirteen repeated diminished-seventh chords that initiate the obsessive rhythms of the movement and lead toward the whirlwind first theme. These thirteen brutal chords effectively obliterate the impression that had been created by one of the most perfect expressions of peace in the second movement: twelve reiterated high A-flats in the free third variation, gloriously "beyond, and above us all" (bars 65–68). The harsh tonality and driving rhythms of these *ff* chords create a devastating bleakness in no way counteracted by the material of the movement per se. The tonality is implacably in F-minor and related minor keys. (Tovey points out two small patches of major tonality, 14 of 361 bars.) After the gloriously measured pace of the second movement, this movement is a furious *moto perpetuo* of storm-driven themes.

The first theme is not so much a melody as a swirl of rhythmical motion. It dominates the shape and the mood of the movement from its first appearance, in the bass (Figure 9). The second theme too is more of a rhythmic principle than a recognizable melody (bar 76). It makes its insistent power felt, but it in no way alters the mood. Nor does its C-minor tonality provide any relief from the relentless F-minor insistence of the first theme. The closing group brings a return of the first theme itself—*forte*, rather than *pp*, as it had originally been announced. The exposition is brought to a close by rushing diminished-seventh arpeggios that sweep up three octaves and plunge down five octaves, *ff*, leading to a three-bar diminuendo preparation for the development section. The furious rush of rhythm-driven themes and arpeggios has run nonstop from the thirteen opening chords.

Figure 9

The return of the first theme, *pp*, at the beginning of the development continues the furious pace without a hitch. The obsessively familiar material is put through additional pressure until an extraordinary stretch of forty-plus bars (168–211) prepares for the return of the first theme in the recapitulation. This extended "crisis," as Tovey puts it, is themeless. It progresses through arpeggios first broken, then unbroken; through the harmonies of the Neapolitan sixth, the dominant seventh, and the diminished seventh; and through dynamics from *ff* to *p* to *pp*. The solid *pp* arpeggios, which rush from the bass clef to the very peak of the keyboard before plunging slowly to its very depths, bring a tremendous sense of drama, their extreme range of register being enhanced by the fact that the sixteenth notes that have prevailed throughout the movement have turned to eighth notes, reducing the perpetual motion to half its original speed until, during the final descent, these turn into half notes, seemingly bringing the motion to a dead stop.

This crisis induces a suppressed hope that new worlds are possible, that the storm might perhaps be waited out. The result, however, is no different from that of the three-bar diminuendo at the end of the exposition: the principle of storm returns with a vengeance. The return of the first theme at the beginning of the recapitulation restores the perpetual motion and the F-minor tonality. The rush of motion sweeps over the same unrelenting thematic material as before, this time transposing the second theme from C minor to F minor. After the furious closing version of the first theme we now expect to be moving toward the coda. Instead, however, the rushing arpeggios that had ended the exposition now lead back to a repeat of the entire development and recapitulation.

This extraordinary structural deflection turns a movement that was already relentlessly bleak in its melody, rhythm, and harmony even more so. Its length extended by another forty percent, this Allegro becomes one of the longest piano finales yet composed. Its demands are such that some pianists do not observe the repeats. Tovey muses that "Beethoven has unquestionably overlooked the difficulty ordinary mortals must feel in enjoying such a crisis as 168–211 twice in one performance" (p. 186). But the composer's intentions are clear.

The player who does survive the repeat of the development and recapitulation must also maintain a reservoir of strength for the short but incredibly powerful coda which brings this work to its fatalistic end. This coda is introduced not by the striding arpeggios that ended the exposition and the first recapitulation but by a new transition of driving scales within the confines of the treble clef marked *sempre più allegro* and, in their rhythmic accompaniment in the bass, *più forte*. These lead in turn to a new melody, strangely inexpressive, marked *presto*. In Blom's words, "It is as if all restraint were lost and any random thought were snatched in a frantic effort to drown the wild fancies that have been rushing in on us in this finale. But they come back again faster than ever and crowding more closely together, for it is [the first theme] which the final page gathers furiously into a hurricane of dramatic force."[11]

Beethoven's unprecedented decision to repeat the development and the recapitulation, though not the exposition, of the third movement transforms the expressive possibilities of the sonata-allegro form as much as had his equally unprecedented decision not to repeat the exposition of the first movement of the *Appassionata*. Here the mirror repetitions that in his classical predecessors tended to emphasize overall order and repose—even in such a vehement work as Mozart's G-minor Symphony—emphasize instead those sections of the work that are the most tense, disturbed, and discontinuous. This driven sonata-allegro movement thereby comes to feel like an unwieldy, obsessed rondo whose refrain keeps returning again and again but without the release or repose of contrasting episodes. In contrast to the C-minor rondo of Opus 13, this finale measures the distance Beethoven had traveled along his "new path" by 1805.

The *Appassionata* reveals that Beethoven had "finally arrived at a conception of a sonata where all three movements have been formulated as one" (Rosen, p. 399). As Howard Truscott puts it, "A tragic drama is enacted and completed in the first movement. The slow movement is in suspension throughout, and the finale is an emotional echo of the first." That echo is retrospective. "The emotional residue of the first movement is here frozen into a great tragic tableau, which comes to no solution except that 'this burden shalt thou carry.' Its triumph is in the strength wrested to enable the load to be carried."[12] Beethoven wrested that strength from the sonata-allegro form and from the depths of his soul.

As we have seen, the principle of storm that permeated the first movement of the *Appassionata* is even more harsh, ruthless, wild, and dynamic in the third. In *Wuthering Heights* the same is emphatically true of the eighteen years and fifteen chapters that follow the death of Catherine. For now Heathcliff intrudes on the calm of his adversaries even more implacably than before. Whereas his vengeance and anger while Catherine was alive were modified by his love for her, his vengeance and anger for eighteen years after her death are seemingly unrelenting. In chapter 17, after nearly trampling Hindley Earnshaw to death, he drives his wife Isabella from the Heights, her knife-pierced ear dripping blood. He wreaks vengeance not only upon Hindley, his old persecutor, but upon Hareton, Hindley's son. He is equally cruel to Linton Heathcliff, his own son, born of Isabella after her departure, and to Cathy Linton, daughter of Edgar and Catherine, born of Catherine on the morning she died. Through his cruelty to these children he continues to revenge himself upon their uncle and father, Edgar Linton.

It is in the shadow of his brooding presence that Cathy Linton, Linton Heathcliff, and Hareton Earnshaw carry on the love triangle in chapters 20–33 whose structure resembles the one carried on between Heathcliff, Catherine, and Edgar in chapters 4–15, though it differs, of course, in emotion. After Heathcliff forces his son, Linton, and Cathy's daughter, Cathy, to marry so that he will be doubly assured of inheriting Thrushcross Grange, the love of Cathy and Hareton begins to bloom in the very face of Heathcliff's vengeance until he finally feels a "change" approaching and enters the spiritual world that will be the subject of the chapter to come. Preceding that change are eighteen years of protracted grief (March 1784 to March 1802) for Heathcliff and for all who come in contact with him.

In chapter 16 Heathcliff seems to share for a brief moment in the calm that envelops the Grange on the morning of Catherine's death. When Nelly finds him outdoors in the park he is leaning "against an old ash tree, his hat off, and his hair soaked with the dew that had gathered on the budded branches" (p. 138). When Nelly expresses a wish that Catherine "may wake as kindly in the other world" as her life has closed in this one, however, he cries out vehemently, "May she wake in torment!" After "stamping his foot, and groaning in a sudden paroxysm of ungovernable passion . . . he dashed his head against the knotted trunk; and, lifting up his eyes, howled, not like a man, but like a savage beast getting goaded to death with knives and spears" (p. 139). Heathcliff's eighteen years of vengeance are underway before chapter 16 can end.

One measure of the brutality of that vengeance is the account Isabella gives Nelly in chapter 17 of her harrowing departure from the Heights. The psychic storm she endures before leaving is appropriately matched by the unseasonable springtime snowstorm that has obliterated the "infinite calm" in which Catherine had died. "That Friday made the last of our fine days, for a month. In the evening, the weather broke; the wind shifted from south to northeast, and brought rain first, and then sleet and snow" (p. 140). Heathcliff's near murder of Isabella is prompted by the coolness with which she "pulls out his nerves" with "red hot pincers," as she tells Nelly (p. 143). She begins the fearsome battle by taunting him for being driven away from Catherine's grave by the snow. "And that's a poor love of yours that cannot bear a shower of snow!" (p. 146). Marriage to Heathcliff has brutalized Isabella, while sharpening her powers of sarcasm and scorn. Her only defense is to return his aversion verbally—and to run for her life from the physical retaliation it provokes.

76

Another measure of the adult Heathcliff's brutalizing power is the reception he gives to Linton, his own son, upon Linton's first arrival at Wuthering Heights in chapter 20. Nelly, on Heathcliff's orders, has brought the thirteen-year-old boy from Thrushcross Grange. "God! what a beauty! what a lovely, charming thing!" Heathcliff exclaims. "Haven't they reared it on snails and sour milk, Nelly? Oh, damn my soul! but that's worse than I expected—and the devil knows I was not sanguine!" This is the inspection motif with a vengeance. Moments later, Heathcliff asks, "Where is *my* share in thee, puling chicken?" as Linton lifts "his great blue eyes to inspect the inspector" (p. 169).

Linton Heathcliff's only consolation, as his father's had been years before, is in being loved by Catherine—in this case Cathy Linton. Heathcliff despises both youngsters, but encourages their courtship for his own purposes. Linton and Cathy, like Heathcliff and his Cathy, are happiest when dreaming of the out of doors, away from their various persecutors. Linton Heathcliff is sickly, how-ever, so they do not actually get outside very often. Their most enduring re-sponse to nature actually occurs indoors, he in an armchair, she in a rocking chair. It is winter, and they are dreaming of summer. As each projects "a perfect idea of heaven's happiness," they define their opposing personalities. As Cathy tells Nelly, "he said the pleasantest manner of spending a hot July day was lying from morning till evening on a bank of heath in the middle of the moors, with the bees humming dreamily among the bloom, and the larks singing high up over head, and the blue sky and bright sun shining steadily and cloudlessly." Cathy prefers "rocking in a rustling green tree, with a west wind blowing, and bright, white clouds flitting rapidly above; and not only larks, but throstles, and black-birds, and linnets, and cuckoos pouring out music on every side . . . and the whole world awake and wild with joy. He wanted all to lie in an ecstasy of peace; I wanted all to sparkle, and dance in a glorious jubilee" (pp. 198–99).

Such moments of peace are much easier for them to achieve in imagination than in actuality. Whenever they are outdoors in a condition of peace, Heathcliff intrudes. Three scenes in volume 2 actually embody their contrasting visions of peace. In chapter 22 Cathy, walking with Nelly, climbs a tree on a glorious day and rides in a "breeze-rocked cradle" (p. 186). But her descent, on the other side of the wall, leads to her first conversation with Heathcliff, much to Nelly's chagrin. In chapters 26 and 27 Cathy and Nelly twice encounter Linton Heath-cliff inert on the heath. On the first occasion he is so abject in mood and manner that he cannot even recall the earlier discussion in which he had voiced the "idea of happiness" he is currently enacting physically. He appears slightly more animated when the three meet the next week at the same spot, but their

outdoor calm is interrupted by Heathcliff, who entices them all to Wuthering
Heights, where, as part of a premeditated plan, he imprisons them. He wants
Cathy and Linton to marry so that he, as Linton's father, will be certain to inherit
Thrushcross Grange as soon as his son dies, as happens in chapter 30. No
wonder he winces as he interrupts Mr. Lockwood on the first page of the novel
by saying, "Thrushcross Grange is my own, sir."

Once indoors Heathcliff's vengeance and cruelty become even harsher and
more ruthless than before. On the same page where he tells Nelly, "I have a
mind to be hospitable to-day," he also confides these feelings about his son and
his daughter-in-law-to-be: "It's odd what a savage feeling I have to anything that
seems afraid of me! Had I been born where laws are less strict, and tastes less
dainty, I should treat myself to a slow vivisection of those two, as an evening's
amusement" (p. 215). When Cathy grabs the key in an attempt to escape, he
subdues her with "a shower of terrible slaps on both sides of the head, each
sufficient to have fulfilled his threat, had she been able to fall" (pp. 215–16).
The temporary dream of peace on the moors has been irrevocably shattered by
Heathcliff. For his son Linton all that remains is "rushing deathwards."

Cathy agrees to marry Linton on condition that Heathcliff will allow her to go
home to visit her father, Edgar, who is dying. When he does die in chapter 28,
however, she can only leave the house by escaping through her mother's former
window at the Heights. Linton Heathcliff, in his short history as a husband,
shows himself to have become as brutalized by Heathcliff as his mother Isabella
had been. When Cathy claims possession of Thrushcross Grange, her childhood
home, he tells Nelly that "it's mine—papa says everything she has is mine. All
her nice books are mine; she offered to give me them . . . but I told her she had
nothing to give, they were all, all mine" (p. 223). When Linton dies in chapter
30 and Hareton begins to hazard his first signs of affection toward Cathy by
helping her reach for her books, Nelly's narration of the past history of Wuthering Heights and its inhabitants comes to an end: "Thus ended Mrs. Dean's
story" (p. 236).

At the beginning of chapter 31 Mr. Lockwood, having decided to spend the
next six months in London, visits the Heights to inform Heathcliff of his plans.
Here he witnesses the spat between Cathy and Hareton that results in Hareton's
throwing her books into the fire, preparing for the resumption of the comedy of
manners in the form of their courtship in chapters 32–34. Mr. Lockwood also
sees in Heathcliff "a restless, anxious expression" he has never seen before,
preparing for the "change" about which Nelly will tell him when he returns in
November. That Lockwood himself has not yet been essentially changed by

Nelly's extraordinary story is indicated by the fact that he still fantasizes, as he leaves, about the charming young mistress of the Heights. " 'How dreary life gets over in that house!' I reflected, while riding down the road. 'What a realization of something more romantic than a fairy tale it would have been for Mrs. Linton Heathcliff, had she and I struck up an attachment, as her good nurse desired, and migrated together into the stirring atmosphere of the town!' " (pp. 240–41).

The closing words of chapter 31 have brought us full circle: from the tragic love triangle among Catherine Earnshaw, Edgar Linton, and Heathcliff; to the echo of that triangle among Catherine Linton, Linton Heathcliff, and Hareton Earnshaw; to the absurd love triangle among "Mrs. Heathcliff," Mr. Lockwood, and "the clown at his elbow" comically projected in the Lockwood introduction. The tragic residue of the Heathcliff-Catherine love story has nearly played itself out.

Catherine's death at the beginning of chapter 16 ended the living phase of the tragic love story, a phase which was relatively active, hopeful, and dynamic in spite of the external and internal obstacles confronting her and Heathcliff. By contrast, the second phase of the Heathcliff-Catherine love story is retrospective, vengeful, and despairing. From the moment Heathcliff bashed his head against the tree in chapter 16, the "tragic passion has been rushing deathwards" in a perpetual motion running eighteen years. Heathcliff himself is not yet dead, but Hindley Earnshaw and Isabella Linton, in the first wave, and Edgar Linton and Linton Heathcliff, in the second, have been rushed to their early ends. We can say of these eighteen years, relative to the living love story, what Truscott says of the third movement of the *Appassionata* relative to the first, that the emotional residue is "frozen into a great tragic tableau, which comes to no solution except that 'this burden shalt thou carry.' " Emily Brontë has wrested this burden into a fictional structure whose emotional storm is even bleaker than that of the living love story, a structure whose emotional climate matches that of the finale of the *Appassionata*.

The main theme of the third movement differs from the main theme of the first movement much as the adult Heathcliff differs from the young Heathcliff. Both themes are announced very quietly, *pp*. But this theme, in its furious pace and obsessive rhythms, incorporates the principle of storm from the very beginning. It has no self-weakness comparable to that of its first-movement counterpart; it extends itself in large striding sequences that are impervious to outside forces and unthreatened by internal timidity. This theme can be announced very quietly because it knows its own strength from the first, leaving its more explosive manifestations for crises that require them—as when it returns with a vengeance, *forte*, near the end of the exposition. Its *pp* reannouncements at the beginning of the development and recapitulation lead to more immediate crescendos and *sforzandos* than before, setting up its final return, faster and louder than ever, in the coda. This theme experiences no dramatic transformations comparable to those of its first-movement counterpart; it simply becomes ever more strongly its own implacable, self-contained self. It also differs from its first-movement counterpart in having no consoling second theme.

The adult Heathcliff differs from the young Heathcliff in much the same way. Although he embodies psychic storm throughout chapters 17–31, he more often than not arrives on the scene quietly. Even Isabella says, "He is quieter now than he used to be, if no one provokes him; more sullen and depressed, and less furious" (p. 144). Before the emotional storm that erupts in chapter 17 he approaches Wuthering Heights quietly in the snow—until, being locked out by Hindley and taunted by Isabella, he explodes into rage. He is quiet and self-contained in chapter 22 when, after Cathy descends from the tree, he tells her that her cousin Linton is dying and needs her help. He appears just as calm when he accosts Nelly, Cathy, and Linton on the heath in chapter 27—before going on to imprison them at the Heights. Unlike the passive child who at first had no defenses against his traumatic introduction to the Heights, the adult Heathcliff can announce himself quietly because he knows that he can unleash psychic violence at will. He is now impervious to any force that would attack him from without; nor does he reveal any self-weakness that might be felt from within. In these chapters he experiences no overt transformations comparable to those of his youth; nor does he find the consolatory equivalent of the living Catherine.

Perhaps the main difference between the sonata-allegro structures of the first and third movements of the *Appassionata* is the tremendous sense of fatality that pervades the third. The first movement, fateful enough in itself, nevertheless brought dramatic changes to the material of both themes in the exposition, in the development, in the recapitulation, and in the coda. Here the material of the main theme remains essentially unchanged in the exposition, in the development, in the recapitulation; then again in the development, recapitulation, and coda. Whereas the first movement ended quietly, with the first theme having been stripped of its trill and rendered a "ghost" through the process of attack and transformation, this movement ends as brutally as it began, the thirteen ominous diminished-seventh chords at its beginning being resolved, harmonically, by the furious "hurricane" which pushes the main theme, *presto* and *ff*, through to its final F-minor cadence. Whereas the first movement contained contrasting themes and contrasting harmonies, expressive of drama and hope, this movement embodies the unvaried extension of psychic storm.

A comparable sense of fatality characterizes chapters 17–31 of *Wuthering Heights*. Characters are born, characters die, characters leave the Heights, characters arrive there, but all are oppressed by the controlled, relentless psychic storm emanating from Heathcliff. The crises in this section do not rival those of the living love story in suspense. In chapter 7 one did not know what would happen between Heathcliff and Catherine when they inspected each other following her stay at Thrushcross Grange. In chapter 10 one did not know exactly what would happen when Heathcliff returned after three years away. There was a strong sense of fatality, to be sure, in chapters 4–15, but one never knew in advance exactly how the contrasting forces would work themselves out. Here, however, there is relatively little drama or suspense. For eighteen years Heathcliff seems to prevail, with no one strong enough to oppose his plans or effectively stand up to him. For all involved, there is "no solution except that 'this burden shalt thou carry.'" Every time the pain and tension seem to reach their maximum level, a new perverse deflection of Heathcliff's will carries it even further. These chapters eventually attain an inhuman sense of pain and tension akin to that found in the third movement, when the already unendurable material is deflected back to retrace the same ground, the same crisis once more. The brief, contrasting views of peace articulated by young Cathy and Linton manifest themselves no more lastingly than does the mighty crisis that produces a deceptive pause, near the end of the development, in the storm of the third movement. In each case, all calm is consumed in the resumption of storm.

In chapters 17–31, as in the third movement, the drama of the great tragedy is past. Instead we live with the fierce residue. Rolland's summary of the motions of the spirit of the F-minor finale applies equally well to the story of the adult Heathcliff: "A wind of madness blows over the heath of the old Lear; it is the desperate *lamento* of broken loves, hopes, friendships, ambitions" (p. 148). After the death of Catherine, Heathcliff's life is such a *lamento* for eighteen years. From chapter 17 through chapter 31 he is the human embodiment of the principle that Rolland feels is the ultimate "hero" of the *Appassionata:* "the naked Force of the Elements of Destruction" (p. 169). The violence with which Heathcliff lets the "winds of madness blow," however, does not entirely obliterate his consuming love for Catherine—as Nelly's account of the "change" that overcomes him shortly before his death makes clear. That change will be addressed in the chapter to come.

Organic Form

The *Appassionata* is an extremely early example of organic form in Viennese music, *Wuthering Heights* a rather late example in English fiction, but each is a stunning expression of the concept.[13] In both arts, the term *organic form* evolved in response to transformations that nineteenth-century Romantic artists brought to the forms of their eighteenth-century predecessors. It denotes an artistic structure that seems to be shaped by the intrinsic dynamics of psychic energies themselves—as opposed to one evidently derived from a preconceived, conventional mold. Internal to a work, the concept applies to the psychic energies themselves, to the structure by which they are given shape, and to the relation between the energies and the structure. External to the work, the concept implies (a) divergence from the conventional forms of an artistic tradition and (b) adherence in some way to the "organic" form of nature itself. The "whole created cosmos" of the *Appassionata*, as much as that of *Wuthering Heights*, gives masterful expression to all these aspects of organic form.

Rolland writes that "were it only by reason of the psychical contents of [its] interior drama, the *Appassionata* would be something exceptional" (p. 170). The interior drama of the Heathcliff-Catherine love story is equally exceptional. In our comparison of the emotional strife found in the sonata and in the love story, the "organic" nature of the "psychical contents" has been most evident in the treatment of theme in the first movement and in the treatment of character in chapters 4–15. The brutal transformations undergone by the leading themes and characters; the extent to which those themes and those characters are related to, even derived from, each other; and the tendencies of those themes and characters to be violated from within or without—all these characteristics serve not only to create organic growth within the work itself but to do so in a way that differs sharply from the precedent of each artist's classical predecessors. Stylistically and psychologically, the treatment of theme in the *Appassionata* and of character in *Wuthering Heights* is an important measure of the Romantic transformation of classical equilibrium.

Austen's heroines, like Mozart's themes, tend to be introduced with the strong outlines of their characters already determined. They undergo experience which enriches their character (and our understanding of it) but which, however stressful, does not transform that character into something different in its essentials. Elizabeth Bennet in *Pride and Prejudice* is a typical example. At the beginning of the novel she is brilliant, witty, loving, proud, and attractive. At the end of the novel she is one year older, somewhat less proud, otherwise much the same. She has undergone considerable stress in volume 2 owing to Darcy's shocking proposal and subsequent letter, but while her response to that stress heightens her experience and deepens her character, it does not essentially change her character. In three volumes, her character has changed much less in essentials than has that of Heathcliff or Catherine in a dozen chapters. The man she marries, Fitzwilliam Darcy, changes even less than she. Even Emma Woodhouse, who changes more than do most Austen heroines, is essentially static in comparison to Heathcliff or Catherine. The man she marries, George Knightley, is even more static than Darcy.

Mozart's treatment of musical themes is comparable to Austen's treatment of character. As noted in Chapter 1, the theme that begins the orchestral exposition of Mozart's Piano Concerto No. 9, K. 271, returns essentially unchanged to begin the solo exposition, the development, the recapitulation, and the coda. The stability of each of these returns far outweighs the motivic and harmonic pressure experienced in the development section. This concerto, of course, is one of Mozart's earliest and most effervescent masterpieces. But even his most agitated, vehement, and pre-Romantic works reveal a comparable treatment of theme. The main theme of the G-minor Symphony, K. 550, is clearly stated and repeated in the opening bars, stated again in the counterstatement, and presented three more times in the exact repeat of the exposition. It experiences brutal stress in the development section, but it is not thereby transformed, for it returns unscathed in the recapitulation, regaining the pristine grace with which it had expressed its anguish in the exposition and its repeat. As for the contrasting second theme, it undergoes no pressure comparable to that experienced by the second theme of the *Appassionata*. This theme, lyrical and harmonious in the exposition, is repeated in the exact repeat of the exposition; it then returns in its pristine beauty and integrity in the recapitulation, having been transposed into the tonic key, but otherwise unchanged.

The treatment of character in Austen and theme in Mozart consistently reveals a psychology in which the concept of a personality or a theme is essentially inviolate. Whatever growth or change takes place in the process of a narrative or a movement may deepen the experience of the character or theme but it in no way violates or transforms its essential nature. The concept of character in *Wuthering Heights* and theme in the *Appassionata* is radically different. What Maynard Solomon, writing of the *Eroica* Symphony, observes of Beethoven's themes is eminently true of Brontë's characters: "The result is music which appears to be self-creating, which must strive for its existence, which pursues a goal with unflagging energy and resoluteness—rather than music whose essence is already largely present in its opening thematic statement."[14] This is the psychology of organic form, of Romantic transformation, and it intensifies the texture of the artistic fabric at the same time that it transforms the characters and themes.

Consider the transformations undergone by Catherine Earnshaw Linton. Not only do they far exceed those experienced by any Austen heroine; they are revealed in language worlds away from Austen's diction. Catherine, in her one-page account of her dream in chapter 12, speaks of a "wrenching" change, of "paroxysms of despair," of "groveling" before an "abyss," of "maddening" under injuries, of a "burning" wish to be outdoors, to be "half savage, and hardy, and free." Such extremes of heart and mind pervade *Wuthering Heights;* in Austen's fiction they are nonexistent. The force and vehemence of the diction here corresponds to the melodic mutilation and exaggerated dynamics found at the pressure points of the *Appassionata,* beginning with the counterstatement.

In a local sense, such passages of deep psychic drama exemplify the vehement Romantic transformation of Brontë and of Beethoven; in a larger sense, they exemplify their Romantic equilibrium as well. For these passages of extreme stress are given long-range as well as short-range meaning by the contexts in which they occur. In the works of such Romantics as Chopin and Poe, such intense and extreme states are often made to stand in and of themselves—as in a prelude, say, of seventeen bars, or a dream narrative of ten pages. But Catherine's dream occupies only one page of 266 in the novel, and the counterstatement only eight bars of 262 in the movement. Impressive as these moments are in isolation, they are even more so in their overall structural context.

Earlier we discussed several of the ways in which the extreme tension of bars 16–23 of the *Appassionata* relates to much of the music that precedes and follows the counterstatement. Briefly, let us do the same for the "psychical contents of the interior drama" of Catherine's dream in chapter 12. Her dream begins in her "oak-panelled bed at home," the bed in which Mr. Lockwood had been confined in chapter 3. One of the disturbing, unresolved ambiguities Mr. Lockwood had encountered during his introduction to the Heights was a series of names scratched on the window ledge and "repeated in all kinds of characters, large and small—*Catherine Earnshaw,* here and there varied to *Catherine Heathcliff,* and then again to *Catherine Linton*" (p. 25). This confusing multiplicity is clarified by Catherine's dream in chapter 12 when one realizes that the three names that puzzled Lockwood correspond precisely to her psychic split: Catherine Earnshaw ("I was a child; my father was just buried"), Catherine Heathcliff ("my all in all, as Heathcliff was at the time"), and Catherine Linton ("converted at a stroke into Mrs. Linton"). This delayed clarification of earlier ambiguity is a dramatic example of the organic form with which the "psychical contents" of this novel are expressed; the result is art that "seems to be self-creating," deriving from material whose essence is discovered with "resolute strife," rather than being "largely present in its opening statement."

After speaking of the "psychical contents" of the *Appassionata*, Rolland goes on to say that the sonata is exceptional "also in virtue of the unity of its form . . . its never-relaxing tension, its rigorous logic, the athleticism of this body that has no drapery, no ornaments, that is all muscle and solid frame" (p. 170). Such unity of form, never-relaxing tension, rigorous logic, and athleticism are equally exceptional in *Wuthering Heights*. It is the combination of psychic eruption and organic unity of form that makes these works such unique embodiments of Romantic equilibrium within their separate traditions. Barzun pointed out that true Romanticists "abandon the ready-made formula" of their classical forerunners "because its excessive generality gives it too loose a fit." We have seen Beethoven and Brontë intensify and muscularize the formula from within. Barzun speaks of the "distortion or asymmetry" characteristic of Romantic forms. [15] Beethoven and Brontë distort the classical forms, but they wrestle the residue into a new kind of expressive symmetry.

We have already addressed several of the methods by which Beethoven and Brontë have achieved a new kind of unity of form while giving expression to psychic energies that would have broken the forms of their predecessors. In long-range structure, we have seen Brontë imbed the vehement Heathcliff story within the conventional framework of the Lockwood story, and Beethoven contain the vehemence of the *Appassionata* within the conventional three-movement framework of the classical piano sonata. Within these long-range structures, we have compared the symmetrical distribution of the violent transformations endured by the main themes of the first movement and the main characters of chapters 4–15, these actively tragic sections of each work being balanced by the tragic residue found in the third movement and chapters 17–31, with only the structurally temporary but spiritually nurturing calms of the second movement and chapter 16 to serve as fulcrums. In shorter-range structure, we have seen the one artist use literary motifs and the other musical motifs to unite individual passages and even imaginative planes that would not otherwise seem to be closely related—motifs that come to unify the organic texture of each work as much as the characters and themes do.

These solutions allowed Beethoven and Brontë to preserve the formal unity of their predecessors while transforming it from within. As opposed to the linear, direct narrative sequence of an Austen novel we have the interpenetrating narrative frames, time frames, and imaginative planes of *Wuthering Heights*. As opposed to the linear, direct sequences of a three-movement Mozart sonata we have the fused movements of the *Appassionata*, their internal sequences defying classical expectation with their exacerbated recapitulations, unrepeated expositions, and structural deflections (the third-movement repeat of the development and recapitulation). Such inward transformations of the long-range structural forms have allowed each artist to create a "whole created cosmos" whose shaping force seems to derive from the "psychical contents" and from the contrasting principles of "storm" and "calm" as much as from the structural models of their predecessors.

Perhaps the strongest element of the organic unity of form in each work is the violent symmetry with which the principles of storm and calm are expressed and distributed. In each work the opposition between such principles becomes so heightened that they seem finally to be opposing sides of the same force. In overt structure, the fusion of the second and third movements of the *Appassionata* creates a disruptive ambiguity; in essence, it reveals an indissoluble link between the contrasting principles of calm and storm. Melodically, the stormy counterstatement of the first movement mutilates the uneasy calm of the opening theme; in actuality, it reveals the degree to which the fate of that theme *is* to be violated by its opposite principle in just such a way. In the "frozen tableau" of the third movement, the principles of storm and calm express themselves simultaneously in the main theme, whose major arrivals are always calm, *pp*, in dynamics, but whose perpetual motion and implacable rhythms always embody storm.

This kind of *discordia concors* occurs throughout *Wuthering Heights* on a variety of levels. Structurally, there is the alternation between the worlds of the Lockwood story and the Heathcliff story, which by the end of the novel become closely linked with each other not only in chronology but in meaning. Genealogically, there is the fusion between the two generations of Earnshaws and Lintons, when the first Catherine dies in giving birth to the second: "About twelve o'clock that night was born the Catherine you saw at Wuthering Heights, a puny seven months' child; and two hours after, the mother died, having never recovered sufficient consciousness to miss Heathcliff, or know Edgar" (p. 137). Psychologically, there is the opposition between the "storm" principle as represented by Heathcliff and the "calm" principle as represented by Edgar, an opposition so strong that the opposing principles sometimes merge into the same concept. In chapter 10, for example, they merge into selfishness: "The mild and generous are only more justly selfish than the domineering" (p. 81). Finally, of course, there are the transformations of meteorological storm and calm into social storm and calm that occur throughout the novel. In chapter 5 the calm inside the Heights before Mr. Earnshaw's death is defined by the storm that is blowing outside. Broken by Cathy and Heathcliff's heartfelt grief when they see he is dead, the indoor calm is later reestablished during their mutually consoling articulations of peace.

Storm and calm, strong and weak, loud and soft, high and low, character and character, theme and theme, volume and volume, movement and movement—these are among the living principles that come to be fused and inextricably bound together within the organic, unified forms of these two works. Even so, all of the violent transformation is contained within the classical frame of the Lockwood story and of the three-movement sonata, however much each has been intensified and transformed from within.

A final measure of the strength with which conflicting principles have been made to express unity in the two works is the treatment of geographical setting on the one hand and harmonic setting on the other. Brontë limits her passionate tale to Thrushcross Grange and Wuthering Heights, only four miles apart. These domains originally represent the contrasting principles of calm and storm, respectively. By the end of the work, however, the differences between them become so heightened that one is not sure there is any essential difference after all. Because all of the tension in the work is made to flow within this compressed geographical range, each locale becomes imbued with the passions of the other. To have created such a cosmic contrast within a four-mile range is one of Emily Brontë's great achievements, and much of the vigorous logic that unifies the work can be traced to the restriction to its two adjacent yet contrary locales.

Beethoven treats the harmonic setting for the *Appassionata* in much the same way. The F-minor outer movements contrast with the D-flat-major inner movement. These two tonal areas are treated in such a way as to embody a stark dichotomy of storm and calm. Yet they, like the two fictional locales, become inextricably linked by the end of the work. Primarily they are linked by the thirteen diminished-seventh chords that fuse the second movement with the third. But they are also linked by the power they show over their respective domains. The hymnic second movement never deviates from D-flat major; the tempestuous finale never diverges from F minor and its related minor keys. Even the first movement is unusual in its relentless minor-key character, the consoling theme in A-flat major being followed by the minor of the relative major to close the exposition. Furthermore, the dramatic pressure-point of the first-movement development section occurs when the second theme returns in D-flat major, the tonality of the second movement to come. The dynamics by which that theme is pushed beyond articulate utterance by the pressures of the relentless bass during its most complete self-statement anticipate the dynamics by which the more sustained D-flat-major harmony of the second movement will be dissolved by the brutal chords that initiate the third movement.

The "setting" of each work, then, concentrates the symmetry of the violence at the same time that it expands its meaning. The violence that flows between Thrushcross Grange and Wuthering Heights in the novel transforms them from contrary locales into contrary principles—and mutually interacting ones, at that. This effect is produced not so much by the limitation of setting per se as by the power of the treatment, as comparison with Austen's *Emma* makes clear. That novel is restricted to the village of Highbury and its near environs—a spatial range as narrow as that of *Wuthering Heights*. But within that limited range there are a multiplicity of rival domains that serve to soften, explain, and articulate the contrast between the two main domains of Hartfield and Donwell Abbey, which remain contrasting locales, not contrasting principles, throughout. The treatment of harmony in the *Appassionata* contrasts with that in Haydn and Mozart similarly, the difference being not in the outer range of keys (home, away, home in successive movements) but in the powerful, organic energies generated within the conventional boundaries. By making each movement more harmonically single-minded than was typical of his classical predecessors, Beethoven created a new kind of harmonic concentration in which the contrasting keys come to represent contrasting principles as well. Indeed, the principles contrast so intensely that they ultimately seem extensions of one another, rather than conventional areas of contrast.

As with the treatment of themes and of characters, of motifs and of motifs, of movements and of volumes, the pressures that Beethoven and Brontë brought to bear upon contrasting harmonic and geographical locales came to transform such locales in a way not typical of their classical predecessors. This tendency becomes even stronger in the "unworldly" plane of *Wuthering Heights* yet to be discussed—and in the music of Opus 111, with which it will be compared in Chapter 3.

Rolland's final account of the relation between form and content in the *Appassionata* emphasizes the tense equilibrium of its organic form. That relation is "characterized by the emprise of reason over the forces let loose. The tumultuous elements are purified, confined within the strict forms of the classical discipline. These forms, indeed, are enlarged to admit the entry of a whole world of passions. A sea of blood thunders within them; but the sea is closed with the pillars of Hercules. Beethoven, by a tenacious and superhuman tension of the will, has sealed the hinges and put his shoulder to the gate" (pp. 171–72).

Appropriately, Rolland's final metaphor for the essential form of the *Appassionata*—"a thunderous sea of blood closed with the pillars of Hercules"—resembles the metaphor the reviewer of the *Britannia* used to summarize the essential form of *Wuthering Heights:* "a dark and sullen torrent, flowing between high and rugged rocks." The Romantic equilibrium of each work is found in the strength with which the high, rugged pillars of the organic form manage to contain the dark and thundering sea of emotional content.

It is in such motions of the spirit that the ultimate meaning of each work is found. Dorothy van Ghent's summary of the essential meaning of *Wuthering Heights* applies closely to that of the *Appassionata*, so closely that it is essentially a variation on Rolland's evaluation of the sonata.

> The design of the book is drawn in the spirit of intense compositional rigor, of *limitation;* the characters act in the spirit of passionate immoderacy, of *excess.*
> . . . Essentially, *Wuthering Heights* exists for the mind as a tension between two kinds of reality: the raw, inhuman reality of anonymous natural energies, and the restrictive reality of civilized manners, habits, and codes. . . . The tension between these two kinds of reality, their inveterate opposition and at the same time their *continuity* with one another, provides at once the content and the form of *Wuthering Heights.* . . . Only in the fully wrought, fully realized, work of art does form so exhaust the possibilities of the material that it identifies itself with these possibilities.[16]

One would be hard pressed to name a novel or a sonata in which such possibilities are so profoundly exhausted as in *Wuthering Heights* or the *Appassionata*. In their brute, raw energy, in their muscular organic form, and in the tense equilibrium between the energy and the form, these two works invite comparison with each other as much as with any works in their separate artistic traditions.

This is not to say, of course, that their achievements are unrelated to those of their classical predecessors in their separate fields. Consider, for example, Tony Tanner's description of the essence of *Pride and Prejudice*. According to Tanner, the novel "shows us energy and reason coming together, not so much as a reconciliation of opposites, but as a marriage of complementaries. Jane Austen makes it seem as if it is possible for playfulness and regulation—energy and boundaries—to be united in a fruitful harmony, without the one being sacrificed to the other." Tanner's analysis applies equally well to Mozart's Piano Concerto No. 9, a work in which Rosen finds a comparable union between "freedom" and "submission to the rules."[17] *Wuthering Heights* and the *Appassionata* supplant the playfulness with passion and the freedom with fate, at the same time heightening the tension between the energy and the boundaries. The *Romantic* equilibrium of Brontë and Beethoven is found in the added vehemence and rawness they bring to the energy; their Romantic *equilibrium* is found in the added strength and rigor they bring to the boundaries.

Response to Nature

In discussing the organic form of the *Appassionata* and *Wuthering Heights*, I have purposely withheld consideration of the extent to which these works can be said to "adhere in some way to the 'organic' forms of nature itself." Thus far we have discussed in a general way the extent to which both works embody the contrasting principles of storm and calm; in doing so we have cited Rolland's image of the second movement as "a zone of anti-cyclone between two typhoons." Certain music critics, taking the comparison literally, would term it illegitimate. They would argue that we have no evidence that that is what Beethoven intended by the piece, or that there is no single bar or passage in the work that can be said to represent a "typhoon" and nothing else. Such objections, however, miss the point. They assume that Rolland means that the *Appassionata* is *about* a typhoon.

Rolland's description of "a zone of anti-cyclone between two typhoons" is accurate not because typhoons exist in the music but because the work itself embodies the principles of elemental strife with a period of calm in the center. To embody such principles, of course, is not *all* that the *Appassionata* does, but is an essential part of what it does. Any analysis of the work that overlooks the principle of elemental strife (however that principle is expressed in words) would be overlooking the principal motions of the spirit that have given the work meaning for generations of human beings who have responded to it.

This is not to say that metaphorical descriptions of musical works are always valid. They can be particularly dangerous if intended as literal descriptions of what is happening *in* the music. Schindler quotes Czerny's idea that the *Appassionata* depicts "ocean waves on a stormy night when from the distance a cry for help is heard."[18] William S. Newman reproduces this nineteenth-century effusion: "Dismal shadows rise, as it were, out of the lowest depths; soft wailings issue from the heart, and fate is heard knocking at the door. Suddenly a mighty storm breaks forth, then there is painful trembling, and in the second theme in A-flat major, there arises a wonderful sympathetic strain of happy consolation" (p. 522). This is heavy going, to be sure. But the reader who eschews such a response entirely in order to embrace the "objective" analysis of a Hans Keller, or even a Heinrich Schenker, may well be in danger of losing the baby with the bathos. Even the passage Newman quotes, sentimental as it is, responds to primary features of the music.[19] It is not by definition a mistake to use metaphor to describe the emotional or spiritual essence of a great musical work; the mistake is to respond to such metaphor as if it were literal discourse.[20]

This can easily be shown by reference to the *Britannia*'s metaphor for the "impetuous force" of *Wuthering Heights*. We have already compared this "dark and sullen torrent, flowing between high and rugged rocks" with Rolland's "tumultuous seas of blood closed with the pillars of Hercules." Some would argue that such metaphors are more appropriate for novels, which can actually depict such torrents and rocks, than for "pure" music, which cannot. But *Wuthering Heights* is as lacking in actual "dark and sullen torrents" as the sonata is lacking in "tumultuous seas of blood." Nor would the presence of such torrents in the literal world of the novel necessarily enhance the force of the metaphor. The sullen torrents of the novel, like the tumultuous seas in the sonata, are emotional, psychological, and spiritual, not topographical. To banish metaphorical language from the criticism of either art would be to lose access to the motions of the spirit that generate much of the meaning that music and literature have. This is especially true in the case of artists such as Beethoven and Emily Brontë.

Early in this study we cited Beethoven's assertion that his musical ideas are "roused by moods which in the poet's case are transmuted into words, and in mine into tones, that sound, roar, and storm until at last they take shape for me as notes." The "organic form" of his most nature-oriented compositions results from such a shaping process. Language drawing upon the forms of nature is appropriate for the criticism of such compositions not because it corresponds literally to details from nature portrayed within its notes but because it corresponds to the spirit with which its notes express a response to nature. *Wuthering Heights*, no less than the *Appassionata*, is exceptional in the way in which it expresses, not nature itself, but a human response to it.

Beethoven's Sixth Symphony, the *Pastoral*, is the most programmatic of his works because of the literal indications he put in the score. The successive movements are actually entitled "Awakening of cheerful feelings on arriving in the country," "Scene by the brook," "Merry Assembly of Countryfolk," "Lightning, Thunderstorm," and "Shepherd's Song: Happy, grateful feelings after the storm." In addition to these general indications, there are moments in the music—birdcalls, thunder—which directly imitate identifiable sounds in nature. Yet it is the re-creation of a human response to nature rather than a literal representation of the sounds of nature itself that Beethoven intended and achieved. In his notebooks he stated that "all painting carried too far in instrumental music loses its effect." He said of the Sixth Symphony that it is "more an expression of feeling than a painting." He felt that this feeling was "so strongly expressed" that the spirit of nature would be recognized by the listener "even without the description" Beethoven himself provided.[21]

The spirit of nature, of course, has been recognized in many of the works for which he himself did not provide descriptive terms. Three of his piano sonatas have come to be known as the *Moonlight*, the *Pastoral*, and the *Tempest*. Each of these works contains "motions of the spirit" somewhat comparable to the conditions with which it has been programmatically associated—otherwise their labels would probably not have remained so strongly affixed. But this does not mean that these works are *about* moonlight, pastures, or even tempests.[22] Moreover, the experience of nature in Beethoven is often felt just as strongly in works which have no specific programmatic connection with nature—whether affixed by Beethoven or anyone else. The *Appassionata* and the *Waldstein* are perhaps the most striking examples among the piano sonatas. Robert Simpson points to the second movement of the first of the last quartets, Opus 127: "The last full variation, with its great striding arpeggios marching skywards past the slow soaring of the theme, the air alive with the singing of birds, surpasses even the 'Scene by the Brook' in the 'Pastoral' Symphony as a response to nature."[23]

"Response to nature"—rather than description of it—is the key phrase in understanding the function of nature in Beethoven's music. Any composer with a certain facility can walk out in a field or a storm and reproduce in a recognizable way some of what is heard—as the Romantic age was to make all too clear. Beethoven's experience and love of nature allowed him to internalize the motions of its spirit; his transforming genius allowed him to communicate, not the sensations of nature, but his human response.

Emily Brontë possessed a similarly rare transforming genius. Curiously, in *Wuthering Heights*, too, it is the spirit of nature and of Emily Brontë's response to nature that dominates the "landscape" of the novel, not the details of the landscape itself.[24] In Beethovenian terms, it is the feeling and not the picture that dominates. Consider the two kinds of storm presented in the Lockwood introduction. One is the literal storm that transforms the landscape into a "billowy, white ocean" and obliterates the landmarks by which he had earlier negotiated the path from the Grange to the Heights. The other, more typical of the novel as a whole, is Lockwood's description of "wuthering" as a provincial adjective. In that description the "north wind" does not actually blow. Rather Lockwood "guesses its power . . . by the excessive slant of a few stunted firs at the end of the house; and by a range of gaunt thorns all stretching their limbs one way, as if craving alms of the sun" (p. 14).

Descriptions of the second kind, in which the spirit of the wind and its emotional effects are presented figuratively, are by far the most numerous and most powerful examples of nature in the novel. Here the emotional force of the wind is expressed through the personification of thorns: "gaunt," "limbs," "as if craving alms of the sun." Later in the novel the process is reversed: the wind is embodied in a man, the "stunted" object is a boy. The man is Heathcliff, who says "with particular gusto" to Hareton, "we'll see if one tree won't grow as crooked as another, with the same wind to twist it" (p. 154). People, plants, animals, sun, wind, clouds—all are interrelated in *Wuthering Heights*. The spiritual and emotional qualities of any one of them can invade and shape the qualities of any of the others.

Two concrete examples will suffice for showing how nature tends to be felt more than pictured in *Wuthering Heights*. When Catherine speaks with Nelly about the difference between Edgar Linton and Heathcliff, she uses metaphors *from* nature—not pictures *of* nature—to explain herself. After memorably telling Nelly that the two men's souls are as different "as moonbeam from lightning, or frost from fire," she compares her love for Linton to "foliage in the woods," her love for Heathcliff to "the eternal rocks beneath." The reader does not see the moonbeam or the frost, the foliage or the eternal rocks, yet they are among the strongest presences in the novel because they are so strongly felt. This is one of the great differences between Emily Brontë and many second-rate Romantic writers, who set their characters in elaborate natural settings but do not imbue them with the feelings or the spirit of nature. She differs from them in the same way that Beethoven differs from those Romantic composers whose tempests embody the details rather than the spirit of storm.

A second example from *Wuthering Heights* that feels nature more than it paints it is Cathy Linton's contrast between her vision of peace and that of Linton Heathcliff. At first blush, his "ecstasy of peace," inert on the moors, and her "glorious jubilee," rocking in a rustling green tree, would seem to be nature-painting of the most literal sort. But, as Cathy says, she is describing *ideas of happiness*—not nature itself. She is giving, in Beethoven's words, "more an expression of feeling than a painting." The feelings are those of Cathy and of Linton as they, indoors during the winter, imagine themselves in nature. The result is a picture not of nature but of two youngsters whose felt response to nature defines their contrasting personalities more accurately than literal discourse could ever do.

A final example of how nature is felt more than pictured in the novel is not really an example at all. Readers of *Wuthering Heights* often picture Heathcliff and Catherine together on the moors, but as a matter of fact, no such scene is actually pictured in the book. The only "picture" we have of them actually together on the moors comes during her delirium in chapter 12, when the feathers of her pillow cause her briefly to remember how she and Heathcliff had trapped birds when young. This particular scene, however, is not what most readers picture when they "see" the young lovers together in the wild. Similarly, we tend to picture Heathcliff alone on the moors in a storm, even though the book never actually presents him in this way. In fact, nearly the only times we see him alone are in scenes of retrospect years after the fact—as he tells Nelly of his reaction to Catherine's death or of his visits to her grave. It is the spirit of his solitude that is felt constantly throughout the book, not the physical manifestation of it. Likewise, it is the spirit of the storm within him that is felt to blow throughout the pages of the novel, seldom the north wind itself. Emily Brontë, for whom nature itself was at least as important as it was for Beethoven, has internalized it, and so have her characters. That is why she is able to give us not so much picture as feeling.

A striking measure of the manner in which these two artists convey the spirit rather than the details of nature is found in their treatment of register (high and low on the keyboard) and of altitude (high and low on the earth). The two main themes of the first movement of the *Appassionata* both reveal great extremes of register, especially in the context of Beethoven's classical predecessors. The first theme spans a range from low to high of two octaves in less than four bars. Because it moves dramatically down before beginning its two-octave ascent (which is actually spanned in less than two bars), it conveys a strong feeling of movement from low to high and of the power required to move so "far." The second theme also moves in its first bar from the bass up to the treble, and reaches high above the treble clef when restated a few bars later. This sense of great spaces being spanned is intensified throughout the movement in the treatment of both themes.

By the arrival of the coda, these two themes, intrinsically displaying a wide range of register from low to high, have been heard at the very top and the very bottom of the keyboard's range. During the development the second theme was pushed higher and higher above the treble clef by the rising bass notes. At the beginning of the coda the first theme was pushed far below the bass clef by the "hot pulse" of octaves in the treble. In each case the height or depth of the theme is emphasized by the depth or height of the accompanying notes that are doing the pushing. This range of register is further emphasized later in the coda when the second theme returns in its highest version yet—from which it again disintegrates. Now follow twenty bars of themeless storm running from high to low, concluding before the return of the "fate" motif with eight bars of *ff* arpeggios that plunge violently from high D-flat all the way to the C below the bass clef. It is this passage that causes Rolland to write of "the cavalcade, that mounts towards the tempest-lashed heights, striding from top to bottom of the piano in fiery arpeggios, in a frenzy that knows no respite, till it halts abruptly on the dialogue of Destiny" when the "fate" motif returns, first *ritardando*, then *adagio*, then *ff* (p. 158).

One does not have to force a connection between Rolland's phrase and the literally storm-lashed heights in the novel in order to see that the fiery drive combined with great contrasts between high and low produce similar kinds of intensity in both works. High and low are most literally embodied in the novel by the difference in altitude between Wuthering Heights and Thrushcross Grange. This difference is dramatically felt in Mr. Lockwood's descent from the Heights to the Grange in chapter 3. But it is the social and emotional differences between high and low that produce the real tension, the actual altitude, in the novel. Indeed, few of the "tempest-lashed heights" in *Wuthering Heights* are strictly geographical.

When young Heathcliff arrives, first at Wuthering Heights, then at Thrushcross Grange, he is lashed at by Mrs. Earnshaw, Hindley, Cathy, and Nelly, by Mr. and Mrs. Linton, Edgar, and Isabella. In return, he lashes out at the high-handed tyranny of Hindley; at the high-class marriage of Catherine and Edgar; at the highborn Isabella, after he marries her; even at the high-strung cowardice of his own son Linton. In addition, the lowborn Heathcliff aspires for the relatively highborn Catherine, who herself aspires with half her being toward the even higherborn Edgar. When Cecil says that the "whole created cosmos" of *Wuthering Heights* is animated by the living principles of storm and calm, it is dynamics such as these of which he speaks. The "tempest-lashed heights" in *Wuthering Heights*, as much as those in the *Appassionata*, are primarily metaphorical, not literal.

Not only the range of vehement emotion but the range of social scale is much greater in this novel than in any of Jane Austen's, which are without "tempest-lashed heights" of the geographical, emotional, or social varieties. There are, of course, fine gradations of social class within the upper-middle-class boundaries of Austen's world, but these are not probed in such a way as to radically challenge the entire class system, as it is in *Wuthering Heights*. Emily Brontë's intense exploration of social register demands symbolic interpretation of a kind not required by Austen's fiction.

Likewise, Mozart's melodies and his treatment of them do not normally push the extremes of register to the extent that Beethoven's habitually do. Again, the vehement first movement of Mozart's G-minor Symphony provides a telling contrast with the *Appassionata*. Whereas the main theme of the *Appassionata* spans well over two octaves in four bars, the first theme of the G-minor Symphony moves less than one octave in the same space. Whereas Beethoven's theme moves in great leaps and with irregular rhythm, Mozart's is mostly stepwise in motion, and regular in rhythm. The second theme of the Mozart movement contrasts in the same way with that of the *Appassionata*. Whereas Beethoven's consoling major-key second theme moved well over an octave in the first bar, and moved even higher when immediately restated, the consoling major-key second theme of the G-minor Symphony moves less than an octave in its first eight bars, with almost none of the intervals being more than a step.

Mozart's piano sonatas do use the full range of his keyboard, often in imaginative ways, but they do not assault the extremes of his instrument with the vehemence that Beethoven does in the *Appassionata*. High and low on the keyboard do not necessarily indicate a condition of storm, either emotional or psychological. But Beethoven's dramatic exploration of register in the *Appassionata* makes metaphors such as "tempest-lashed heights" appropriate. Alfred Brendel, a leading interpreter of the sonatas, writes that "among the most important gifts a Beethoven player can have is the power to visualize in an almost geographical sense, the entire panorama of varying dynamic levels embodied in a work—like looking at a landscape and taking in at a glance its valleys and mountaintops."[25] Readers need a comparable imaginative power when interpreting *Wuthering Heights*, not so much because of its actual landscape as because of its metaphorical ones.

We began this section by suggesting that organic form in music or fiction adheres "in some way" to the organic forms of nature itself. The adherence in Beethoven and Brontë is in the feeling for nature's forms more than in the picturing of them. That is why *Britannia*'s image of "a dark and sullen torrent, flowing between high and rugged rocks" and Rolland's image of "tumultuous seas of blood closed with the pillars of Hercules" are striking metaphors for the organic form of each work, even though none of these images are literally present in the works themselves.

Earlier in his study Rolland used a related metaphor for the essential form of the *Appassionata*. Reviewing all of Beethoven's piano sonatas, he finds that "no other of his sonatas shows to the same degree the union of unrestrained passion and rigid logic; we have to go to *Tristan* to find another such torrent of fire in a bed of granite" (p. 147). This fire-and-rock metaphor, no less than its water-and-rock counterpart, speaks to the elemental strife and to the essential form of the sonata. It too applies to *Wuthering Heights*.

David Cecil plays on this metaphor when he describes the implacable emotions of Brontë's characters: "unchanging as the hills, fierce as lightning." Within the novel itself the metaphor crops up in the images Catherine uses to contrast Heathcliff's essence (and by extension her own) with that of Edgar. The "lightning" and "fire" she contrasts with Edgar's "moonbeam" and "frost," the "eternal rocks beneath" she contrasts with the "foliage in the woods," are the most enduring images of fire and granite in the novel. But her language is no more literal than Rolland's. She too is speaking not of actual flame and rock but of conditions of the soul.

Early in this chapter we quoted Rolland to the effect that "the most intoxicating ecstasy in nature" is "an ecstasy controlled by the mind." He was referring to the majestic repose of the *Waldstein* Sonata, but his concept applies as well to the impetuous force of both the *Appassionata* and *Wuthering Heights*. It is Beethoven's and Brontë's abilities to feel nature through the heart and to express those feelings through the mind that make their passionate responses to nature so intoxicating. Legend has it that Beethoven composed the finale of the *Appassionata* in a rainstorm and that splotches from that storm can be seen on the score. This legend has telescoped two different events in the history of the sonata, but this particular confusion matters relatively little. It is the spirit of the music, not the spots on the score, that testifies to his response to nature.[26]

Intimations

Before leaving Beethoven's middle period, it is necessary to look briefly at his condition in life at the time he composed the *Appassionata*. Rolland points out that Beethoven's deafness had "worsened since the period—two years before—of the Heiligenstadt Testament. . . . The unhappy man had been compelled to recognize that his trouble was permanent." He quotes a letter from Stephan von Breuning: "You cannot imagine the indescribable (I ought to say frightful) effect that the loss of his hearing has had . . . on that passionate temperament! He shuts himself up within himself; he often distrusts his best friends." That distrust shows in a letter Beethoven wrote at the time: "and now, an end to friendship!" In Rolland's words, "Beethoven creates a vacuum around himself. He is too big. He has developed too rapidly. . . . The world and he glare defiance at each other, like strangers" (pp. 148–51).

The motions of the spirit by which Beethoven responded to the loss of his hearing correspond to some degree with those by which Heathcliff responds to the loss of Catherine, a delicate issue to be addressed more fully in Chapter 5. Here our concern is with the degree to which the *Appassionata* itself (and several of its musical neighbors) seems to express a response to that intolerable loss. Naturally, one must be wary of assuming a direct link between Beethoven's compositions and the conditions of his life at the time he wrote them. The buoyant Second Symphony, completed about the time of the Heiligenstadt Testament, is a sufficient warning. So are two glorious pianistic neighbors to the *Appassionata:* the *Waldstein* Sonata, Opus 53, and the Fourth Piano Concerto, Opus 58. Even so, one feels that the *Appassionata* represents, even more than most works by Beethoven, a passionate outcry from the depths of the soul. That is why Rolland chose to "evoke the storm-charged atmosphere, the black and burning sky under which [it] was conceived; it will help us the better to grasp the meaning of the work, and the somber fury of the first sketches." Rolland, like Tovey, points out that these sketches were even bleaker than the final version of the sonata, lacking any equivalent of the consoling second theme.

The Fourth Piano Concerto, Opus 58, is gracious and buoyant. Yet its tense second movement contrasts with the outer movements as sharply as the second movement of the *Appassionata* contrasts with its outer movements. This movement, like its counterpart in Opus 57, is an Andante con moto. But it depicts the condition Rolland wrote of, in which Beethoven and the world "glare defiance at each other, like strangers." Those motions of the spirit are embodied in the opposed forces of the solo and orchestra. Basil Deane argues that "it would be difficult not to feel in the E minor Andante con moto the confrontation between two worlds, in which the aggressive rhythms of the unison orchestral strings are answered and finally overcome by the pleading phrases of the muted piano. Such confrontation is often implicit in Beethoven, but never elsewhere in the instrumental music is it so explicitly stated, and Liszt's view that the movement represents Orpheus taming the Furies is a credible programmatic interpretation."[27] This brutal, even primal confrontation, even though it finally reaches a harmonious resolution, is of a kind not found in Mozart's piano concertos—or in Austen's novels. It makes musically explicit the tenacious, unyielding motions of the spirit by which a Beethoven or a Heathcliff chose to meet his fate.

Beethoven's next-numbered works, the *Rasoumovsky* Quartets, Opus 59, enter even stranger spiritual ground. Here Rolland finds, "for the first time perhaps in Beethoven's music, 'demoniac' elements that will be more pronounced later. The hinges of the soul are grating" (p. 229). These quartets anticipate to an uncanny degree not only Beethoven's "late" period but also Heathcliff's internal suffering, to be addressed in the chapter to come.

Robert Simpson writes of the "sublime instability" of the first quartet. "Harmonic question marks" delay a statement of the "main theme with strongly rooted F-major harmony" until the coda. The harmonic suspense is comparable to that created by the late resolution of the "fate" motif in the *Appassionata*, but here it is even more severe owing to the fact that the main theme is the subject. A comparable suspense is created in the Lockwood introduction of *Wuthering Heights* when the adult Heathcliff sobs to Cathy's ghost to "Come in! Come in!" Those sobs, as we shall see, are not resolved until the very end of the work. Simpson says of the unsettling first movement that "fate does not knock at the door—it stares in through the window." After this, the "disturbed humor and frequent stammer" of the second movement are the "only possible reaction." The F-minor Adagio which follows is "withdrawn music, a private kind of funeral march" whose "rare gleams of major [tonality] serve to intensify the darkness when it returns."[28]

In *Beethoven: His Spiritual Development*, J. W. N. Sullivan suggests that "the 'Fate' that is to be overcome" in the second quartet of Opus 59 "is not some external menace, some threatening and maleficent power, but Beethoven's own loneliness." That loneliness is "enforced and bitter," expressed through "its yearnings, and its outbursts of something very like rage." It is comparable to the kind of loneliness Heathcliff experiences after being deprived forever of Catherine. Sullivan finds, as do others, "something strictly abnormal" in the slow movement of the third quartet of Opus 59. "It is as if some racial memory had stirred in [Beethoven], referring to some forgotten and alien despair. There is here a remote and frozen anguish, wailing over some impossible destiny. This is hardly human suffering; it is more like a memory from some ancient and starless night of the soul."[29] During the eighteen years following Catherine's death, Heathcliff experiences a like anguish, remote and frozen; we do not learn of his "hardly human suffering" until he speaks to Nelly of his visits to Catherine's grave and of the "change" he feels approaching.

Joseph Kerman describes an "unlikely amalgam" in the slow movement of Opus 59, No. 3: "harmonic instability, suggesting disturbance and passion" coexists with "rhythmic and repetitive sameness, suggesting on the contrary dull obsession."[30] Such contrasting conditions coexist in Heathcliff during his "change," divided between his disturbed yearning for Catherine and the dull obsessions of daily existence. In the quartet this spell is broken by the finale. Its "tumult," in Simpson's words, "comes from within, blotting out the despair and nostalgia of the two previous movements, drowning the sense of failure where ordinary means of communication were concerned." It does so by fusing the principles of fugue and sonata-allegro "with a heat that Mozart could never have conceived, generating a defiant, realistic energy." A comparable fusion of fugue and sonata-allegro animates the first movement of Opus 111, composed fifteen years later. By that time Beethoven will have found a way not only to express but to resolve such defiant energy—in the variations of the sonata's second movement. Its motions of the spirit, as we shall see, correspond to those that animate Heathcliff shortly before his death.

Simpson's final metaphor for the essential form of the finale of the third *Rasoumovsky* quartet is another measure of Beethoven's Romantic equilibrium: "With these means Beethoven hammers out his greatest quartet finale so far, fiercely stretching the medium, yet never breaking it."[31]

Chapter Three

Catherine Heathcliff and Opus 111: "This Shattered Prison"

Writing of the *Eroica* Symphony, Rosen describes the manner in which Beethoven, in the middle period, came to ground the extreme tensions of his development sections in his massive, capacious codas (p. 394). The first-movement coda of the *Eroica* is an excellent example; so are the outer-movement codas of the *Appassionata*. One might say that Emily Brontë resolved the extreme tensions generated by Catherine and Heathcliff by grounding their bodies in the earth. The concept is more than a pun: think of its literal meaning in *Wuthering Heights* and its total irrelevance for any of Austen's novels.

Yet the death and burial of the two lovers is not the only resolution of their energies. Nor is the powerful energy-grounding coda the only method Beethoven was to devise to bring an emotionally vehement movement or work to its end. During his "late" period, the principles of fugue and variation were to become a means by which tension could be not so much "grounded" as transcended—a means by which conflict itself could be transfigured into a harmonious state of oneness. Such a transfiguration, foreshadowed in the mysterious coda which ends the first movement of Beethoven's last piano sonata, Opus 111, occurs in the variation movement that concludes that sonata.

Such an ending also occurs in *Wuthering Heights*—twice. It occurs when Catherine dies and then again when Heathcliff dies. Each character's life of conflict is ended by a death of transcendence in which all previous dissonance is subsumed into a harmonious vision of peace. Catherine's vision is articulated at the beginning of volume 2, in chapter 15. Heathcliff's is dramatized (though not fully articulated) at the end of volume 2, in chapter 34. Whereas the first volume of the novel is characterized by savage violence that is unresolved, the second volume, which also contains such violence, resolves it into a higher harmony. The full resolution, however, does not come until the end. Catherine's brief vision of "a glorious world beyond" in chapter 15 is immediately swept up into the psychic violence that ends her "last reunion" with Heathcliff. Even the "infinite calm" which bathes her body—and Nelly's soul—at the beginning of chapter 16 is quickly broken by the onset of Heathcliff's vengeance. Catherine's deathbound vision of peace becomes spiritually permanent when it is matched, eighteen years later, by Heathcliff's answering vision.

Whereas the *Appassionata* (1804–5) was composed only a few years after the Sonata *Pathétique,* Opus 111 was composed two decades later, in 1820–21. Opus 111 resembles the two earlier sonatas in having a stormy minor-key first movement that includes a contrasting second subject and that is followed by a "heavenly" major-key second movement. Its second movement resembles that of the *Appassionata* in its theme-and-variations form and in maintaining a "heavenly" state throughout. But Opus 111 differs from both predecessors in not having a third movement; more particularly, it differs from the *Appassionata* in that its heavenly variations generate from within themselves not the minor-key strife of the *Appassionata*'s third movement but the free-flowing variations that sublimely crown not only Beethoven's last piano sonata but his lifelong attempt to express reality through pedals, ivory, strings, and a sounding board. As Tovey puts it, "the ink with which Beethoven wrote the ethereal end of Op. 111 was hardly dry before he was telling his publisher that 'the pianoforte is, after all, an unsatisfactory instrument'" (p. 297). His meaning is clarified by the late quartets.

"Beethoven's last sonata," as Philip Barford has written, "defines with absolute assurance the two polarities within which his creative consciousness evolved."[1] The first movement embodies the "storm" principle as we have seen it in earlier works; the second movement embodies the principle of "calm." But here the relationship between such principles is different in kind. As Ernest Newman says of Beethoven's late style in general, the antithetical principles that clashed so violently in his earlier styles are now transferred to "another psychical plane," moving the "polar struggle from the outer to the inner world; the drama is henceforth wholly internal."[2] In Barford's words, Beethoven's late style can be seen as "the period of transcended antitheses—or at least as the period marked by the emergence of a new emphasis on what can be experienced above and beyond antithesis" (p. 149). The new "psychical plane," the "wholly internal" drama, and the "transcended antitheses" are all magnificently embodied in the relationship between the stormy first movement and the transcendent second movement of Beethoven's Opus 111.

The "calm" principle in Beethoven's last sonata differs from its counterpart in the *Appassionata* in that it has the last word. But it also differs in kind from the earlier principle of calm. The Andante con moto of the earlier work was, in Tovey's words, "a dream that must be shattered at the first hint of action." The theme and the early variations of the Arietta of Opus 111 seem at first to embody a comparable dream. But a transformation occurs within the movement that converts the principle of calm into something qualitatively different from that in the earlier sonata: a principle at once visionary and active, a principle capable of containing and transforming the principle of storm.

The principle of calm also has the final word in *Wuthering Heights*. And the calm that animates the final visions of Catherine and Heathcliff operates on "another psychical plane" than has the principle of calm elsewhere in the novel. Linton Heathcliff's "ecstasy of peace," inert on the moors, and Cathy Linton's "glorious jubilee," high in a tree, are satisfying counterparts to the principle of storm—as long as they last. But these visions, no less than the theme and variations of the *Appassionata*, are "shattered at the first hint of action." The states of calm ultimately achieved by the elder Catherine and Heathcliff are unworldly, mystical, and eternal. They transcend the social concerns and even the natural environment that have so occupied these two characters during their strife-filled years on earth. Their energies, and their resolution of them, become "wholly internal," wholly spiritual.

Naturally, literary and musical critics have had some difficulty articulating the kind of unworldly calm that is expressed in the Arietta of Opus 111 and in the final visions of Catherine and Heathcliff. Mystical visions are indescribable. They are incomparable. They inhabit spiritual realms rarely probed in either instrumental music or prose fiction. For visions comparable to that in the Arietta of Opus 111, the student of music must turn, more than to other composers, to Beethoven's own late sonatas and quartets. For visions comparable to those embodied by Catherine and Heathcliff, the student of literature must turn, more than to other novelists, to Emily Brontë's own poetry. Indeed, Beethoven's and Brontë's mystical visions, as manifested in their art, compare more closely with each other than with the work of others in their own separate artistic traditions, a truth that has been intuited by the two critics, one from each field, briefly cited in the opening pages of this book.

Philip Barford, in his study of Beethoven's late piano sonatas, turned to Brontë's poem "The Prisoner" for an analogue to the spiritual vision expressed by the sublime variation movement that concludes Beethoven's Sonata, Opus 109. The lines he compares to the music are the following:

Mute music soothes my breast—unuttered harmony,
That I could never dream, till Earth was lost to me.

Then dawns the Invisible; the Unseen its truth reveals.
My outward sense is gone, my inward essence feels:
Its wings are almost free—its home, its harbour found,
Measuring the gulf, it stoops and dares the final bound.

Philip Henderson, in an introduction to Emily Brontë's poetry, turned to the "unearthly blessedness of Beethoven's late quartets" for a spiritual analogue to the same Brontë poem, finding in the same lines cited by Barford "one of the great moments in English poetry."[3] These very lines from "The Prisoner" (written in 1845) anticipate the mystical visions attained by Catherine and Heathcliff in *Wuthering Heights* (1847). After this connection is shown, the vision that animates not only Brontë's poetic lines but her great fictional protagonists can be compared with the motions of the spirit made manifest by the Arietta of Beethoven's Opus 111.

New Departures

In chapter 15, at the beginning of volume 2, Nelly finally gives to Catherine (Mrs. Edgar Linton) the letter from Heathcliff. It is Sunday and the weather is "warm and pleasant." Its calm is rendered in sound: "Gimmerton chapel bells were still ringing; and the full, mellow flow of the beck in the valley came soothingly on the ear." The soothing sound of the beck is made clearer by the absence of a different sound: "It was a sweet substitute for the yet absent murmur of the summer foliage, which drowned that music about the Grange when the trees were in leaf."

Like the weather, Catherine is calm this Sunday morning. In Nelly's eyes, she is "altered" and "doomed to decay." But this "change" is accompanied by an "unearthly beauty": "The flash of her eyes had been succeeded by a dreamy and melancholy softness; they no longer gave the impression of looking at the objects around her; they appeared always to gaze beyond, and far beyond—you would have said out of this world" (p. 131). Catherine's "dreamy" and "out-of-this-world" state, as described, corresponds precisely to the poetic lines, "That I could never dream, till Earth was lost to me." As Catherine listens to the ringing of the bells and to the "full, mellow flow of the beck," she seems to be thinking of Wuthering Heights—"that is, if she thought, or listened, at all." For her "vague distant look . . . expressed no recognition of material things either by ear or eye." The music that soothes her own breast is mute.

When Nelly interrupts her rapture to give her the letter, Catherine is brought back to this world long enough to endure her last reunion with Heathcliff on earth. Nelly tells us that "the two, to a cool spectator, made a strange and fearful picture" (p. 133). Yet Heathcliff, in the heat of the moment, sees the essential reality of Catherine's life: "I have not broken your heart—*you* have broken it—and in breaking it, you have broken mine" (p. 135). She, in turn, sees the essential reality of her impending death. "The thing that irks me most," she muses to Nelly, "is this shattered prison, after all. I'm tired, tired of being enclosed here. I'm wearying to escape into that glorious world, and to be always there; not seeing it dimly through tears, and yearning for it through the walls of an aching heart, but really with it, and in it. . . . I shall be incomparably beyond and above you all" (p. 134). She has achieved this vision only after transcending earthly and material reality: "Then dawns the Invisible; the Un-seen its truth reveals / My outward sense is gone, my inward essence feels."

That Catherine has indeed "escaped into that glorious world" seems to be indicated by Nelly's description of the "infinite calm" in chapter 16. Nelly's vision of "a repose that neither earth nor hell can break" would seem to indicate that Catherine is "incomparably beyond and above." But neither the reader nor Heathcliff can be certain of the permanence of this vision until the change that overcomes Heathcliff shortly before his death. In chapter 34, his re-vision of Catherine verifies her vision and shatters his prison.

The fine weather that prevailed immediately before and after Catherine's death changes abruptly at the beginning of chapter 17. The primroses and cro-cuses are covered by snow, the larks are silenced, the "young leaves" of the "early trees" are "smitten and blackened," and Isabella arrives from Wuthering Heights with a deep cut in her ear. She tells Nelly how Heathcliff has nearly killed Hindley and then thrown the knife that has pierced her ear. The tale of violence and oppression resumes, engulfing the new generation. Young Cathy and Linton have their momentary visions of paradise, the weather is occasion-ally calm, but essentially the next dozen chapters are of human storm and hell.

Only in the retrospect of chapter 29 do we learn that Heathcliff has suffered as much as his victims during all these years. He has suffered, however, on a different psychical plane than they. In that chapter he tells Nelly how he re-cently opened Catherine's grave at the time of Edgar's burial so he could look at her. "I disturbed nobody, Nelly, and I gave some ease to myself." He tells Nelly how Catherine's ghost has "disturbed me, night and day, through eighteen years—incessantly—remorselessly—till yesternight; and yesternight, I was tranquil. I dreamt I was sleeping the last sleep, by that sleeper, with my heart stopped, and my cheek frozen against hers" (p. 229). He tells Nelly of the arrangements he has made with the sexton to loosen, when he himself is buried, the adjoining sides of his and Catherine's coffins, so that then he will "dissolve with her, and be more happy still." And he tells Nelly how, after Catherine was buried, he had dug up her grave on the first night it had snowed. As he was doing so, he heard a sigh "close at my ear" and felt "the warm breath of it displacing the sleet-laden wind." He felt, in short, "that Cathy was there, not under me, but on the earth."

Reliving that moment eighteen years later, he tells Nelly of following her spirit across the moors to Wuthering Heights. When his entrance is opposed by Isabella and Hindley, he "kicks the breath out of" Hindley and hurries upstairs in search of Catherine. (He does not even register the harrowing details that Isabella gives of this same scene in chapter 17, for his whole being is straining toward Catherine.) "I looked round impatiently—I felt her by me—I could *almost* see her, and yet I *could not!* I ought to have sweat blood, then, from the anguish of my yearning, from the fervour of my supplications to have but one glimpse! I had not one" (p. 230). After describing various hallucinatory visions he has had of Catherine since, he tells Nelly, returning to the grave-digging present, "Now since I've seen her, I'm pacified—a little."

Only in chapter 29 do we feel the force of the words Heathcliff had spoken to Catherine when she accused him of killing her in chapter 15: "Do you reflect that all those words will be branded in my memory, and eating deeper eternally, after you have left me?" (p. 133). Only now do we understand the full implications of the words he spoke to Catherine's departed spirit in chapter 16 in the presence of Nelly: "Be with me always—take any form—drive me mad! only *do* not leave me in this abyss, where I cannot find you!" (p. 139). Psychically, this inability to unite with her spirit has underscored his eighteen years of revenge, which extend even beyond his revelations to Nelly in chapter 29. He does not become fully "pacified" until the "change" that overcomes him in chapters 33 and 34, where Nelly describes to Lockwood the events leading to Heathcliff's death.

In chapter 33 Heathcliff finally loses "the faculty of enjoying the destruction" of young Cathy and Hareton. He explains to Nelly that "there is a strange change approaching—I'm in its shadow at present. I take so little interest in my daily life that I hardly remember to eat, and drink." Cathy and Hareton "are the only objects which retain distinct material appearance to me; and that appearance causes me pain, amounting to agony." The agony is that he sees, in their eyes, Catherine's eyes. The resemblance tearingly reminds him of his loss—and it extends everywhere. "The entire world is a dreadful collection of memoranda that she did exist, and that I have lost her!" (p. 255). To be reunited with her spirit is his "single wish, and my whole being and faculties are yearn-

ing to attain it. . . . It has devoured my existence. I am swallowed in the anticipation of its fulfilment" (p. 256). Losing his "outward sense," he is feeling his
"inward essence," much as Catherine did in chapter 15.

Chapter 34, like chapter 15, opens in calm springtime weather. "We were in
April then: the weather was sweet and warm." The sound of the stream is as
audible as it was eighteen years earlier: "Not only the murmur of the beck down
Gimmerton was distinguishable, but its ripples and its gurgling over the peb-
bles, or through the large stones which it could not cover" (pp. 257, 259).
Heathcliff has been out all night. Nelly sees "a strange joyful glitter in his eyes
that altered the aspect of his whole face." He tells her, "Last night, I was on the
threshold of hell. To-day, I am within sight of my heaven" (p. 259). He too has
reached the condition of the poem: "Then dawns the Invisible; the Unseen its
truth reveals / Its wings are almost free—its home, its harbour found."

The following day his "glittering restless eyes" fix on something invisible a
few feet before him. Whatever he is looking at "communicated, apparently, both
pleasure and pain, in exquisite extremes; at least the anguished, yet raptured
expression of his countenance suggested that idea" (p. 261). That night Nelly
hears him pace his room, moaning in the wee hours. "My soul's bliss kills my
body," he tells her the next day, "but does not satisfy itself" (p. 262). His soul is
as ready to shatter its prison as Catherine's was in chapter 15: "Measuring the
gulf, it stoops and dares the final bound." Nelly discovers him dead after the
next night's storm. The shutters are open to the elements, his body washed by
rain. A "life-like gaze of exultation" stares from eyes that will not shut.

In the last two chapters of volume 2, Heathcliff attains a condition of peace
that answers and completes the condition achieved by Catherine in its first two
chapters. On the last page of the novel the sky is "benign." No longer does a
"wuthering" storm beat against the Heights; there is now a "soft wind breathing
through the grass." During the one year that has passed since Lockwood first
arrived at the Heights, all of the energies that have threatened his—and the
reader's—equilibrium have been resolved, "grounded," or transcended. Heathcliff's final destiny has revealed that the "principles" of storm and calm, in spite
of their apparent opposition, "are not conflicting." When "free from fleshly
bonds they flow unimpeded and unconflicting; and even in this world their discords are transitory. The single principle that ultimately directs them sooner or
later imposes an equilibrium." Cecil rightly contends that "such convictions
inevitably set Emily Brontë's view of human life in a perspective fundamentally
different from that presented to us by other English novelists. For they do away
with those antitheses which are the basis of these novelists' conceptions."[4]

Mary Visick concedes that "generations of readers" have found Heathcliff's ultimate vision "difficult to accept." But she asserts that by "withdrawing into himself and his vision of Catherine" he "approaches an end which is free of meanness." Comparing his final vision with Brontë's "The Prisoner," she argues that "the figure of Heathcliff embodies his creator's insights into the nature of that love which is stronger than death." As the embodiment of "a single-minded, destroying, and all-consuming love," Heathcliff brought Emily Brontë "very close to the frontiers of what is possible in a novel."[5]

Music critics have long contended, for a variety of reasons, that Beethoven reached, in Opus 111, the frontiers of what is possible in a piano sonata. One way in which he did so is by making uncommonly explicit in the Arietta the kind of motions of the spirit glimpsed by Catherine and Heathcliff in their answering visions of peace. In late Beethoven too, conflicting principles somehow become component parts of a harmony. They flow free and unimpeded, reaching an equilibrium that finally does away with antitheses altogether. Before turning to Opus 111, it will be useful to refer to Sullivan's study of Beethoven's spiritual development for an overview of such dynamics in the composer's late period.

For Sullivan, the central vision that radiates throughout the late quartets is found in the fugue that opens the C-sharp-minor Quartet, Opus 131. He calls it "the most superhuman piece of music that Beethoven has ever written." This music, as he describes it, has much in common with the visions achieved by Catherine and Heathcliff before death. "It is the completely unfaltering rendering into music of what we can only call the mystic vision. It has that serenity which . . . passes beyond beauty. Nowhere else in music are we made so aware, as here, of a state of consciousness surpassing our own, where our problems do not exist, and to which even our highest aspirations, those that we can formulate, provide no key." Sullivan writes of "a way of apprehending life, passionless, perfect, and complete, that resolves all our discords." This "is the last and greatest of Beethoven's spiritual discoveries, only to be grasped in moments of his profoundest abstraction from the world."[6] He grasped an earlier version of it in the variation movement of Opus 111.

Several times in his study Sullivan points to "spiritual" affinities between Beethoven and Shakespeare. But he claims that in the late quartets Beethoven "is dealing with states for which there are no analogues in any other art" (p. 126). Yet his description of the opening fugue of Opus 131 is also a description of the very motions of the spirit we have been tracing in *Wuthering Heights*, which is almost the only English novel whose ultimate vision may bear analogy to the late quartets.

Such motions of the spirit, of course, cannot be permanent in the daily lives of those who experience them. "That this vision was permanent with Beethoven is inconceivable," writes Sullivan. "No man ever lived who could maintain such a state of illumination." In "The Prisoner," Brontë describes the withdrawal of such a vision.

> O dreadful is the check—intense the agony
> When the ear begins to hear and the eye begins to see:
> When the pulse begins to throb, the brain to think again
> The soul to feel the flesh, and flesh to feel the chain!

Catherine felt such agony when she again became conscious of the material world in chapter 15. So did Heathcliff when he returned to the world of earthly reality after his first ethereal pursuit of her spirit. Such agony was no doubt felt by Beethoven, too, whenever the vision receded. Appropriately, the spiritual home that he created in the second movement of Opus 111 can be entered only through the spiritual prison of the opening movement.

Catherine's escape from her "shattered prison" means what it does to us because we know what that prison is. The meaning of the Arietta has the same relation to our knowledge of the opening Allegro. In Barford's words, "the two movements completely symbolize the two primary functions of the mind." The one function is "analysis and synthesis of conflicting elements." The other is "the transcendence of all oppositions." The successive movements therefore "project, in the abstract structure of musical thought, at once the inner conflict and tension of consciousness and the unmoving ground of that conflict and tension" (p. 179). The second movement without the first, the "unmoving ground" without the "inner conflict and tension of consciousness," would be as incomplete as Heathcliff's "sight of heaven" in chapter 34 without the "threshold of hell" the night before—or without the eighteen years of "inner conflict and tension of consciousness" revealed retrospectively in chapter 29.

Spiritual Prison

The first movement of Opus 111, like the first movement of the *Pathétique*, begins with a slow introduction that establishes a mood of conflict, mystery, and drama. This introduction, Maestoso, begins with "left-hand plunges of the diminished seventh in a dramatic and tightly-spaced rhythmic relationship" (Barford, p. 181). The discordant sound and the downward motion are typical of the introduction and of the first movement as a whole. So is the harsh dotted rhythm in the opening bar and the harsh contrast in the opening phrase from *forte* to *piano* (Figure 10). The downward plunge of the opening chords impresses us immediately with a vision of the "low." It is answered in the same bar by a higher figure including a trill (reminiscent of the trill-figure that followed the more quietly plunging opening notes of the *Appassionata*). As the entire group is repeated in higher sequence, the trill figure is sounded above the treble clef in bar 5. But this is the highest phrase to be sounded in the entire introduction. There follows a gradual but dramatic descent, *piano*, which once turns upward again but which finally takes both hands into the bass clef, eventually dissolving into a rumbling well below it. It is out of this deep rumbling that the Allegro con brio ed appassionato finally erupts. In register, the introduction has dramatically driven us low (the opening diminished sevenths), has allowed us to see that "high" still exists (the trill figure, rising in sequence), and has then implacably driven us low again.

Figure 10

After the "thunder" of the bass (the word is Tovey's) leads out of the introduction, the dramatic opening theme of the Allegro, in C minor, stammers forth (Figure 11). The three-note motif x, with its low register, its ff dynamics, and its sf emphasis on its third and lowest note, sets the tone for the entire movement, which it dominates. Its own motion from low, to higher, to lower than its beginning at once condenses the basic motion of register in the introduction itself and anticipates the basic motion that will be found in the movement per se. This motif will dominate the Allegro not only in its own motion from low to high to lower but in its role as a harmonic and rhythmic intensifier.

Motif x invariably provokes impetuous running figures, both high and low. The first of these figures, motif y, completes the opening theme. It is the consequent to motif x (the antecedent), but it is an open-ended consequent that never finds rest. The opening statement of the sharply defined motif x was in itself restless, stammering forth twice before its consequent running figure was heard.

110

Figure 11

That restlessness continues in its fuguelike counterstatements. After first appearing in the bass clef and below (bars 4, 5), motif *x* returns in the treble (13), below the treble (19–20), again in the bass clef (24), and finally above the treble clef (28–29)—all of this violent and emphatic movement occurring before the contrasting second theme (in A-flat major) enters at bar 34. This lyrical theme, *piano*, descends from a high register, returns in an ornamented version, and even manages a restful bar of *adagio*. But the original tempo returns *ff* at bar 39, driving the register dramatically downward in broken arpeggios until motif *x* returns in descending sequence (bars 42, 43, 44) to anchor and dramatize the downward motion. The stormy mood has been restored with a vengeance.

The effect is similar to that achieved by the driving closing theme that follows the "consoling" second theme in the first movement of the *Appassionata*. But the effect is even more "fateful" here, owing to the relentless assertion of a motif we have already heard before. Here, as in most of its appearances during the movement, the third and lowest note of motif *x* is accented with a *sforzando*, making even more emphatic the plunge of the descending sequence. At bar 47 this downward motion is answered immediately by another statement of motif *x* in the treble, but the articulation of the motif here, which is also twice repeated in descending sequence, is cluttered by a rumbling in the bass and chordal accompaniment in the treble. The exposition then moves toward cadence in a long uphill chromatic run in both hands (bars 51–52) whose arrival at high A-flat is immediately and brutally smashed down two octaves by *ff* chords, the effect being as emphatic as a "slam-dunk" in basketball (Figure 12).

Figure 12

Movement from high to low in music, of course, cannot be automatically equated with any particular nonmusical concept. But this exposition, as well as its Maestoso introduction, relentlessly emphasizes not only downward motion but the finality of such motion. So consistent is this motion not only within motif *x* itself but within the unfolding of the entire movement that a "principle" of low-to-high-to-lower is expressed, a principle in which the restless and passionate attempt to ascend is perpetually dashed. The temporary calm of the second theme, high in the treble, intensifies even further the relentless return of the principle of the "low." The final "low blow" of the exposition, the slam-dunk of a cadence following the aspiring chromatic ascent, leads not to the development section but to a repeat of the entire exposition. Retraversal of its aspiring ascents and obsessive descents intensifies one's feeling of inhabiting a prison without exit.

The emphatic aspiring-and-descending three-note motif *x* that dominates the exposition and its repeat also begins and ends the short development section. At the beginning it modulates to G minor and is stated in bare octaves for four bars (56–59). At the end of the development the motif "rises in steep steps over the home dominant pedal" for five bars (Tovey, p. 291). Then in bar 76 the same motif (in bare octaves again) introduces the recapitulation with a harsh *ff* statement that spans four octaves from high to low. The development itself has lacked the strife and ferocity which characterized that of the *Appassionata*—or even that of the *Pathétique*. But here the exposition itself had plenty of development-like dynamics; it remained for the development to take the leading motif into even more mysterious harmonies than before, deepening the mystery with an intensification of the fugal texture.

The recapitulation follows the pattern of the exposition with important modifications. The opening motif no longer stammers forth: its bare octaves spanning four octaves now know their shape and have found their range. After motif *y* begins its impetuous running, leading to more statements of motif *x* high and low, a new transition of unison passagework ushers in the second theme. Now announced in C major, this theme extends, surprisingly, beyond its *adagio* bar. The theme descends into the bass clef for the first time as the extension, in F minor, seems to open up a new world of possibility and of poignant feeling. A new transition leads to the original closing group. In the exposition, this group (motif *x* in descending sequence both in the bass and the treble, the ascending chromatic run, and the emphatic "slam-dunk" cadence) had brutally invaded the short-lived peace of the second theme. Now, owing to the thematic extension and to the new transition, its relentless reality is somehow more spaciously embraced.

The short coda, which brings the impetuous motion of this movement to a mysteriously abrupt yet most satisfying halt, begins with another version of motif *x*, this time welded to the final note of the cadence that ended the re-capitulation. But a sudden diminuendo leads to the quiet *p* and *pp* bars that end this stormy movement, just as the first-movement storm of the *Appassionata* was allowed to recede in its final bars in preparation for the Andante con moto. As the motion slows, the sound softens, and the striving angularity of the motif flattens out into horizontal sequences of chords, the harmonic intensifiers that were so active in the introduction and in the movement per se act in reverse, putting on the brakes so mysteriously that in the last two bars we find ourselves poised on C major, awaiting the calm of the Arietta.

This violent movement, so harsh and relentless in its rhythm, its harmony, its contrast of high and low, of loud and soft, of calm and storm, has many similarities in mood and spirit with the opening movements of opp. 13 and 57. Indeed, Beethoven's sketchbooks show that some of the musical figures of the Allegro were written down "twenty years before the sonata was composed," that is, sometime between the *Pathétique* and the *Appassionata*. Barford is probably correct in supposing that this thematic material "arose painfully into its final form through the stress of subconscious pressures" (p. 129). Perhaps this material achieved its final form only when Beethoven was psychologically prepared to compose a "heaven" fully equal to its "hell."

First-movement similarities with Opus 13 include the C-minor tonality, the slow introduction, and the repeat of the exposition. Yet this movement, no less than the Arietta of Opus 111, displays the distance Beethoven had traveled from his early to his late style. Rosen points out that "most of Beethoven's works in C minor from the *Sonate Pathétique* on rely heavily upon diminished sevenths at climactic moments. Yet none before the Sonata Op. 111 fixes an order for these chords so firmly, . . . derives the principal melodic material so directly from their sonority, and makes such a consistent attempt to integrate the whole movement by their means." First heard in the opening bars, intervals of the diminished seventh "color most of the piece, appear with extreme violence at every important climax, and supply the dynamic impulse for most of the harmonic transformations." They illustrate the "concentration upon the simplest and most fundamental relationships of tonality that characterizes Beethoven's late style most dramatically. His art, with all its dramatic force and its conception in terms of dramatic action, became more and more an essentially meditative one" (p. 444). *Wuthering Heights*, too, for all its dramatic force and action, becomes more and more "essentially meditative" the deeper one penetrates into volume 2.

Martin Cooper emphasizes the meditative nature of this first movement by contrasting its Maestoso introduction with the Grave introduction of Opus 13. From the opening bar of the earlier work, "Beethoven engages in a manifest dialogue, with fortissimo chords in the bass answered by an eloquently pleading phrase in the treble." The diminished sevenths that open in the Maestoso introduction, on the other hand, initiate "a monologue." The young Beethoven had "exteriorized the struggle in himself, dramatizing his 'opponent' as a force outside himself, one whom it was possible to defy or placate." But the late Beethoven recognized that "this opponent was his own dark shadow, a rejected aspect of his own self still sharing with him a common identity."[7] Heathcliff, in his own "late" phase, turned from his external opponents to internal monologue.

One difference between the first movement of Opus 111 and its predecessor in Opus 57 is that the exposition, in spite of its relentless and seemingly irresistible drive, is repeated. One feels that Beethoven is more abstracted from the harshness he is expressing here than he was in the *Appassionata*, where the drive and immediacy of the painful emotion swept the exposition past its expected repeat and into the even more heightened strife of the development section. In Opus 57, the main theme, suffering one brutal transformation after another throughout the movement, was never allowed to return in its original form. In Opus 111 the main theme *is* repeated exactly in the repeat of the exposition; moreover, the simple fundamental shape of motif x is omnipresent throughout the movement, always identifiable in its strife, strength, and tight integrity, whether it is heard high or low, in simple or complex texture. It has the compact, anguished insistence of Heathcliff's search for Catherine's spirit—until his "essentially meditative" concentration finally lifts him onto a new imaginative plane.

In the first movement of Opus 111, the short, mysterious development and coda sections intimate that the relentless condition of conflict and strife is not now to be overcome through heroic struggle, as it was in the development and coda sections of the *Appassionata*. Rather the condition must be endured in all its mystery until some change occurs to transform its meaning. The first movement does not disclose what that change will be. Even the recapitulation, however, suggests that some kind of transformation may be in the offing. The new consolation brought about by the F-minor extension of the second theme feels qualitatively different from the theme in its first version—as qualitatively different as the new consolation Heathcliff expresses in his poignant recollections to Nelly in chapter 29 of his visits to Catherine's grave. This new emotion seems to open wide the possibility of a new solution to the "inner strife and tension of consciousness" expressed in this movement, even though in the present context of the recapitulation there is no choice but to embrace the world dominated by the finality of the closing theme. Yet the very "slam-dunk" that ends the recapitulation with its relentless descent is fused onto the coda, with its quiet calm and mysterious harmonies suggestive of transformations to come. One might say of the coda, as Heathcliff says of himself in chapter 33, "there is a strange change approaching. I'm in its shadow at present." The revelation awaits in the Arietta.

Breaking Free

Whereas the Allegro of Opus 111 is a meditation on the discord of the diminished-seventh chord, the Arietta is a meditation on the concord of the C-major chord. The movement itself is marked Adagio molto semplice e cantabile. The songlike theme that provides the basis for its subsequent variations expresses as much immobility and peace as did the "hymnic" theme of the Andante con moto of the *Appassionata*. In structure this theme, like its earlier counterpart, is divided into two sections of eight bars apiece, each of which is given an immediate repeat. In melody, the theme begins with a descending three-note motif (motif z) that resembles motif x of the first movement in its downward destination, but differs sharply in its manner of arriving there: motif x moved abruptly up and emphatically down; motif z drops immediately down and repeats the note it lands on (Figure 13). After lingering on that restful third note (a dotted quarter-note), this opening motif is immediately heard again, but at a slightly wider interval (now beginning on D rather than C, but again landing on G, the "dominant" of the key of C major). The first eight bars of the theme are in C major throughout. The second strain of the theme touches on A minor in bars 9–12 but returns to C major in the closing bars, which consist mainly of cardinal tonic chords. By the end of the movement, this static, immobile, songlike

Figure 13

theme will have been lifted onto "another psychical plane" through a complex process of breaking free and bonding together.

Variations 1 and 2 become increasingly animated and increasingly high in register, as had the successive variations of Opus 57. They also maintain the rigid structural pattern of eight bars (repeated) plus eight bars (repeated). In its third variation, however, the slow movement of Opus 111 enters a world completely different from that of the earlier Andante con moto. Variation 3 features such extremes of syncopation and animation that it can barely be contained within the variation form. Variation 4 is stranger yet—even more animated in pulse and even more extreme in its range of motion. It is followed, not by another formal variation or by a direct return of the theme, but rather by a seemingly improvised development or fantasy that breaks entirely away from the original formal structure.

Tovey calls the freer concluding section of the movement a coda (bars 96–146) and an epilogue (bars 146–177). These sublime sections of the Arietta serve a structural function equivalent to the one served by the stormy third movement of Opus 57; they complete the slow movement by engulfing it, thereby revealing its ultimate essence. The fate of the Andante con moto of the *Appassionata* was to embody a principle of calm that would be swept away by a return of the principle of storm. The fate of the Arietta of Opus 111 is to transcend itself—and in doing so to transform and to contain within its cosmic calm even the storm which preceded it.

Although the spiritual destination of this movement is found in the coda and the epilogue (and especially in the celebrated climax beyond a trill that hovers before an abyss of five octaves), the theme and the first four variations provide the necessary foundation for the spiritual activity to come. Dramatic changes in register, pace, rhythm, and dynamics carry us from the immobility of the theme itself, to the glorious animation of variations 1 and 2, to the breaking free of variations 3 and 4.

Whereas the progression in register throughout the first movement is decidedly and cumulatively downward, the motion reverses itself throughout the Arietta. The theme itself (Figure 13) lies almost wholly within the treble clef, its accompaniment in the bass clef and below. The first half of the theme stretches upwards in bars 5–6 (at the same time that the bass goes lowest), but there is no sense yet of unearthly spatial range. Variation 1 (Figure 14) maintains this simple division between a melody in the treble and an accompaniment in the bass. Its rocking melody in the treble, however, rises and falls more freely than the relatively inert theme. The register in variation 2 is more complex. From the beginning, its melodic line alternates between the bass and the treble. By the end of the variation the melody is straining higher and higher, as emphasized by two isolated chirps high above the treble (bars 44–45).

In variation 3 the movement between registers becomes much more dramatic. Abruptly descending figures in the treble are boldly juxtaposed with upthrusting figures from the bass. In bar 51 the descent begins on a high G, by far the highest note heard so far in the movement. Repeated notes on high C and high D further dramatize the new heights reached in this variation—as does, of course, the repeat of the first eight bars. The second strain of variation 3 also reaches much higher than its earlier counterparts, though here the high-low contrast is not as extreme as in the first half of the variation.

In variation 4 the contrast between high and low is expressed in an entirely new way. Both hands play the first strain in the bass clef and below (Variation 4A). They then play a free repeat in the treble clef and above (Variation 4B). This total disjunction of register then repeats itself, with eight more bars in the bass (bars 81–88) and eight more in the treble (bars 89–96). At the end of bar 96, where one might expect another variation to begin, the high ethereal melody continues into the coda, leading eventually to the trill that trembles before the abyss of five octaves. While taking us higher and higher, these four variations have increasingly emphasized a distinction between high and low until the two have become, in the dichotomous world of variation 4, opposing principles or "worlds." During the trill that will lead to the five-octave abyss, these two principles will paradoxically become one. But that is to anticipate.

Figure 14

The progression of pace from the theme through the first four variations can be more quickly summarized. The *adagio* tempo remains essentially the same throughout, but the pace continually quickens. The theme, stated in a leisurely ⁹⁄₁₆ time, seems almost immobile, especially in the last four bars. In variation 1 each main beat is divided by three, imparting a flowing motion. The main beats are further subdivided in variation 2, quickening the pace considerably. A further subdivision makes the notes of variation 3 four times as fast and four times as numerous as in the theme itself. Variation 4 increases the pace even more, the deepest pulse in the bass vibrating at twenty-seven notes per bar.[8]

As the register and the pace become more extreme, the rhythm becomes more complex. It is regular in the theme itself, the three main beats of each bar being clearly felt in both the bass and the treble. Variation 1 introduces a cross-rhythm, each beat in the treble getting a long-short stress over syncopated triplets in the bass. Variation 2 is characterized more by two-part polyphony and four-part harmony than by cross-rhythms per se, though the melodic motion has the effect of a strong "dotted" rhythm at its accelerated pace. In variation 3 the previously latent tendency toward harsh rhythmic disruption finally explodes. The "dotted" rhythm effect is magnified by the even faster pace, by the abrupt contrasts between high and low, by the strange cross-rhythms, and by the strong *sforzandos* on weak beats, these becoming relentless by the end of the first strain. Bars 53–55 (the equivalent of bars 5–7 of the theme) have all their accents on off-beats. Variation 3 anticipates the syncopations of twentieth-century jazz.

The rhythm of variation 4 is stranger still; not wilder (for that could hardly be), but more mysterious. In the low opening sections, deep in the bass, rapid thirty-second notes keep up a steady unmoving repetition on two alternating notes. Over this unvaried throbbing the mutilated melody is sounded in sixteenth-note chords that create a strong impression of arrested motion. This rhythmic juxtaposition is even stronger in the second version of the low section, owing to the increased poignance of the melodic mutilations. In the two high, ethereal sections of the variation, however, all flows free and easy. Both times the thirty-second-note pulse that had vibrated deep below the bass rises high above the treble clef, taking the original theme high above its original pitch and presenting "its main lines through an infinite variety of quivering ornament" (Tovey, p. 294). Here the accompanying sixteenth notes in the left hand are pointedly regular in rhythm, strengthening the ease of the flow.

One similarity between variation 4 and the original theme is a restricted dynamic range. The theme is *piano* throughout, with a crescendo in bars 13–15 returning to *piano*. Variations 1 and 2 also occupy a *piano* range animated by occasional crescendos. But variation 3 begins *forte* and remains so throughout its first strain, the dynamic contrast intensified by the off-beat *sforzandos*. Its second strain also begins and ends *forte*, two abrupt changes to *piano* dramatizing its force. Variation 4, in sharp contrast, begins *pp*. It remains *sempre pp* throughout both transitions from the mutilated, syncopated bass to the flowing, quivering treble. As with register, pace, and rhythm, these contrasts in dynamics, rather mild in the theme itself and the first two variations, are extreme and intense in variations 3 and 4. Before discussing the rest of the movement—the part which has a less formal structure—it will be useful to compare the musical phenomena so far discussed with certain spiritual phenomena in volume 2 of *Wuthering Heights*.

The simplest, most natural visions of peace in volume 2 are expressed by Linton Heathcliff and Cathy Linton in chapter 24. Each vision projects an individual alone in nature. His differs from hers much as the theme of the Arietta differs from its first two variations. The comparison can be developed with some precision in terms of register, rhythm, pace, and dynamics.

Linton Heathcliff's "ecstasy of peace" is, even more than the theme of the Arietta, essentially immobile in rhythm and pace. He envisions himself "lying from morning till evening on a bank of heath in the middle of the moors." The sky he envisions is as immobile as he: the "bright sun" shines "steadily and cloudlessly." The sounds he imagines, like the musical melody and its accompaniment, are divided into simple high and low. Above him are "the larks singing high up over head." Near him on the heath are "the bees humming dreamily about among the bloom."

Cathy Linton's "glorious jubilee," like variations 1 and 2, is much more intense in register, pace, and rhythm. She is high in a green tree, just as these variations are increasingly high in register, but not yet unearthly. She hears music on "every side," not just high and low. Variation 2 is thick with polyphonic effects and four-part harmony; she hears "not only larks but throstles, and blackbirds, and linnets, and cuckoos pouring out music on every side." The pace of her vision exceeds Linton's languid immobility as much as the pace of these variations exceeds that of the theme. Her "rocking in a rustling green tree" compares with the animated rocking rhythm of variation 1. But at the same time that she rocks, she sees that the wind is blowing, that the clouds are "flitting rapidly," and that the great swells of long grass are "undulating." Her simultaneous mixture of multiple motions and sounds corresponds to the multiple rhythms and voices in variation 2.

Cathy's vision of peace, though more intense than Linton's, still remains essentially earthbound: the tree in which she rocks has roots in the ground. For the increasingly unworldly motions of the spirit embodied in variations 3 and 4, we must turn to the experience of Catherine and Heathcliff. These variations do not embody peace itself so much as a violent and then a yearning departure from earthly constraints toward a peace that is to be reached only in the coda and epilogue of the Arietta. In this sense, variations 3 and 4 resemble, respectively, Catherine's violent shattering of her prison in chapter 15 and Heathcliff's yearning search for her spirit after her body is dead and in the ground.

For Catherine and Heathcliff the "perfect idea of happiness" is to be to-gether—if not in life then in death. They are last together in life in chapter 15. As we have seen, Catherine, at the beginning of the chapter, appears to "gaze beyond, and far beyond—you would have said out of this world." But the arrival of Heathcliff's letter returns her briefly to the "shattered prison" she is about to escape. Their final reunion, including mutual accusations of murder and Catherine's last loss of consciousness, compares, as we have seen, with the brutal coda that completed the first movement of the *Appassionata* by putting the two main themes through their last violent transformations. On the spiritual level, however, this same scene allows Catherine to articulate to Nelly her con-sciousness of being about to escape from the prison she is now in the process of shattering. In the exhilarating tension between these two levels of consciousness we experience something like the wild extremes of register, rhythm, pace, and dynamics that explode in variation 3 of the Arietta.

The abrupt range from high to low in the music—with the violent downthrusts answered by equally violent upthrusts—can be said to parallel the way in which Catherine is violently transported from "out of this world" back into it by her final encounter with Heathcliff. The "pace" of that encounter has the acceler-ated quality of variation 3—four times the notes and four times faster. From the moment that Catherine waits with "straining eagerness" for Heathcliff to enter the room until the moment she finally collapses from exhaustion, the increased pace is not so much in physical movements—though these are often dramatic—as in emotional intensity, which is at a fevered pitch throughout.

> In a stride or two [he] was at her side, and had her grasped in his arms.
>
> He neither spoke, nor loosed his hold, for some five minutes, during which period he bestowed more kisses than ever he gave in his life before, I dare say; but then my mistress had kissed him first, and I plainly saw that he could hardly bear, for downright agony, to look into her face! The same conviction had stricken him as me, from the instant he beheld her, that there was no prospect of ultimate recovery there—she was fated, sure to die. (p. 132)

Here the accelerated "pace" is mental, emotional, and spiritual, a pace that is accompanied by actual physical motionlessness. Throughout their last meeting Heathcliff and Catherine communicate with their "inner essences"; it is these that have increased to an intensity barely bearable.

The harsh *forte* dynamics which begin the third variation and prevail through-out, intensified by *sforzando* accents and by two sudden appearances of a more tender *piano*, also correspond to the intense spiritual states embodied in the last meeting between Heathcliff and Catherine. His first words—"Oh, Cathy! Oh, my life! how can I bear it?"—are uttered "in a tone that did not seek to disguise his despair" (p. 132). He "cries," she "moans," he "says wildly," she "sobbed," and then "they were silent—their faces hid against each other, and washed by each other's tears" (p. 135). The words themselves, and their ideational content—"You have killed me," "I love *my* murderer—but *yours!*—How can I?"—show as much as the vehement verbs descriptive of their speech the almost inhuman force with which they address each other. So does the punctuation, as full of exclamations and broken dashes as variation 3 is of exclamatory *sforzandos*.

This brings us to rhythm, perhaps the strongest parallel between Catherine's last reunion with Heathcliff and variation 3 of the Arietta. The human heart is the body's rhythmic pacemaker, and alterations in its activity are noted with great care in those parts of the novel that describe the manner in which Catherine and Heathcliff approach, recede from, and finally gain their visions and conditions of "unearthly peace." The alterations not only in the heartbeat but in the breathing of both characters as they yearningly break out of this world and into the one toward which they aspire closely parallel the rhythmic alterations that Beethoven employs in the variation movement that listeners find "unearthly" and "sublime"—often without knowing why. The comparison that follows may suggest one reason, at least, why variation 3 of the Arietta feels "unearthly" to us.

In the middle of the vehement, tense reunion in chapter 15, Catherine is "recalled to a sense of physical weakness by the violent, unequal throbbing of her heart, which beat visibly and audibly under this excess of agitation" (p. 133). In rhythm, her physical condition compares closely to the heavy syncopations of variation 3: "violent, unequal throbbing" describes the musical motion in a precise, even technical way. If variation 3 were heard outside the context of the Arietta as a whole, one would think it wild, bizarre. In context, however, its unequal rhythms animate the heart of one of the most sublime variation movements, by general consensus, ever written for the piano. A similar paradox is created by the "violent, unequal throbbing" of Catherine's heart. If chapter 15 were read out of context, we could only see Catherine and Heathcliff as two individuals in extremely bizarre physical and psychological states. *In* context, however, we understand the aberrant behavior. In a final manifestation of Catherine's psychic split, her heart beats so "visibly" that Nelly can see it and so "audibly" that Nelly can hear it, but at the same time she is "yearning through the walls of [that] aching heart" toward the "glorious world" beyond. She is both deliriously happy and deliriously agitated at being once more with— and soon evermore apart from—Heathcliff.

All of the intensifications of rhythm, pace, dynamics, and "register" embod-ied by Catherine in chapter 15 serve to bring her right to the edge of her "shat-tered prison"—but not yet beyond it. The ultimate condition she envisions in the aside to Nelly—"I shall be incomparably beyond and above you all"—is achieved only after her death. In much the same way the intensities of rhythm, pace, dynamics, and register embodied in variation 3 come as near as possible to shattering the "prison" of a variation movement that moves in methodically equal segments of eight bars each, each of them repeated exactly. Variation 4 begins to actually transform that pattern toward a new structure and vision, a process further intensified by the coda and epilogue that grow out of it.

In chapter 16 Nelly looked at Catherine's calm body and imagined "a repose that neither earth nor hell can break." Heathcliff broke that repose when he bashed his head against a tree, initiating eighteen years of revenge. In chap-ter 29, however, he approaches that repose on a new imaginative plane when he tells Nelly of the sensations he has experienced while pursuing Catherine's spirit. These sensations, initiated by his visits to her grave, are as far beyond the range of ordinary human experience as the mysterious, haunting sensations of variation 4 are beyond the range of ordinary musical experience. Passages of music and fiction that are "beyond the ordinary" do not necessarily have signifi-cant affinities with each other. But Heathcliff's extraordinary spiritual pursuit does compare with variation 4 of the Arietta in its expression of a suspended, yearning, bifurcated consciousness.

Variation 4 first begins to shatter the prison of the preceding variations by avoiding the repeat signs. The first eight bars, low in the bass clef, are an-swered, not by a repeat of themselves, but by the quivering, ethereal flow in the treble. This bifurcation between the low and the high extends beyond the mere separation of registers: the accompanying changes in pace, rhythm, and melody carry the music toward a new imaginative, as well as structural, plane. The second half of variation 4—the new, more poignant throbbings in the bass, answered again by an ethereal flow high in the treble—increase one's sense that the music of this movement is about to transcend the structure that has so far contained it. This impression is further confirmed when the second stretch of ethereal passagework continues uninterrupted into the coda.

The first, sudden transition from the halting, suspended motion in the bass to the ethereal flow in the treble creates a strong sense of psychological release. As noted above, the pace and rhythm of the two hands low in the bass are curiously contrary. In the left hand, deep below the bass, steadily vibrating notes are moving very rapidly (twenty-seven notes per bar) but going nowhere at all. The mutilated melody in the right hand is delivered, technically, at nine notes per bar; actually it moves much more slowly than that. The strongest of the nine beats in each bar (1, 4, and 7) are silent. And most of the chords that play fragments of the melody on beats 2, 5, and 8 are tied to the same chords on the following beat (3, 6, and 9). This means that only three clear pulses are struck in the right hand for every twenty-seven in the bass. The effect is like juxtaposing the motion of a heart that is beating three times too fast with the motion of one that can hardly beat at all.

It is in this halting, suspended context that the ethereal flow in the treble is so exhilarating. As the ornamented version of the original theme climbs high above its original treble register, breaking free of the unnatural depths to which its mutilated remains had been confined in the opening of variation 4, the left hand provides steady accompaniment in the treble clef. For two-thirds of one bar (75) the left hand actually matches the right hand's glorious motion in pace; otherwise it offers more prosaic support. The psychological relief created by the clarity of articulation, the certainty of movement, the regularity of rhythm, and the wonderful high register gives one the temporary feeling that the goal of the entire sonata has been achieved.

The sense of psychological relief induced by this ethereal flow compares to the relief Heathcliff feels when he first comes into contact with Catherine's spirit. In the retrospect of chapter 29 he recalls the night immediately following her death, during which he dug for her body in the ground. As he "delved" downward with "all his might," his spirit, suspended, awaited the outcome. When the two sighs convinced him that "Cathy was there, not under me, but on the earth," he tells Nelly, "a sudden sense of relief flowed from my heart and through every limb. I relinquished my labor of agony, and turned consoled at once, unspeakably consoled" (p. 230). The flowing sense of relief and the unspeakable consolation that animate Heathcliff's spirit as he pursues Catherine's spirit across the moors make all the more unbearable the loss, the withdrawal of vision when he is not able to find her. His heart, he tells Nelly, "ought to have sweat blood, then, from the anguish of my yearning." His nerves, these eighteen years since, have been kept "at such a stretch that, if they had not resembled catgut, they would, long ago, have relaxed into the feebleness of Linton's" (p. 230).

The effect of this withdrawal of vision is comparable to the return, in the middle of variation 4, from the high ethereal flow in the treble to the halting, suspended motion in the bass. Now the mutilated melody is even more painful than before. Still syncopated, this version has enough melodic shape and rhythmic pulse to be extremely poignant. The tied chords in the right hand now vary in pitch, each descending pair articulating a melody and a rhythm that is not only suspended, but broken.

In the sonata this poignant loss of vision lasts eight bars only: it is supplanted by an immediate return of the notes that flow high and fast and easy. In the novel Heathcliff's loss of vision has lasted eighteen years (though neither Nelly nor the reader has known about it until chapter 29). By returning to Catherine's grave, he has once more approached the "unspeakable consolation" he had felt before: he has again found the "tranquility" and "ease" that have eluded him since he had first pursued her spirit across the moors (p. 229). As we have seen, the ethereal musical flow that concludes variation 4 bridges over into the coda and finally into the epilogue. Similarly, the ethereal level of consciousness that Heathcliff reveals and regains in chapter 29 extends into the concluding chapters of the novel, where his spiritual quest will end.

We noted above that Catherine's transitional state in chapter 15 and the strange energies of variation 3 would both seem bizarre if encountered outside of the larger fictional and musical contexts in which they occur. The same is certainly true of Heathcliff's transitional state in chapter 29 and of the bifurcated world of variation 4. Out of the halting rhythms and mutilated melodies of variation 4 have come the "unspeakable consolation" of their ethereal extensions. Out of Heathcliff's anguished pursuit of Catherine's spirit has come his translation to a psychological and spiritual plane in which union with her spirit will actually become possible. In each case a suspended psychological impasse has been twice translated into an exhilarating ethereal flow. The energies thereby unleashed are seeking a kind of expression which the "prison" from which they emanate can no longer contain.

Before following these energies into the world of mystical consummation, it will be well to briefly review the comparisons made above between the visions (and versions) of peace in volume 2 of *Wuthering Heights* and the Arietta of Opus 111. In each case the visions of peace arrange themselves in an ascending hierarchy from the simple and natural toward the complex and ethereal. In each case the respective visions become increasingly intense in register, rhythm, pace, and dynamics as they move from the earthbound to the unworldly. These parallel hierarchies of vision have taken us from the immobile "ecstasy of peace" of Linton Heathcliff and of the theme of the Arietta, to the "glorious jubilee" of Cathy Linton and of variations 1 and 2, to the "shattered prison" of Catherine and of variation 3, and to the arrested motion and "unspeakable consolation" of Heathcliff and of variation 4. Each parallel stage has revealed striking similarities in register, rhythm, pace, and dynamics. But the value of these musical and fictional comparisons inheres more in the spirit of the visions than in the details of their expression.

Consider, for example, the bifurcated worlds of Heathcliff and variation 4. More attention might have been given to a curious similarity of "register." In the halting, suspended section that begins the variation, both hands are low on the keyboard, in the bass clef and below. As Heathcliff digs toward Catherine's grave, his two hands are likewise low, below ground level. Such a comparison of low with low, however, means little when taken by itself. Nor is it necessarily strengthened by another curiosity: the fact that one of the principal early reviewers of Opus 111 heard "the sounds of the grave" and even "the digging of the grave" in the music of the Arietta.[9] It is not Heathcliff's digging itself that may be compared to the music, but rather his psychological and spiritual condition as he "delves" toward Catherine, as he hears her sigh and follows her spirit, as he poignantly loses his vision of her presence, and as he regains that vision after visiting her grave once more. Both in chapter 29 and in variation 4, the low, halting, suspended episodes are given meaning and definition by the "unspeakable consolation" of the higher, ethereal episodes that ensue. Each sequence embodies a psychological process of suspension and then of flow, followed by loss and then renewal. This process in the novel is a precondition for the spiritual harmony to be achieved in the closing chapters; in the music it is a precondition for the mystical fulfillment to be achieved in the coda and the epilogue.

Joseph Kerman, writing about Beethoven's late quartets, acknowledges a danger faced by the writer who tries to do justice to their motions of the spirit: his language may appear at times to approach the terms of "an extramusical program." In his view the proper use of nonmusical language is not to refer to an imagined "series of events or pictures, whether biographical or not," but rather to refer to "the musical image of an underlying psychological process that is generalized and essentially inchoate."[10] Such an "underlying psychological process" has brought the music of variation 4, at the threshold of the coda, like Heathcliff at the threshold of the last chapter, to a condition in which "measuring the gulf, it stoops and dares the final bound."

Spiritual Home

Tovey summarizes the first four variations of the Arietta, and anticipates the coda and the epilogue, in the following words:

> In spite of the novel kinds of subdivision, the progress of the present variations has been the merest straight line of *air et doubles* like the Andante of Op. 57. . . . Hitherto Beethoven's static and ecstatic visions in this sublime mood have been aloof from action. . . . But now in Op. 111, and afterwards in the Ninth Symphony, the E-flat Quartet, Op. 127, and the C-sharp-minor Quartet, Op. 131, Beethoven finds ways of modulating which bring action harmoniously into the contemplative vision. (p. 294)

In the coda of Opus 111 the contemplative vision is animated by the principle of "action" in a number of ways. Rhythmically, action is embodied in the glorious trills that begin in bar 106 and reach a climax in bar 117, as they approach the abyss of five octaves. Harmonically, it takes the form of modulations strong enough to cause a change in the key signature by the beginning of bar 116. Motivically, it takes the form of a dialogue between the bass and the treble over motif *z*, a dialogue in which the two voices—or principles—that were separate in variation 4 now merge into glorious union. Each of these embodiments of contemplative "action" in the coda—the rhythmic, the harmonic, the motivic—corresponds to motions of the spirit by which Catherine's contemplative vision is finally answered and validated by Heathcliff's "active" response. As the mystical union in the novel is not rendered with such completeness as its counterpart in the Arietta, it will be well to briefly summarize what the novel does in fact reveal about that union.

In chapter 3 Mr. Lockwood had dreamt that the ghost of Cathy Earnshaw/Heathcliff/Linton was trying to invade his room at Wuthering Heights. After pulling its wrist on the broken glass so that it bled, he had cried out in fear—and awakened to find Heathcliff in his room. When Lockwood called the ghost a "changeling" and a "wicked little soul," he was surprised to see Heathcliff immediately fall into a fit of "irregular and intercepted breathing," struggling to "vanquish an access of violent emotion" (p. 32). Then the startled man had watched in disbelief as Heathcliff "got on to the bed and wrenched open the lattice," sobbing "Come in! come in! Cathy, do come. Oh, do—*once* more! Oh! my heart's darling, hear me *this* time—Catherine, at last!" Lockwood cannot understand "the gush of grief" (p. 33). Neither can the reader—until chapter 29. Then we realize that the spector which inspired Lockwood's cruel dream and Heathcliff's strangled sobs is the one reality for which Heathcliff has been searching these eighteen years.

In chapter 16, immediately after Catherine's death, Heathcliff had implored, "Do not leave me in this abyss where I cannot find you" (p. 139). But she *had* left him there—despite the temporary consolation of his first visit to her grave, which, after the vision withdrew, only served to intensify his agony. His second visit to her grave, in chapter 29, serves as a bridge to the change he describes to Nelly in chapter 33. It is then that he says, "I cannot continue in this condition! I have to remind myself to breathe—almost to remind my heart to beat! . . . I have a single wish, and my whole being and faculties are yearning to attain it. They have yearned towards it so long, and so unwaveringly, that I'm convinced it *will* be reached—and *soon*—because it has devoured my existence" (p. 256).

In chapter 34, on an April morning, the "change" has occurred. Heathcliff, who has been out all night, does not describe it in so many words. The reader is not informed of its cause, only of its effects. These are dramatically revealed in his physical appearance and biological condition. Young Cathy reports him *"very much* excited, and wild and glad!" Nelly sees the "strange joyful glitter in his eyes" and notes that sometimes he "breathes as fast as a cat," whereas other times he "stops breathing, during half a minute together." In addition, "his frame shivers, not as one shivers with chill or weakness, but as a tight-stretched cord vibrates—a strong thrilling, rather than trembling" (p. 258). On the night he paces the floor of his room, Nelly hears him "frequently breaking the silence by a deep inspiration, resembling a groan." The only word she can make out is "the name of Catherine, coupled with some wild term of endearment or suffering, spoken as one would speak to a person present—low and earnest, and wrung from the depths of his soul" (p. 261).

The morning after, he roams "to and fro . . . in a state approaching distraction; his heavy sighs succeeding each other so thick as to leave no space for common breathing between." Now he says, "I'm too happy, and yet I'm not happy enough. My soul's bliss kills my body, but does not satisfy itself" (p. 262). In the context of his search, there can be but one explanation for these extraordinary motions of his body and spirit: he has found Cathy. And she has heard his cry. And answered it. His inner essence is with hers.

The rare spiritual union he has achieved, combined with its rare bodily manifestations, provides an excellent analogy for describing one aspect of the spiritual exchange that occurs during the extraordinary "trill-abyss" of Opus 111. I do not offer this analogy as the final word about the music but as one way of perceiving its motions of spirit. Under the trill that begins in bar 106, the left hand announces motif *z*, low in the bass (Figure 15). The *forte* emphasis on the first note creates the effect of a searching question. The quieter, higher response in the treble immediately in the next bar has the effect of a reassuring answer; it is another version of motif *z* (flatter in its first interval but identical in its rhythm and repeated third note) that is extended, modulated, and finally inverted (bar 110). In bar 110 the bass answers with a new version of the motif, rising closer

Figure 15

to the treble, modulating *its* voice, and increasing the span of its opening interval. The treble (played by the left hand) now answers in kind, descending toward the bass voice and then dissolving into the celebrated triple trill through which the treble voice ascends toward the peak of the famed five-octave abyss. Beginning at bar 116 the bass answers across the abyss, transforming motif *z* into a calm answer that is no longer questing but that has arrived at union, a union that is expressed, paradoxically and sublimely, in the two-part bass-treble harmony five octaves apart in bars 118 and 119. In these bars, as Barford writes, all sense of distance has been dissolved through the great spaces that have been opened up in the keyboard—and in the spirit.

The musical process summarized above is, on the motivic level, a process of question-answer-question-answer-resolution. It corresponds to the process by which the earthbound Heathcliff calls out to Cathy, hears her reassuring answer, calls out once more, is answered once more, and dissolves into a perfect union. A listener who wished to personify the psychological process underlying the musical exchange could think of motif *z* in the bass asking *"Where* are you?" and the treble answering "Here I am . . . am . . . am . . ." Then follows a calmer "Where are you?" higher in the bass, answered by "Here I am" lower in the treble, after which the two voices simultaneously announce "Here we are" across the span of five octaves. I do not mean to suggest, of course, that these particular words "belong" in any literal way with these particular notes. Their function is to articulate the process of question and answer, of seeking and finding and found, expressed in the music itself.[11]

The union of the bass and treble across the abyss resolves the "principles" of high and low so at odds in variation 4 (not only in register but in rhythm and pace). It has been prepared by the voicing in the transition to the coda. The high treble figuration had maintained its rapid flow beyond the technical end of variation 4 and through to bar 99. Beginning in bar 100, however, the rapid pulse had returned to the bass, where the left hand now pursues the treble in syncopated upthrusts. These produce the painfully sublime answers in the treble (bars 103, 104, and 105) that dissolve into the trills under which the dramatic question-answer-question-answer-resolution occurs. The left hand, then, even after descending from its second stint of ethereal pursuit in variation 4, has this time remained animated by its vision, as has Heathcliff after his second encounter with Catherine at the grave.

Barford, echoing Thomas Mann's Kretschmar and many others, has called bars 106–19 "the profoundest moment in all music, a still emptiness transcending thought and emotion, which finally brings home the significance of the deep spacing which is apparent throughout the entire movement." At the point where "the long trill trembles on the edge of an abyss five octaves deep," forward "momentum is almost completely lost" and the music becomes symbolic of "the experienced inner spaces opened up in contemplation."[12] So it is when the momentum of Heathcliff's life gives way to his final vision of union with Catherine. The drive toward vengeance that has animated his adult life is gone. He does not care to raise his hand against young Cathy or Hareton. He does not eat or sleep. He "shivers as a tight-stretched cord vibrates." And then, one strange night, the deep low groans overheard by Nelly, earnest and wrung from his soul, seem to be answered by Catherine. The abyss that has separated them since chapter 16 is finally bridged.

Heathcliff's paradoxical condition might well be called one of "extreme rapidity and immobility" at the same time. These are the words Rosen uses to describe the condition of the trill in bars 106–17 of the Arietta. His analysis summarizes perfectly our earlier discussion of pace and rhythm throughout the first four variations.

> The trill is the culminating point in the rhythmic scheme of the movement. A long trill creates an insistent tension while remaining completely static; it helped Beethoven both to accept the static form of the variation set and to transcend it. . . . The fourth variation reaches an almost undifferentiated pulsation, enforced by the continuous *pianissimo* and by the omission of the melody note from the opening of every beat. The trill represents the complete dissolution of even this rhythmic

articulation: the movement reaches the extremes of rapidity and immobility. Its importance in the rhythmic structure of the movement as a whole accounts for the length of the trill and for its sonorous transformation into a triple trill. (pp. 447–48)

No more dramatic—or suspended—context than the trill could have been provided for the question-answer-question-answer-resolution exchange of motif z between the bass and the treble. Significantly, the cessation of the trill in bar 117 is accompanied by a modulation to a new key. At the nearest edge of the abyss, responding to the modulatory pressure already expressed during the exchange of motif z under the suspense of the trill, the key signature changes from that of the second movement (C major) back to that of the first (C minor, now transformed to E-flat major). It is in this new harmonic setting that the consuming union occurs.

Following the unworldly bond that is achieved across and beyond the trill, nearly sixty free-flowing bars remain in the Arietta (there are no more repeats). Melodically, the spiritual climax that has just occurred is crystallized in the form of two new variations on the original theme of the movement, one of them powerful in its simple skeletal vehemence, the other ethereal in its delicate, consuming bliss. Harmonically, the Arietta returns emphatically to its "home" key of C major.

The same modulation to E-flat major that lifted the music onto a new psychical plane during the two-part low-high union that bridged the abyss now makes possible the harmonically dramatic extension of that bridge into the fifth variation. This extension, in Barford's words, takes the form of a "magical progression through the diminished chords heard in the first movement. It steals upon the ear like the voice of memory whispering on the heights of the soul. It even leads, at bar 129, as in the introduction, to a B-flat minor chord and thence to A flat; but this is gloriously swept away in the ecstatic C major of the fifth variation" (pp. 187–88). This diluted evocation of the strife of the first movement allows us to feel the extent to which the second movement has now transcended that strife—just as Heathcliff's final encounters with young Cathy and Hareton reveal his transcendence of discord. [13]

Variation 5, an unornamented and unrepeated version of the original theme, seems, in Rosen's words, to be "discovering the essence" of the theme rather than "decorating" it. Here, as in many of Beethoven's late theme-and-variation movements, "there is a progressive simplification as the variations proceed"— the shape of the theme in its final manifestations becomes "more and more

131

skeletal in nature" (pp. 436–37). Variation 5, more than any of its predecessors in the Arietta of Opus 111, reveals motif *z* to be the skeletal essence of the theme itself. Although the motif had begun the melody of the theme in the opening bars of the movement, it had been all but obliterated in the four variations that followed. Its return here as the essential shape of variation 5 is all the more forceful following its prominence in the motivic exchange under the trill.

In variation 5 the new skeletal version of the theme rings out in the treble (Figure 16). In the bass, the musical texture is complicated by strong vibrations that build to a strong crescendo by the end of the variation (bars 130–46). This rumbling in the bass is identical in pace to the strange vibrations in the bass in variation 4; here, however, this pulse, rather than vibrating without direction, distributes itself in thrusting groups of three. One might expect that such a rapid, upthrusting, increasingly loud rumbling in the bass would obscure the melody in the treble. But its effect in variation 5, paradoxically, is only to enhance the melody. This is true even at the end of the variation, where the vehemence in the bass resembles Heathcliff's "heavy sighs" on the morning after his unworldly exchange with Catherine, these "succeeding each other so thick as to leave no space for common breathing between": hear the Ashkenazy recording.

var. 5

Figure 16

Conflicting principles in the music, as in the novel, are now fully complementary. Barford calls variation 5 both "glorious" and "ecstatic." The glorious calm of the skeletal theme in the treble derives its ecstatic power from the accompanying storm in the bass, just as the glorious calm of Heathcliff's skeletal yearning for Catherine derives *its* ecstatic power from the stormy vehemence that propels it. In the storm within the calm of variation 5, and in the magical progression through diminished chords that immediately precedes the variation, the Arietta has now incorporated within its "unmoving ground" the "inner conflict and tension of consciousness" that had dominated the Allegro con brio ed appassionato. In doing so, it has reversed the process by which the storm of the third movement of the *Appassionata* had swallowed up the calm of the second movement. In the world of the *Appassionata*, as in the tragic world of Catherine's and Heathcliff's love on earth, the principles of storm and calm had, in Cecil's words, got "in each other's way. They [were] changed from positive into negative forces; the calm [became] a source of weakness, not of harmony, in the natural scheme, the storm a source not of fruitful vigor, but of disturbance" (p. 301). In variation 5, as in Heathcliff's final days, harmonious calm and vigorous storm are fruitfully conjoined.

Just as variation 4 had extended itself into a transition to the coda, so does variation 5 extend itself into a transition to the epilogue. At the end of the variation per se its stormy propulsive figure ascends into the treble, against which accompaniment motif z descends three times in the bass (bars 151–53). Then the propulsive figure returns to the bass, while motif z ascends to the treble. This episode recalls the closing group of the exposition of the first movement of Opus 111. There motif x, breaking the calm of the second theme, was heard in descending sequence low in the bass and then high in the treble against a rumble of passagework first in the treble, then in the bass. The first-movement episode had dramatized the return of storm and discord following the one glimpse of calm and concord in the exposition; its counterpart in variation 5 dramatizes the capaciousness of a calm and concord that can incorporate storm and discord. We have already noted that variation 5 embodies, in Barford's words, an "ecstatic C major." So ecstatic is its extension toward the epilogue that it incorporates a number of accidentals, including some prominent C sharps, with no sense of discord.

The final variation on the opening theme, which begins what Tovey calls the epilogue of the Arietta, brings a new and more perfect vision of peace (bars 161–69). As at the beginning of the coda, a continuous trill creates a dramatic sense of expectation. Here, however, there are no dynamics of question-and-answer, for what needs to be, is. The continuous trill is high above the treble, under which we hear the skeletal shape of the original theme, beginning with motif z. Under them both is the same rapid pulse (twenty-seven notes per bar) that had vibrated in the bass in variations 4 and 5 but which is here centered in the treble clef (Figure 17). In dynamics, this three-layered simultaneity of sound and motion embodies a hushed calm, *pp*, a striking contrast to the breathless crescendo at the end of variation 5. In register, the three-layered motion occupies the treble clef and regions above, thereby offsetting the downward motion of the entire first movement and setting into relief the high registers already reached in the ethereal sections of variation 4 and in the triple trill that had trembled before the abyss in the coda. In rhythm and pace, this three-layered

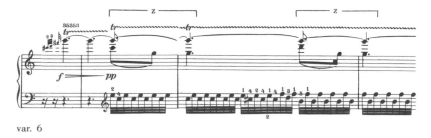

var. 6

Figure 17

motion is "a synthesis of all that went before": it combines the fastest measured motion in the movement (the rapid pulse from variation 4) with the slowest (the theme itself), with both "suspended under the unmeasured stillness of the trill" (Rosen, p. 448). The result is a feeling of redemption and release, as in the last weightless motions of Heathcliff's spirit, in which his "soul's bliss kills [his] body."

Rosen points out that Beethoven's use of trills in the Arietta converts this "typical ornamental device" into an "essential element of large-scale structure." No less than the diminished sevenths in the first movement, the trills in this movement are "essentially meditative in character," revealing the degree to which the late Beethoven's "exploration of the tonal universe was an act of introspection" (p. 448). The same might be said of Brontë's presentation of Heathcliff's shivering, "not as one shivers with a chill or weakness but as a tight-stretched cord vibrates—a thrilling, rather than a trembling."[14] Heathcliff's condition is not intended to ornament a passing feeling on the level of plot; rather it permanently lifts him, and the story, onto a new psychical—and structural—plane.

Overlapping with the end of variation 6, still accompanied by trills, is a four-bar transition featuring, again, motif *z* (bars 168–71). Here the motif is twice stated and twice varied, the variations being achieved by a C and a C-sharp that are added before the three-note motif itself (here taking the form of D-G-G; Figure 18). To Kretschmar in Mann's *Doctor Faustus*, "this added C-sharp is the most moving, consolatory, pathetically reconciling thing in this world. . . . 'Now for-get the pain,' it says. 'Great was—God in us.' ''Twas all—but a dream,' 'Friendly—be to me.' Then it breaks off."[15] This transition completes the redemptive process initiated by the variation itself. Kretschmar's summary of its essence corresponds to the final phase of Heathcliff's "soul's bliss."

The trill, after twelve consecutive bars of "unmeasured stillness," now articu-

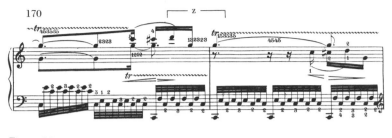

Figure 18

lates into the ethereal flow that was heard in variation 4. Now, as before, the left hand manages to match the glorious motion of the right hand high above the treble; here, however, their joint motion continues for two-plus bars (172–74; Figure 19) rather than two-thirds of one bar, as before. This two-part run is a sign that the pursuit is at an end, that the pursuing figure from the bass has achieved union, at last, with its object. The two hands never play the same notes, but their rhythm, pace, dynamics, and direction are identical. This simultaneous motion, because it is more continuous and complete, provides even more consolation than its counterpart in variation 4.

The rapid runs end in bar 175 when the right hand drops below the treble clef to announce, *forte*, motif *z*. And now the two hands "play" with this motif in

Figure 19

perfect harmony. The left hand immediately echoes it below the bass clef, not as an answer but as a continuation. The bass holds its low notes while the treble states motif z in a high register. Once more we have the unity across the separate registers that was so dramatic in bars 118–19 of the coda. Then, as the treble descends, the bass rises, sounding finally an inversion of motif z, the last note of which, harmonized with the right hand, now in the bass, becomes the most commonplace sound in music, the C-major chord.

A Final Sealing of the Bond

If the end of one of the most sublime sonatas ever written is a commonplace C-major chord, the end of one of the most sublime novels ever written is commonplace too. A commonplace man, Mr. Lockwood, watches commonplace creatures, moths, flutter over graves on a moor. The hushed *pp* in which the powerful Arietta ends corresponds to the quiet that descends upon Wuthering Heights and its occupants following Heathcliff's death. In volume 2 the unresolved violence of volume 1 has finally been contained, exorcized, and transformed. Early in volume 2 Nelly had sensed, as she gazed at the "infinite calm" of Catherine's finite body, an "eternity . . . where life is boundless in its duration, and love in its sympathy, and joy in its fulness." Now, at the end of the volume, Lockwood is able to project such a vision across the entire landscape. This final vision incorporates not only the meteorological calm which now suffuses both the Heights and the Grange, but multiple layers of human calm: below the ground, the physical union that awaits Catherine and Heathcliff; above the ground, the alleged two-part runs of their spirits; at ground level, the upcoming marriage of Cathy and Hareton.

None of the human characters, dead or alive, have reached their final vision of eternal joy easily, or even without nearly superhuman struggle. But the novel insists again and again, and especially in volume 2, that if violence, hatred, and revenge are central to what it means to be human, so can those principles of "storm" be enveloped and neutralized by an equally human, if at the same time unearthly, principle of "calm." To return to Cecil's analysis, "the world of our experience is, on the face of it, full of discord. But that is only because in the cramped condition of their earthly incarnation these principles [of storm and calm] are diverted from following the course that their nature dictates, and get in each other's way" (p. 301). During Heathcliff's last phase, as during the storm within the calm of variation 5, these principles finally flow "unimpeded and unconflicting." Early in this study we quoted Solomon's contention that Beethoven's most significant compositions embody a process by which the terrors of "death, destruction, anxiety, and aggression" are "transcended within the work of art itself." The contrasting movements of Opus 111 have embodied such a process, as have the contrasting volumes of *Wuthering Heights*.

Just as the principle of calm in volume 2 of *Wuthering Heights* subsumes the principle of storm in volume 1, so are the characters and images that embody the principle of storm in volume 1 transformed in volume 2. In this sense, the novel we have found to exist on at least three different imaginative planes is ultimately the expression of a single, integrated cosmic vision, as is Beethoven's Opus 111. We have already spoken of the way in which the unearthly calms achieved by Catherine and Heathcliff in their answering visions of peace are intimately connected with the earthly storms each had endured during most of her and his waking lives. But even the comic frame within which their passionate tale is set contains such extremes. The literal storm that prolonged Lockwood's initial arrival at Wuthering Heights has been supplanted by the actual calm that bathes his final visit. Internally, Lockwood's latent disposition toward cruelty and violence has been supplanted by active kindness.

Lockwood's dream in chapter 3 revealed him to be potentially as cruel as any character in the novel: "Terror made me cruel; and, finding it useless to attempt shaking the creature off, I pulled its wrist on to the broken pane, and rubbed it to and fro till the blood ran down and soaked the bed-clothes." Lockwood is always trying to "shake the creature off," whether it be the specter in chapter 3, the dog in chapter 1, or the young lady at the seaside from whom he withdrew before arriving at the Heights. On all such occasions his terror makes him cruel, yet by the end of the novel he shows repeated tenderness toward young Cathy and Hareton as he refuses to disturb them when they go out for a walk on the moors or when they return and look at each other in the moonlight. Such restraint would hardly be worthy of note were it not for the abominable condescension with which he had treated these same youngsters in the opening chapters. Lockwood has overcome some of his latent pride and cruelty in the story—as have, more dramatically, young Cathy and Hareton in learning to love each other, and more dramatically yet, Catherine and Heathcliff in regaining their love.

Comedy and tragedy are one, the novel seems ultimately to tell us, as human beings are one—even human beings so disparate on the surface as Lockwood and Heathcliff, whose tense juxtaposition in the opening pages produces so much humor and suspense. We have analyzed *Wuthering Heights* in terms of its comic frame, its tragic core, and its "unearthly" resolution. But in spite of these three imaginative planes it is, structurally, metaphorically, and spiritually, a "whole created cosmos." There is no person, image, or idea on any one of these planes that does not have its counterpart on the others. As perfectly as the three opening chapters in 1801 and the three closing chapters in 1802 mark off an introduction and a conclusion presided over by Lockwood, so at the same time do they introduce and conclude three different love stories: the tragic, sublime tale of Catherine and Heathcliff; its comic, hearty counterpart in the younger generation; and a comic inversion of that counterpart (Lockwood's infatuation with "Mrs. Heathcliff"). The multiple planes of this book can be separated for the purposes of analysis. But ultimately they all draw back together in a seamless whole, more irregular on the surface than an Austen novel, but just as flawless in its deep poetic structure.

A final glance at the motifs of windows, imprisonment, and inspection so prominent in volume 1—and eventually transformed by their treatment in volume 2—will help to show how this is so. In volume 1, as we have noted, windows tend to be closed, inspiring anxiety, anger, and terror in those inside or outside. In volume 2 this pattern is reversed. In chapter 15, at the beginning of the volume, Catherine gazes "beyond, and far beyond—you would have said out of this world." She does so "in a loose, white dress, with a light shawl over her shoulders, in the recess of the open window" (p. 130). After her death in chapter 16, Heathcliff enters an open window at the Grange in order to "bestow on the fading image of his idol one final adieu," in the course of which he rips Edgar's "curl of light hair" out of Catherine's locket, replacing it with a "black lock of his own" (p. 140). Throughout the rest of volume 2, most of the open windows are at Wuthering Heights. Its windows are opened to warn Heathcliff in chapter 17, to allow Cathy Linton to escape in chapter 28, and, more harmoniously, to welcome Lockwood back to the Heights in chapter 32. In chapter 34 Nelly provides the final image of an open window, as Heathcliff's dead body, washed by the elements, is seen beneath the swinging lattice of his room at the Heights.

In a similar manner, the various prisons that confined characters in volume 1 tend to be "shattered" or transcended by the end of volume 2. Young Cathy overcomes her prejudice against a servant and Hareton overcomes his wounded pride and they achieve a union on earth. The older Catherine, in the first chapter of volume 2, and Heathcliff, in the last, transcend the prison of life itself, shattering as they do so the various social, emotional, and psychological prisons that had denied them a union on earth. The final prisons to be shattered will be their wooden coffins (the ultimate "lockwoods"), owing to the arrangements Heathcliff has made with the sexton.

Even the inspection motif of volume 1, so brutal throughout the lives of most characters, but particularly as endured and then inflicted by Heathcliff, becomes resolved and transformed in the final chapters of volume 2. In chapter 29 Heathcliff carries this motif onto a new plane when he convinces the sexton, who is digging Edgar's grave, to remove the lid from Catherine's coffin so he can see her. "I saw her face again—it is hers yet—he had hard work to stir me; but he said it would change, if the air blew on it, so I struck one side of the coffin loose, and covered it up" (p. 228). In chapter 33, he elevates the inspection motif to the level of hallucination. "I cannot look down to this floor, but her features are shaped on the flags! In every cloud, in every tree—filling the air at night, and caught by glimpses in every object by day, I am surrounded with her image!" (p. 255). In chapter 34 the sight of her apparition, invisible to others, carries him beyond the "threshold of hell" to "within sight of [his] heaven" (p. 259).

The final variation upon the inspection motif is made by Nelly. Her inspection of Heathcliff's corpse returns the reader to the comic and tragic planes of the novel that Heathcliff and Catherine have now, apparently, transcended. "I peeped in. Mr. Heathcliff was there laid on his back. His eyes met mine so keen and fierce, I started; and then he seemed to smile. . . . I tried to close his eyes—to extinguish, if possible, that frightful, life-like gaze of exultation, before any one else beheld it. They would not shut; they seemed to sneer at my attempts, and his parted lips and sharp, white teeth sneered too!" Heathcliff's unshuttable eyes are the ultimate open windows, the ultimate shattered prisons.

Nelly sees that "his face and throat were washed with rain; the bedclothes dripped, and he was perfectly still. The lattice, flapping to and fro, had grazed one hand that rested on the sill; no blood trickled down from the broken skin, and when I put my fingers to it, I could doubt no more—he was dead and stark!" (p. 264). This last inspection transforms the imagery of Lockwood's encounter with the ghost girl in chapter 3. There Lockwood had scraped the girl's hand against the broken glass, making his imagined bedclothes drip with imagined blood; here Nelly touches Heathcliff's actual hand, its skin broken but bloodless, his bedclothes washed not with blood but rain. On the physical level, Nelly's final inspection of Heathcliff's body in chapter 34 answers her final inspection of Catherine's body in chapter 16. On the spiritual level, Heathcliff's "soul's bliss" in chapter 34 answers Catherine's in chapter 15.

No less than in Jane Austen's world, though in a very different way, have the tensions which have threatened the equilibrium of the characters—and of the novel—been resolved, "grounded," and transcended. One measure of the equilibrium of *Wuthering Heights* is the similarity between its ending and that of a typical Austen novel: not only will the marriage of Cathy and Hareton on New Year's Day 1803 reverse the dynamics of pride and prejudice these characters embodied in the opening chapters; it will also cement a permanent bond between Wuthering Heights and Thrushcross Grange, the two conflicting locales throughout the novel. One measure of the novel's *Romantic* equilibrium, on the other hand, is the difference between its ending and that of the typical Austen novel. The kind of equilibrium finally attained by Catherine and Heathcliff requires motions of the spirit that have no counterpart in Austen's fictional world, operating upon a psychical plane that finally obliterates even the dramatic distinction between the Heights and the Grange.

The "whole created cosmos" of Opus 111, in its deep poetic structure, is as unified as *Wuthering Heights*. We have already noted in a general way the manner in which the calm of its second movement completes and subsumes the storm of the first. Let us now look more closely at the relation between the motifs that dominate each movement.

Motif x, violent in its up-and-then-down motion, presides over a movement similarly violent. Motif z is calm in its downward motion and presides over a movement similarly calm. Yet they have much in common. Each is a three-note motif. Each moves in a downward direction. The second motif may even be seen as a transformation of the first, a transformation in which the middle note, the one that had struggled up against the inevitable, now discovers that downward motion can bring peace. After all the upward striving in the first movement that had resulted only in being thrust down, not only for the core motif but for entire sections of the structure, the opening bars of the Arietta twice trace out the peaceful descending motion of motif z. Although it is lost sight of as a separate entity during variations 1, 2, 3, and 4, motif z is omnipresent throughout the coda and epilogue. After its announcement in the bass under the trill in bar 106, it initiates the exchange with the treble that bridges the trilling abyss, the skeletal vehemence of variation 5 and its extension, the ethereal delicacy of variation 6 and *its* extension, and the last playful exchange between treble and bass in the closing bars. It dominates the sublime consummation of the Arietta as much as motif x had dominated the meditational storm of the Allegro con brio ed appassionato.

The peace ultimately achieved by motif z in the coda and the epilogue is enriched by all the variations of register, pace, rhythm, and dynamics undergone by the original theme in variations 1, 2, 3, and 4. It is also enriched by the persistent upward striving that, crystallized in motif *x*, had preceded it in the first movement. The coda and epilogue obviously provide the consummating variations on the theme and leading motif of the Arietta itself; in addition, they provide transformations of material from the preceding Allegro. The relationship between these two movements is even closer than has so far been suggested.

Discussing the first movement, we noted that the strange, subdued harmonies of the development and coda suggested that its conflict was likely to be overcome, not by fierce heroic struggle, as in the *Eroica* or the *Appassionata*, but by some kind of transcendence toward a new psychical plane. And we noted that the poignant F-minor extension of the second theme during the recapitulation had brought a brief glimpse of a new world of emotion and spirit which, though unable to sustain itself in the context of the recapitulation, strongly suggested changes to come. Spiritually, the Arietta itself has made manifest the condition to which the development, the coda, and the poignant extension within the recapitulation had aspired. In doing so, however, the Arietta has revealed something more. It has revealed that its own leading motif, motif *z*, was actually anticipated in the first movement.

In the harsh Maestoso introduction, the mood had lightened only once, shortly before the "thunder" in the bass which introduces the Allegro per se. The new mood had expressed itself in a short melodic arc in the right hand, *piano*, which, after ascending stepwise in bars 11 and 12, had come to rest in a descending three-note motif whose shape and rhythm anticipate motif *z* in the Arietta (bars 12–13, Figure 20). Beginning in bar 13 the same arc ascends again, this time from the bass clef. Again it closes in the descending three-note motif (bars 14–15), whose final chord extends itself toward the "thunder" in the

Figure 20

bass. When one hears the sonata for the first time, bars 11–15 serve primarily as a melodic and dynamic contrast to the powerful dissonance and angularity of the rest of the Maestoso introduction. But these bars also anticipate the transforming calm—and its leading motif—that will finally prevail in the Arietta. As this descending motif is played in the treble and then in the bass, its inversion (anticipating the inversion of motif z that will end the sonata) is heard deep in the bass (bars 12–13 and 14–15). This wide spacing between the motif and its inversion is the sonata's first anticipation of the spacing that, in the Arietta, will reach its climax at the edge of the trilling abyss.

A second first-movement anticipation of motif z comes during the F-minor extension of the second theme during the recapitulation. As we have noted, a new world of poignant feeling opens up when the second theme moves low into the bass for the first time. In the retrospect of the Arietta we see that its descending melody consists of anticipations of motif z. After the dotted half note (bar 108 in the bass, Figure 21), this theme consists of three versions of a descending three-note motif whose shape and rhythm, like that of the motif in the Maestoso introduction, anticipates motif z (bars 108–10).[16] Its third statement, inverted, leads to a high ornamental answer in the treble. Twice before (in the exposition and at the beginning of the recapitulation) this ornamental figure had seemed, in melody and register, a natural extension of the theme itself. Now, following the motivic descent of the theme into the bass, it causes two voices, low and high, to bridge temporarily an abyss of the kind that will open up much more gloriously and sublimely in the Arietta. This temporary bridging

Figure 21

across the registers is another way in which the poignant F-minor extension of the second theme anticipates the greater consolations to come in the Arietta.[17]

The symbiotic relationship between motif x and motif z, and the subtle anticipation of motif z at dramatic moments of contrast within the stormy first movement, reveal that Beethoven's use of reiterated motifs to bring sublime unity out of the harshest possible contrast is, in Opus 111, as striking, pervasive, and inspired as Brontë's use of reiterated literary motifs in *Wuthering Heights*. One measure of the organic form of each work is the extent to which these subtle motivic relationships become evident only after one has assimilated the emotional and spiritual burden of the entire work. Not until Heathcliff's confession to Nelly in chapter 29 can one understand the strangled sobs to Catherine's ghost in chapter 3; not until Nelly's final inspection of Heathcliff's body in chapter 34 can the dissonant energy of Lockwood's dream-encounter with the same ghost be exorcized. Not until the transcendent meaning of motif z is established in the coda and epilogue of the Arietta can one perceive—by retrospective extension—its presence within the introduction and recapitulation of the stormy first movement.

In Opus 111, as in Opus 57, Beethoven has created a "whole created cosmos" out of materials of maximum contrast. The polarized materials of this sonata include its motifs (x and z), its themes (stormy in the Allegro, hymnic in the Arietta), its tonalities (C minor and C major), and its use of register (the principles of high and low as they contrast within and between each movement). As in the *Appassionata*, these highly polarized materials have expressed themselves as contrasting principles of storm and calm. Here, however, those principles, though they clash cruelly, finally manage to flow together "unimpeded and unconflicting." Here, as on the mystical plane of *Wuthering Heights*, a "single principle that ultimately directs them" has managed to "impose an equilibrium" upon the discord. The equilibrium finally achieved is as complete as that which is found in comparable compositions by Mozart, but it is different in kind.[18] Beethoven's Romantic style resembles Mozart's classical style in its concern for achieving equilibrium; it differs in the means of attaining it. More vehement in its expression of raw emotion, as the *Appassionata* testifies, Beethoven's style tends, ultimately, to be more mystical in its resolution of conflict, as evidence Opus 111.

Spiritually, Barford argues, Opus 111 expresses a "consciousness which contains all antitheses as they occur, as being contains becoming, space form, time rhythm, silence harmony, stillness movement" (p. 180). This chapter has argued that *Wuthering Heights*, too, expresses such a consciousness. Within the cosmos of the sonata, notes, motifs, themes, tonalities, and rhythms have found such expression. Within the cosmos of the novel, words, motifs, characters, settings, and actions have found such expression. In the lives behind the art it is Ludwig van Beethoven and Emily Brontë who have been roused to such a consciousness—and who have shaped its still motion, its mute music, into active art.

In an earlier essay Barford termed Beethoven's last piano sonata "a final sealing of the bond between the spiritual and the sensuous."[19] The phrase can be applied in a somewhat morbid way to the merging of Heathcliff's and Catherine's bodies beneath the earth. It can also be applied to Heathcliff's last days, in which all his sensuous movements (speech, sight, hearing, breathing, heartbeat) are governed by a spiritual principle working through his sensory mechanism but from outside it. The phrase also applies to Emily Brontë herself, whose first and last novel was *Wuthering Heights*. She was dead within a year of its publication, at the age of thirty. Her sensuous life was at an end, but a spiritual bond was sealed with posterity, a bond that will link her novel, as it links Beethoven's last sonata, with the lives of receptive human beings as long as our sensuous species remains capable of recognizing and assimilating spirit.

Part Two

THE NOVELIST
AND THE COMPOSER

The "motions of the spirit" compared in Part 1 are valuable primarily for their own sake, for the meaning the art of Beethoven and Brontë has for those who encounter it, whether for personal enrichment or more academic aims. But the Romantic equilibrium each artist expresses also raises questions about the lives behind the art, about the sources of the emotional power and psychic energy each was able to generate and harness. There is a natural, legitimate interest in wishing to explore conditions in the lives of the two artists that may have made possible the similarities in their art.

I hold with René Wellek that "causal explanations and even historical antecedents do not accomplish much" in explaining the genesis of great works of art. "We must leave something to chance, to genius, to a constellation of circumstance."[1] Beethoven and Brontë both managed to forge into lasting form certain possibilities made available by their separate artistic traditions. If the Beethovens had not produced a second son named Ludwig, the transition from classic to Romantic in Viennese music would have taken a much different form than it did. If the Reverend and Mrs. Brontë had produced Anne and Charlotte but not Emily, the nineteenth-century English novel would not have manifested itself in a work whose psychic energies and artistic control compare with Beethoven's musical achievement in the ways traced above. Here I wish to explore some of the elements of chance and genius, some of the constellation of circumstance that made possible the similarities between the second Ludwig's and the only Emily's art. Doing so may help to explain the time lag of several decades between his stylistic achievement and hers.

One possible explanation for the similarities in Beethoven's and Brontë's art is a similarity of character, of personal gestalt. In *The Creative World of Mozart*, Paul Henry Lang posits two kinds of artist. The one kind "circle their domain with their first steps; every circle brings them to known territory, yet every circling results in new discoveries and conquests."[2] Mozart fits this category and so does Jane Austen—as was shown in part 2 of the predecessor to this book. From Concerto No. 9 through Concerto No. 27, from *Pride and Prejudice* through *Persuasion*, these two artists refined and deepened the domain they had circled with their first steps.

Beethoven and Brontë fit Lang's second category: those "who develop constantly by stepping out of their frame and following a new direction." Each pushed inexorably into new psychic frontiers, leaving behind, in particular, the social conventions that both Mozart and Austen allowed so gracefully to frame the world they chose to explore. Rosen argues that "Beethoven is perhaps the first composer for whom this exploratory function of music took precedence over every other: pleasure, instruction, and even, at times, expression" (p. 445). The same might be said of Emily Brontë. As early as 1842 the exploratory mode of her character was evident to Constantin Heger, her gifted professor in Brussels; he made the celebrated assertion that she might have been "a great navigator. Her powerful reason would have deduced new spheres of discovery from the knowledge of the old; and her strong, imperious will would never have been daunted by opposition or difficulty."[3] His tribute applies to the novel she wrote as well as to the student he knew.

Another possible reason for the similarities in Beethoven's and Brontë's art is the personal response of each to nature. Philip Barford briefly touched on this in his footnote comparing "The Prisoner" with Beethoven's late sonatas: "So different in culture, in talent, in environment, there is yet a common element in the Yorkshire novelist and Beethoven. They both knew the elemental life of nature and exulted in lonely walks in the country. Both derived creative inspiration from the contact of the earth, and neither cared a rap for wind or weather" (p. 175). In nature, Basil Deane points out, Beethoven found "the artistic and spiritual refreshment which others might have found in religion, in intimate friendships, or in contacts with fellow artists."[4] The same is true of Emily Brontë. Charlotte tells us that "her native hills . . . were what she lived in, and by, as much as the wild birds, their tenants, or as the heather, their produce."[5]

Biographical accounts of both artists connect the art they created with specific outdoor locales. On a walking excursion in the Austrian countryside in 1823, Beethoven told Schindler, "This is where I composed the scene by the stream" in the *Pastoral* Symphony; "the yellow-hammers up there, and the quails, the nightingales and the cuckoos round about composed with me."[6] This passage calls to mind Cathy Linton's "glorious jubilee" in which "larks, and throstles, and blackbirds, and linnets, and cuckoos" were "pouring out music on every side." We have no Schindler to identify for us the exact spot upon which Emily Brontë was inspired to create that particular vision, but there is no lack of evidence of the importance of the Yorkshire moors to her creative process.

Charlotte Brontë's testimony informs us not only that "my sister Emily loved the moors" but that she transformed the reality of the moors with the power of her own imagination (giving us, in Beethovenian terms, not a picture of nature but a response to it). "Flowers brighter than the rose bloomed in the blackest of the heath for her; out of a sullen hollow in a livid hill-side, *her mind could make* an Eden" (italics mine). "If she demand beauty to inspire her, she must bring it inborn; these moors are too stern to yield any product so delicate."[7] Rolland describes the same inborn habit in Beethoven. "Even the exterior nature that he sees becomes immediately incorporated with [the universe of the Self], loses its own character, takes the form and the odour of the Beethoven cosmos. Imitation . . . is in Beethoven an extremely attenuated faculty, or it is strangely transformed by the nature of the glance, always partial, always passionate, always charged with his own weighty interior life, that he directs upon things" (p. 54).

This similarity in the two artists' mental disposition leads to another: the personal, natural religion developed by each. We have already compared their mystical visions as manifested in their art in our previous chapter. Some sources of those visions can be traced to their lives as well. When Philip Henderson observed that Brontë's "peculiarly personal type of religion finds a parallel in the yearning and crucifixion and unearthly blessedness of Beethoven's late quartets," he also made a biographical comparison between the faith of each artist. For Henderson, Brontë's poem "No coward soul is mine" expresses a faith "of the same order as that expressed in the lines which Beethoven took from an essay of Schiller's on oriental religions and kept permanently framed on his desk: 'I am all that is, that was, that will be.' "[8] In that poem, one of Brontë's last, the speaker rejects the "thousand creeds / That move men's hearts" and locates faith in the "God within my breast / Almighty ever-present Deity."[9]

The above similarities in character with regard to exploratory drives, love of nature, the transformative power of the glance, and personal religion all relate closely to similarities in Beethoven's and Brontë's art. Still, those similarities do not explain how either individual managed to transform the biographical facts or tendencies into lasting art. Furthermore, some aspects of their two lives seem deeply incompatible. Among these are the conditions of their artistic productivity and the nature of their relations with society at large.

For Beethoven the three imaginative planes explored in Part 1 correspond with the three well-documented "periods" of his life. In this sense the Sonata *Pathétique* expresses not only his personal adaptation of the classical forms of Haydn and Mozart but also his attempt to come to terms with Viennese social conditions, which he bent in order to accommodate his independent spirit. Similarly, the *Appassionata* is not only a further intensification of classical forms but also a reflection of his struggle against deafness and his identification with Nature, the latter now seeming to have supplanted society itself as the focus of his being. Finally, in Opus 111, he approaches the spiritual as well as stylistic home for which he had been questing, far removed in time as well as in essence

149

from such early works as Opus 13. Students of Beethoven's art and life have so often traversed the common ground between the "periods" of his life and his art that there is no need to do so here.

Brontë's fiction cannot so easily be linked with comparable stages in her life. First of all, the three imaginative planes of *Wuthering Heights* exist simultaneously in one novel; they are not spread out over thirty years of writing. Second, some imaginative states in the novel are difficult to connect to Brontë's personal life at all—especially the extreme harshness and violence of certain parts of Heathcliff's story. Third, Emily Brontë short-circuited the process by which Beethoven became accepted by Viennese society and then gradually and irremediably withdrew from it. Her short life of thirty years includes little or no sustained intercourse with social institutions. Her experiences at the boarding schools of Cowan Bridge and Roe Head were brief and unpleasant. She did accompany Charlotte to Brussels for nine months when she was twenty-three, an experience about which I will have much to say in the pages that follow. But apart from that she lived what seems to have been her entire life behind the doors of the Haworth Parsonage or walking on nearby moors. (In Charlotte's words, "Except to go to church or take a walk on the hills, she rarely crossed the threshold of home.")[10] Perhaps this self-absorbed abstraction from societal life from an early age, buoyed by the intimate family life at the Parsonage, is what allowed her to explore, by the age of twenty-eight (the age at which Beethoven composed Opus 13), certain aspects of nature and spirit with an absorption Beethoven would not attain until his middle and late periods.

Another circumstance that may have contributed to her exploratory absorption is the fact that she had Beethoven's own example before her. Two important but sparsely documented aspects of her biographical life are her reading and her music-making. As the next chapter will show, Emily Brontë was a devoted amateur pianist who was drawn to the works of Beethoven at the very time she was creating *Wuthering Heights*. In addition, she was an avid reader throughout the decade in which the details of Beethoven's legendary life had first been made available to English-language readers (in Moscheles's 1841 edition of Schindler's *Life of Beethoven*).

In the Introduction we noted the historical anomaly of Beethoven's achieving his Romantic equilibrium near the beginning of the Romantic age in Viennese music, whereas Emily Brontë achieved hers near the end of the Romantic age in English fiction. In spite of this time lag, these two artists expressed the comparable "motions of the spirit" traced in Part 1 above. In the chapters to come, it will become clear that the 1840s were, for Emily Brontë, as well as for many of her English (and Belgian) contemporaries, an "Age of Beethoven." Her assimilation of his music and his legend during that decade left a strong mark on her psyche. After establishing the broad outlines of this "constellation of circumstance," our task will be to speculate upon its possible influence on her prose masterpiece.

Chapter Four

Emily Brontë and Music

T he general outline of Emily Brontë's involvement with music, as
sketched out in Winifred Gérin's biography, has been known for some time. In
the early 1830s, as a teenager, Emily began studying the piano at home in the
Haworth Parsonage; she soon played, in the words of Ellen Nussey, "with precision and brilliancy."[1] In 1842 she studied piano at the Heger Pensionnat in
Brussels and even gave piano lessons to some of the younger students. After
returning to Haworth, Emily acquired a new piano. Now, according to Ellen
Nussey, "the ability with which she took up music was amazing; the style, the
touch, and the expression was that of a professor absorbed heart and soul in his
theme" (p. 40). In the final years of her life (and coincident with the writing and
publishing of *Wuthering Heights*) her playing seems to have been particularly
important to her father. Gérin reports that "Emily's playing on the little upright
in his study became so intimate a language between these two silent people that
when she was dead he could not bear its presence there, and had it carried
upstairs out of sight" (pp. 155–56).

Even this bare outline of what is known about Emily Brontë's experience at
the keyboard suggests that music meant something to her—and to those who
knew her. Yet no attempt has ever been made to analyze her cumulative musical
experience or to speculate on the influence it may have had on her development
as an artist. The following analysis of the music she is known to have studied
and played at Haworth—as well as the music she is likely to have studied and
heard in Brussels—will demonstrate that music was an important part of her
general artistic experience. It will further reveal that Emily Brontë was particularly drawn to the music of Beethoven, her experience of which may well have
been a catalyst in the artistic growth that resulted in *Wuthering Heights*.

Haworth before Brussels

On 24 November 1834, when Emily was sixteen, she wrote a note that is
one of the few surviving items from her correspondence. In it she confesses that

"Anne and I have not done our music exercise which consists of b major" (Gérin, p. 39). Their teacher, expected that day, was Abraham Stansfield Sunderland, the Keighley organist. According to Gérin, his connection with the Brontë family had begun in May, when he inaugurated a new organ at the Haworth church. "Being a piano teacher much in demand among local families, Mr. Sunderland was now engaged to teach the Misses Brontë, whose many preserved albums of music, inscribed and dated by their teacher, show that they began to study seriously in that year. There was no piano at the parsonage at the time of Ellen Nussey's first visit in 1833, but she related that a little later 'there was the addition of a piano,' and added that 'Emily, after some application, played with precision and brilliancy. Anne played also, but she preferred soft harmonies and vocal music.'"

Gérin's account emphasizes the extent to which music-making at the Parsonage was a family affair. She notes that Patrick Brontë, no less than his children, "passionately loved music." Handel was "the chief favourite of the whole family" and "his entire oratorios 'arranged for Two Performers' were gradually added to their repertoire." Emily and Anne performed the oratorios. "Unhappily for Charlotte, who loved music as much as her sisters, her extreme shortsightedness prevented her from making any headway with her piano practice and she had to give it up" (Gérin, pp. 40–41). Their brother Branwell loved music too. Although he aspired to be a painter, he played the organ at the Haworth Church and the flute in the home. He seems to have approached music with the same Romantic enthusiasm that characterized the rest of his life. "Branwell was acquainted with the works of the great composers . . . and although he could not perform their elaborate compositions well, he was always so excited when they were played for him by his friends that he would walk about the room with measured footsteps, his eyes raised to the ceiling, accompanying the music with his voice in an impassioned manner, and beating time with his hand on the chairs as he passed to and fro" (Gérin, p. 58).

Emily too was "acquainted with the works of the great composers." She, moreover, *could* "play their elaborate compositions well," especially after her year in Brussels. Gérin says of her solo playing only this: "Her music books show that she played Beethoven, Mozart, Haydn" (p. 156). It is now time to look at the music she played by these, and other, composers—and to speculate as to when, why, and with what result she played it.

The music books that are preserved today at the Haworth Parsonage include music that Emily Brontë acquired both before and after her residence in Brussels. Three of these books are bound volumes of sheet music acquired primarily in the 1830s. Most of the solo music in these volumes belongs to Emily—much of it inscribed with her name, dated, and carefully marked for fingering.[2] Her solo music in these volumes includes a little Beethoven, some Mozart, and no Haydn; most of the composers are lesser known, or unknown, today. The works she played in the 1830s tend to feature brilliant passagework, dramatic contrasts between loud and soft, and every manner of *con espressione* emphasis. Many of them have "stormy" or "pathetic" introductions; many are very explicitly programmatic. The most prevalent large-scale musical form is the theme and variations.

The themes and variations in Emily's early music books illustrate one of the two directions taken by the form in the nineteenth century: "a debasement that consisted of technically brilliant variations on catchy operatic tunes or 'national' airs." Such variations, Rey Longyear points out, "became the stock-in-trade of the touring virtuoso."[3] For exposure to the other direction taken by the form—termed "ennoblement" by Longyear—the young pianist would have to wait until her visit to Brussels in 1842.

Typical of the themes and variations Emily played in her teens is R. Andrews's "Introduction and Variations to the Admired Air 'Jennies Bawbee.'" Printed by Ward and Andrews of Manchester, the title page is initialed "RA" (no doubt R. Andrews himself) and inscribed "Miss E. Brontë" with a date in the 1830s.[4] Careful notations for fingering (perhaps supplied by Mr. Sunderland) appear throughout the long score—eleven oversized pages. The composition begins with a dramatic thirty-four-bar Maestoso introduction. The halting rhythms, contrasting dynamics, and powerful crescendos reflect the undoubted influence of Beethoven's pianistic style. A brilliant written-out cadenza *ad lib*, presto, leads to the theme itself, in C major, Adagio con espressione. The first variation is fairly calm, the second Brillante. Variation 3 is a Minore in C minor, modulating to F sharp in its central section. The next variation, Majore (Brillante), returns to C major. Variation 5 is a Marcia marked Maestoso. A brilliant, extended Polonaise (four oversized pages) concludes the work.

A similar work, likewise marked for fingering throughout, is "Mr. Macdonald, An Original Air with Variations." It, too, begins with an extensive, dramatic introduction. The theme itself is an Andantino con espressione with heavy pedalling, contrasting dynamics, sections marked *ad lib*, and additional indications of *con espressione*. The seven variations are marked Con delicatezza, Dolce, Siciliana, Brillante, Minore, Allegretto, and Pollacca. This variation set too runs eleven oversized pages. Its publisher, Sykes and Sons, chose to make the dedicatee of this work, the then-celebrated composer J. B. Cramer, more prominent on the title page than the composer, indicated only by two florid initials (which appear to be I. G.).

A more ambitious set of variations, by T. Latour, is entitled "Imitations of Many of the Most Eminent Professors in Twenty-Six Variations." A twenty-nine-page score, fingered throughout, this work begins with an Andante theme that is subjected to variations "à la Corri," "à la Woelfl," "à la Pleyel," "à la Cramer," "à la Dussek," "à la Viotti," "à la Steibelt," "à la Clementi," etc. Latour gives the final variation, Brillante, his own name. That Emily Brontë did the technical homework necessary for playing such a piece is attested by two well-marked sets of Czerny exercises: *Cent exercises* (Opus 13g) and *Die Schule der Geläufigkeit* (Opus 299). Other variation sets in the early music books are by Dussek ("God Save the Queen"), G. Kiallmark ("Auld Lang Syne"), Henri Herz ("O' mon cher Augustine"), and Henry Purcell ("Ground with Variations").

A second prominent category in the early music books is the fantasia, usually of the "characteristic" variety corresponding to a nonmusical program. One such work is I. G. Moscheles's "Napoleon's Midnight Review and the Sea." This work begins with a brooding Andante patetico introduction, followed by "Napoleon's Midnight Review." Beginning *pp* and *sotto voce*, this section introduces a *cantabile* melody which, after being subjected to modulation and dynamic intensification, leads to an Allegro agitato. "The Sea," Allegro vivace, emerges without a break from the Allegro agitato and continues for nine (oversized) pages, a number of which are marked for fingering.

The same bound volume of scores includes J. B. Cramer's "Beauties of Neukomm, A Characteristic Fantasia in which are Introduced The Stormy Petrel, Count Balthazar, and The Sea Rover." This work, too, begins with a dramatic introduction: an Allegro maestoso. It is followed by a spacious Aria movement, by an Allegretto, and by a Rondo, the later movements fused by an *ad libitum* bridge. Beyond the elaborate title of this fantasia no further programmatic indications are given in the score, which is inscribed "E. J. Brontë" and contains a number of marks for fingering.[5]

Among the waltzes and other dance movements Emily played in the 1830s the names of some major composers appear. She owned two sets of waltzes by Mozart. A set of three waltzes for piano is inscribed "Miss E. Brontë" with a date that appears to be 11 Nov. 1835. A collection of twelve waltzes for piano (with accompaniment for flute or violin; did she play these with Branwell?) is carefully fingered for piano in both the bass and treble clefs. Beethoven and Carl Maria von Weber are the prominent names in several separate issues of *Sykes's Favorite Waltzes for Pianoforte*, each issue being inscribed "Miss E. Brontë" and the legible dates reading 1836. Emily's early music books also include waltzes by L. Merveilleux du Plantis, *contre danses* by Henri Herz, quadrilles by R. Andrews (arranged from airs by Paganini), and "Gems of the Opera," a series of "Airs, Waltzes, and Marches" arranged by Corri. The duet music she played with Anne includes three original waltzes by R. Andrews, quadrilles by Henry Smith, and a grand triumphal march by Ferdinand Ries, the student of Beethoven.

The next category of music, piano transcriptions made from operatic overtures, includes only six works, but these are of high artistic value. Emily played keyboard arrangements of three of Mozart's greatest overtures: *The Marriage of Figaro, Don Giovanni,* and *Così fan Tutte*. She also played the overtures to Mozart's *La Clemenza di Tito,* Beethoven's *Men of Prometheus,* and Weber's *Preciosa*.

A final category, full-length sonatas, includes but three works. One is a two-movement sonata by Nicolai, Opus 3, marked Allegro and Rondo. The second sonata, missing its title page and therefore the name of the composer, is in three movements: Allegro, Andantino, and Rondo. A third sonata, "The Battle of Prague, a Favorite Sonata" by Kotzwara, is the most blatant piece of program music in the collection. Like most of the multimovement fantasias and themes-with-variations Emily played, this "sonata" begins with a mood-setting introduction, in this case a slow march. Among the subsequent movements, marked Largo, Grave, Quick Step, Allegro, and Andante, is one marked not for tempo but simply for its program: "Prussians" and "Imperialists." Throughout the score are programmatic indications ranging from "flying Bullets" to "Go to Bed Tom."

Two miscellaneous works round out this summary of the music the young novelist to be played at Haworth in the 1830s. The first is an arrangement for solo piano of J. C. Bach's Fourth Concerto, Opus 13. Although the score indicates movements marked Allegro, Andante, and Andante con moto, the title page emphasizes the fact that "The Yellow-Hair'd Laddie" is introduced. Diabelli's Duet in D (evidently played with Anne) is a nineteen-page work marked Allegro moderato, Andante cantabile, and Allegretto (Rondo).

With only a few exceptions, these keyboard works require more brilliance than musicality, more technique than spirit. Even so, for an amateur to have played them with "precision and brilliancy" when only in her teens certainly would have required considerable ability and application. Stylistically, the music Emily Brontë played at Haworth in the 1830s contrasts sharply with the music Jane Austen played at Steventon and at Chawton in the 1790s and 1810s (summarized in appendix 1 of *Jane Austen and Mozart*). Austen played music primarily of the classical period—even though Romantic music had made considerable inroads, even for amateurs, by the 1810s. Brontë's music in the 1830s is decidedly Romantic, the "classical" period being represented primarily by the Mozart waltzes and overtures she played.

The greatest similarity in the music the two novelists played is the presence of waltzes, marches, quadrilles, and *contre danses*. But in the larger forms their music diverges considerably. Most of Austen's large-scale works are multimove-ment sonatas (or "lessons") by such classical-tending composers as Koželuch, Hoffmeister, Haydn, Schobert, Sterkel, and Pleyel. Kotzwara's "Battle of Prague" appears in her collection too, but it is an exception to the generally nonprogrammatic thrust of her instrumental music. In Brontë's early music books the exceptions are the works *without* the programs. The programmatic nature and the exaggerated dynamics of the large-scale works she tended to play—the characteristic fantasias and the debased variations—found little place in the symmetrical, balanced, restrained music favored by Austen.[6]

I outline these musical differences in style because they correspond to ob-vious, overt stylistic differences in the fiction that Austen and Brontë wrote. *Pride and Prejudice*, like most of the three-movement sonatas that Austen played, begins immediately with the clear, balanced articulation of a theme (the opening sentence). *Wuthering Heights*, like most of the large-scale music played by Brontë in the 1830s, begins with a dramatic, extended, mood-setting intro-duction. In Austen's fiction, as in most of the music she played, transitions are carefully prepared, abrupt shocks avoided. In Brontë's novel, as in much of *her* music, the opposite tends to be true. Austen's novels achieve their charac-teristic expression of feeling through the restraint with which large-scale struc-tural elements are used to bear—rather than bare—the emotion; the same tends to be true of the instrumental music she played. In *Wuthering Heights*, as in the music Brontë played in her teens, the expression of feeling erupts vehe-mently from the very surface of the work. Examination of the music she played in the 1840s, at home as well as in Brussels, will suggest further comparisons with the novel she wrote.

Haworth after Brussels

Emily Brontë lived and studied in Brussels from February until November 1842. As her musical studies there have not yet been (and may never be) docu-mented, our most precise measure of her experience with music in the Belgian capital is found in the music she acquired and played after her return to Haworth. Its quality—emotional, artistic, spiritual—far surpasses that of the music she played in the 1830s. This difference strongly suggests that her musical experience in Brussels not only expanded her repertoire but also transformed her taste.

Two major musical acquisitions mark the years immediately following her return from Brussels. The first was a new upright piano, placed in Patrick Brontë's study. The second was *The Musical Library*, an impressive eight-volume anthology of instrumental and vocal music published as a collected edition by Charles Knight in 1844.[7] Both acquisitions would have been major investments for the Brontë family. Both undoubtedly figured in the sisters' plans to open a small boarding school at the Parsonage: a circular printed up for this project in 1844 indicates the fees that students would pay for piano lessons and use of the instrument.[8] Plans for the school fell through, but Emily had the use of the new instrument and *The Musical Library* for the rest of her short life. After surveying the music itself we will be able to imagine the artistic and spiritual experience she would have gained by playing it on her new piano.

The eight volumes of *The Musical Library* are equally divided between instrumental and vocal music. The editor indicates that the purpose of the entire undertaking was to "afford the same aid in the progress of the musical art, that literature had so undeniably received from the cheap publications of the day. . . . Before this work appeared, the exorbitant sums demanded for engraved music amounted to a prohibition of its free circulation among the middle classes." The four instrumental volumes had the additional purpose of supplanting exactly the kind of music Emily had played in the 1830s. "When this publication was projected," the editor writes, "the piano-forte music then most prevalent, or most fashionable, had reached the very acme of frivolity." This music was "devoid of feeling and taste, requiring from the performer nothing but a certain degree of manual dexterity." The goal of *The Musical Library*, however, is to bring "forward again composers of the highest merit, who were little, if at all, known to many of the present generation. It has enabled thousands who never before had such an opportunity offered them, to form some acquaintance with the great symphonies, quartets, &c, of Germany," etc.

By today's standards the editor succeeded admirably in selecting music "of no ephemeral character, not depending for effect on fashion, or any temporary cause, but excellent *per se*, and such as will be admired so long as a just discrimination and a good taste in the art shall prevail."[9] The four instrumental volumes contain some 170 works—all for piano or piano transcription. The composers most often represented are Handel (25 works), Beethoven (20 works), Haydn (19 works), and Mozart (15 works). Other composers include Corelli, Boccherini, Couperin, J. S. Bach, Gluck, Schobert, C. P. E. Bach, Clementi,

Dussek, Pleyel, Steibelt, Krumpholz, Weber, Moscheles, Spohr, Rossini, and Mendelssohn. Of these works Emily Brontë marked twenty-two for special attention in the table of contents.[10] The works she played would not necessarily be limited to the ones she marked, but those she did mark are certainly a strong indication of the music she liked: four are by Beethoven, three by Handel, two by Haydn, and two by Clementi. She marked single works by Gluck, Mozart, Dussek, Geminiani, Koch, Pleyel, Pinto, Righini, Winter, and Woelfl.

The most consistent preference in the works she marked is for Beethoven symphonies. Of four possible selections, she marked three: movements from the Second, the Sixth, and the Seventh Symphonies.[11] (Her fourth Beethoven choice was "Variations on Paisiello's Air: 'Quanto e bello.'") From Handel she marked the Musette from the Sixth Grand Concerto, the Overture to *Alcina*, and the chorus "From the Censor" from *Solomon*. The two works by Haydn are symphony transcriptions; the two Clementi works are piano sonatas. Obviously, such music is worlds away from the bulk of what she acquired and played in the 1830s. It is usually, though not always, more demanding technically than the display music she played a decade earlier; it is consistently more demanding artistically. It also reveals some important structural and stylistic differences.

"Debased" variations had figured prominently in the early music books. The variation movements she chose from *The Musical Library* tend to be less brilliant, more substantial. The one work she marked by Pleyel is a Concertante. It begins with a theme-and-variations movement that is followed by a short Adagio and a concluding Menuetto-Trio. The variation movement begins immediately with the theme itself, an aria marked Andante grazioso. The theme is perfectly symmetrical: eight bars plus repeat followed by eight bars plus repeat. All three variations remain comfortably within this pattern of symmetrical double repeats. The style of this movement is much closer to that of a series of Pleyel variations played by Jane Austen than it is to the "debased" variations that Brontë played in her teens.[12]

The variation movements by Beethoven in *The Musical Library* also depart from the "frivolity" of her earlier music. His "Variations on Paisiello's Air," which she marked in the table of contents of volume 3, is similar in overt structure to the "debased" variations she played a decade earlier: the theme is followed by three variations in the home key, then a Minore, a Majore, and two final variations, the latter Più moto. This work, however, begins with the theme itself rather than with a dramatic introduction. Throughout the variations themselves there is more emphasis on musical content and less on technique than was true of such works as "Jennies Bawbee" or "Mr. Macdonald." Brontë may also have played three other Beethoven variation sets, unmarked in the table of contents. They are the slow movement, Andante with Variations, from the Piano Sonata, Opus 26; the Air with Variations from the Fifth Quartet, Opus 18; and "Air Russe" with Nine Variations.

The programmatic character piece, usually with a brilliant mood-setting introduction, had also been prominent in the early music books. There is *some* comparable display music in *The Musical Library*, but it is not nearly so predominant. One work marked in the table of contents is Charles Koch's "Rondeau à L'Allemande," Opus 55, a work that does begin with a mood-setting "Introduzione" before breaking into an Allegro, filled with accidentals, that rushes on for five oversized pages. Also marked is Dussek's "The Consolation, An Andante with an Introduction," Opus 62. After the poignant introduction, the theme, Andante con moto, modulates into an extended Minore section answered by an even longer Maggiore. A third such character piece marked in the table of contents is G. F. Pinto's Romance, Opus 3, a one-movement larghetto marked Quasi andantino affettuoso, e sempre legato. This piece is shot through with accidentals and crescendos and it modulates dramatically, but beyond the title there is no further indication of its nonmusical content.

The Musical Library strongly emphasizes purely instrumental music rather than program music. The Clementi sonatas Emily marked are typical. Opus 6 is in two movements, Presto (with the Prestissimo omitted) and Andante con moto, ma con espressione. Opus 7 is in three movements: Allegro assai, Mesto, and Rondo (Allegro). A third Clementi sonata, though not marked in the table of contents, has been dog-eared as if to mark its place in the book. Its three movements are Allegro, Larghetto con espressione, and Rondo. In addition to these entire sonatas are a number of self-contained movements from larger keyboard works. Among these Emily marked the Adagio from Woelfl's Sonata, Opus 25; the Musette from Handel's Sixth Grand Concerto; and the Opening, Slow Movement, and Finale of Geminiani's First Concerto. One Beethoven sonata movement she did not mark in the table of contents has many splotches on the score, as if it has been studied and perhaps even left open to the elements. It is the slow movement, Largo appassionato, of the early sonata, Opus 2, No. 2.[13] Also included in *The Musical Library* is the delightful Menuetto of Beethoven's Sonata, Opus 10, No. 3.

The symphony transcriptions in *The Musical Library* also consist primarily of selected movements. The Haydn works Emily marked for special attention were the Opening and Finale from Symphony No. 18 and the Andante of a Symphony in D. The selection she marked from Beethoven's Second Symphony included the second movement, Larghetto (with Adagio introduction), and the third, Scherzo-Trio. The bottom of the last page of the Larghetto, where one would turn the page to the Scherzo, is torn—the only torn page I noticed in the four volumes. The selection from the Seventh Symphony is the sublime second movement, the Allegretto. In addition to being marked in the table of contents, its first page has been folded down as if to mark its place in the book. The selections from the Sixth Symphony, Beethoven's *Pastoral*, are from the first and third movements. They are presented in the score simply as Allegro ma non troppo, Allegro, and Allegro, with no hint of Beethoven's own programmatic descriptions ("Awakening of cheerful feelings on arriving in the country" and "Merry Assembly of Countryfolk"). The one symphonic selection by Beethoven that Emily Brontë did not mark in the table of contents is the most programmatic, as listed: the *Marcia funebre*, from *Sinfonia eroica*.

The predominance of "pure" instrumental music, whether originally for piano or as transcribed from symphonies, is the biggest difference between the music Emily played in the 1840s and that which she played a decade earlier. The one constant in her early and later music books is her proclivity for keyboard transcriptions of operatic and instrumental overtures. Among the overtures she marked for special attention in *The Musical Library* are those for Mozart's *Idomeneo*, Handel's *Alcina*, Mehul's *Le jeune Henri*, and Winter's *Marie Montalban*. Beethoven's overture to *Fidelio* is not marked in the table of contents, but there are a number of splotches on the score which suggest that it, like the Largo appassionato from the early sonata, may have been studied and perhaps exposed to the elements.

Her marks in *The Musical Library* indicate that Emily's approach to the piano had greatly matured in the ten years since she confessed to not practicing the b-major scale. The music she marked for special attention in the 1840s is more serious, more profound. There is much less emphasis on Romantic display, much more on musical content. Although much of her music remains Romantic in style, classical composers and classical forms are now more strongly represented, both in number and quality of works. The sonatas by Clementi and the symphony movements by Beethoven and Haydn all have solid roots in the classical style that a decade earlier had been represented in her music books primarily by waltzes. Even so, there are very few complete multimovement works in the classical forms (as there were, for example, in Jane Austen's music books); apart from the Clementi sonatas, most of the music tending toward the classical in *The Musical Library* consists of selected movements, not entire works.[14]

Now that we have surveyed the contents of *The Musical Library*, Ellen Nussey's comment about Emily's playing after her return from Brussels takes on added meaning. The music that Emily marked for special attention in *The Musical Library* requires being played "heart and soul." Her new rosewood piano, as well as her recent training in Brussels, must have helped her to play it with "the style, the touch, and the expression of a professor." Biographically, two aspects of her musical life in the Parsonage during the last five years of her life are of particular interest.

First, there is the pleasure her playing evidently gave to her father, whose eyesight had worsened to the point of blindness during the 1840s. When on her death her father had the little upright removed from his study, Charlotte was not pleased, and expressed her "shock" in a letter of 1851. But Patrick Brontë's biographers, Lock and Dixon, express their own shock at Charlotte's insensitivity to the "hours of delight" he had received from Emily's playing on the instrument, now "a sore reminder of his daughter."[15] One wonders what music Emily played for her father during her last years. From the works marked in *The Musical Library*, at least three Beethoven movements, owing to their spiritual value, would certainly seem to be likely candidates: the expansive Larghetto of the Second Symphony, the joyous opening movement of the *Pastoral*, and the soulful Allegretto of the Seventh Symphony. To the head of a literary family who was losing his eyesight, the music of a composer who had lost his hearing might have had special poignance and meaning.

Whichever works she actually played for her father on their new piano in the mid-1840s, Emily was doing something else at the time: writing and then publishing *Wuthering Heights*. According to Charlotte's "Biographical Notice," Emily began writing the novel sometime after the autumn of 1845.[16] Considering its power and complexity, many critics argue for an earlier starting date. But whenever Emily actually began the novel she is certain to have done most of the writing sometime between 1844 and its publication in 1847—that is, during the very period when her playing seems to have meant so much to Ellen Nussey, Patrick Brontë, and, no doubt, herself.

It is possible that the music Emily played "heart and soul" in the mid-1840s had no relation to the novel she wrote, these simply being two simultaneous heartfelt activities. Or perhaps her intense musical experience did play a part in the artistic and spiritual activity that resulted in the creation of her literary masterpiece. This question can be addressed after summarizing what is known, what is not known, and what can be surmised about her musical experience in 1842, the year she spent in Brussels.

Brussels in 1842

Emily Brontë and her sister Charlotte, accompanied by their father, left Haworth for Brussels on 9 February 1842, arriving in the Belgian capital on the evening of February 14. Their avowed purpose was to acquire, at ages twenty-three and twenty-five, respectively, the educational training that would prepare them for setting up their own boarding school in England. They enrolled at the Heger Pensionnat, planning to stay six months. In July, however, they decided to stay another half-year. Their studies were interrupted when the death in October of their aunt, Miss Branwell, necessitated their departure for Haworth. Charlotte returned to Brussels in January 1843 and remained a year. Emily did not return.

Emily's nine months in Brussels were occupied primarily with study—so much so that she and Charlotte stayed on at the pensionnat straight through the "grand vacation" in August and September. For information about Emily's life in Brussels, as at Haworth, we must rely almost wholly on the testimony of others: nothing survives in her own hand. In May Charlotte writes: "Hitherto Emily and I have had good health, and therefore have been able to work well." She adds that "Emily works like a horse" in learning French, overcoming many obstacles. In July Charlotte writes that "Emily is making rapid progress in French, German, music, and drawing. Monsieur and Madame Heger begin to recognize the valuable parts of her character, under her singularities." In the same letter she reveals the plan to stay another half-year, owing to Madame Heger's offer to employ Charlotte as an English teacher and "to employ Emily some part of each day teaching music to a certain number of the pupils" (Gérin, pp. 123, 133).

Mary Taylor was an English acquaintance of the Brontë sisters also resident in Brussels. On 24 September she wrote that "Charlotte and Emily are well . . . not only in health but in mind and hope. They are content in their present position and even gay and I think they do quite right not to return to England" (Gérin, p. 134). In early October, however, Martha Taylor, Mary's sister, died of cholera; she was buried in Brussels on 14 October. Two weeks later, on 29 October, Miss Branwell died in Haworth and Charlotte and Emily left for home. "Miss Emily," M. Heger wrote to Patrick Brontë in November, "was learning the piano, receiving lessons from the best professor in Belgium, and she herself already had little pupils." She "was losing whatever she had of ignorance, and also of what was worse—timidity."[17]

One of Emily's piano students, Louise de Bassompierre, aged sixteen, remembered her fondly all her life. But the testimony of Laetitia Wheelwright, then fourteen, has contributed to the negative picture often presented of Emily's experience in Brussels. Three of her sisters, ages seven through ten, were among Emily's "little pupils." According to Laetitia, Emily would "only take them in play hours so as not to curtail her own school hours, naturally causing many tears." This pianistic tyrant, whenever she did go out for recess, allegedly clung to her sister Charlotte out of fear of contact with anyone else. Emily further angered the Wheelwrights, with whom Charlotte got on much better, by at least once preventing Charlotte from visiting their home on a Sunday, the one day free from study (Gérin, pp. 130–31). Charlotte's own published account of Emily's stay in Brussels stressed her homesick yearning for the moors and her antipathy to the Catholic religion.[18]

Whatever the personal hardships of living in a foreign environment, however, Emily gained a cultural awareness that has been overlooked by too many students of this period of her life. As Romer Wilson has pointed out, she "discovered a world of cathedrals and pictures," learned to "read the masters of French and German literature," learned to "draw for herself, not copies of mezzotints, but the beautiful old trees in the garden," and learned "to interpret the masters of music upon the piano." Without offering any further evidence Wilson connects this cultural exposure with the creativity soon to burst forth in *Wuthering Heights* and the best poems. "Whatever she got in Brussels lay fallow for one year, and then, from 1844 to 1846, Emily wrote the best things of her life. Strength and certainty are added to power."[19] An investigation of "what she got" from "the masters of music" in Brussels will help us to judge what *it* may have added to the strength and certainty of her writing.

The best evidence of Emily Brontë's musical experience in Brussels, of course, would be a precise record of the music she studied, taught, and heard while living there from February to November 1842. Unfortunately, here, as in so many other areas of her life, no such record appears to exist. We have no direct evidence of the piano works she studied in Brussels—or even of the works she taught to others. Even worse, some of what little we thought we knew about her musical studies there turns out to be erroneous. According to Gérin, "Emily studied music with M. Chapelle, M. Heger's brother-in-law, a professor of the Conservatoire Royal of Brussels, the visiting master of the Pensionnat" (p. 133). There seems no doubt that Emily did study with M. Chapelle, who later took English lessons from Charlotte and who probably served as the model for M. Josef Emanuel, the musician in Charlotte's *Villette*. But M. Chapelle never was a professor at the Conservatoire Royal of Brussels, according to the current records there. Nor does he show up in the other major musical archives of the city.[20]

Gérin goes on to report that the progress Emily made with M. Chapelle "was exceptional enough for the Hegers to decide on giving her lessons the next half [year] with the finest teacher in Belgium. The incentive of working with a really great pianist must have reconciled Emily to the new plan" (p. 133). This "really great pianist" (the one M. Heger called "the best professor in Belgium") may well have been a professor at the Conservatoire. But we seem to have no evidence at all as to who he (or she) was. Nor do we know the extent of Emily's study with this person before being called back to England by the death of her aunt. Until more can be learned about M. Chapelle or the other professor, and until some record can be found of the works Emily actually studied in Brussels, the quality of her musical studies there can only be interpolated from the change that occurred in what she played at Haworth. But even that evidence, as we have seen, is eloquent testimony to the quality of the music and training she must have encountered in the Belgian capital.[21]

Just as we lack any record of the actual music Emily studied in Brussels, so do we lack any record of her attendance at concerts. One concert program from Brussels is preserved at Haworth, but it is dated 24 October 1843, when Charlotte, unaccompanied by Emily, was spending a second year in the city. Even so, this program in itself seems to have had meaning for Emily, for it was among the small number of possessions found in her desk at the time of her death.[22]

That Emily herself would have attended some concerts during nine months in Brussels certainly seems likely. In the days before radio or recordings, no talented amateur from the provinces would have passed up an opportunity to hear great music played by first-class musicians in a cosmopolitan setting. More important, Emily was seriously studying music in Brussels. Attendance at concerts is certain to have been encouraged, probably even required, by her professor. Charlotte, not at all a student of music, managed to get to enough concerts in Brussels that they actually influenced her art.[23] Emily certainly attended concerts too, even though we have no hard evidence as to which ones they were. In addition, she would have followed the musical life of the city in such daily newspapers as *L'Indépendant*. A summary of the musical year of 1842 as presented in its pages will provide an overview of the concert life in Brussels during Emily's residence there.[24]

Musical life in Brussels in 1842 was exceedingly rich and varied, much of the activity flowing from well-established musical institutions. The Conservatoire Royal, in a newly refurbished hall, was the center of serious symphonic life. The operatic center was the Theatre Royale, where Bellini's *Norma* premiered that year (other operas included *Lucia de Lammermoor*, *I Puritani*, and *The Barber of Seville*). Two competing societies—the Société Philharmonique and the Société Royale de la Grand Harmonie—sponsored separate series of "grandes concerts vocal et instrumental." These concerts usually combined popular excerpts from orchestral, operatic, and solo works, with the proceeds often designated for the poor or, this year, the victims of a disastrous fire in Hamburg. Brussels also featured numerous concerts by visiting artists on the European circuit, ranging this year from Franz Liszt, who played once, to the sisters Milanollo, violinists who played eight times. A new musical offering in 1842 was a weekly series of chamber music concerts, praised in *L'Indépendant* (March 27) as supplying the only ingredient previously lacking in the city's musical life. In the summer there were outdoor concerts in the park that the Brontë sisters could apparently hear, at times, from their dormitory (Gérin, p. 134). In addition to this regular flow of musical activity there were three very special musical events in July, September, and October, to be discussed below.

Of all the concerts in Brussels in 1842 the ones Emily Brontë is most likely to have attended are the symphonic concerts at the Conservatoire Royal. The critic of *L'Indépendant* points out that the conservatoire concerts were musically the most progressive and accomplished in the city; they were also the least expensive, the price being three francs rather than the customary five. Writing in April, two months after Emily's arrival, he calls attention to the low prices, the serious programs, and the devotion to music rather than "celebrities." The purpose of these concerts, he writes, is not so much to display singers and instrumentalists as to "popularize the knowledge of the masterworks of art." The editor of *The Musical Library* would heartily approve.

There were three symphony concerts at the conservatoire in the early months of 1842. The first, on January 30, two weeks before Emily arrived in town, began with Beethoven's Second Symphony and ended with his *Egmont* Overture. The second, on March 12, began with Beethoven's *Leonore* Overture and ended with his *Eroica* Symphony. The third, on April 24, began with Mendelssohn's *Hebrides* Overture and concluded with Beethoven's Seventh Symphony. Wedged between the overtures and symphonies at these concerts were concertos for piano and for flute; fantasies for orchestra, for piano, for violin, for bassoon, and for cello; and excerpts from operas (*Ana Bolena, Lucia de Lammermoor, Sémiramide, Otello,* and *Orfeo*). A cello fantasie by Servais on the March program, heard between the *Leonore* Overture and the *Eroica* Symphony, was entitled *Hommage à Beethoven*.

By the date of the next regular symphonic concert at the conservatoire, November 20, Emily Brontë had returned to Haworth. Writing on December 1, the critic of *L'Indépendant* calls attention to the fact that this time "there is not a single work by Beethoven." Instead, there is a symphony by Haydn (No. 95) and a Mozart piano concerto (No. 7). He praises the conservatory for not allowing the masterworks "d'une autre époque" (Haydn, Mozart) to fall into an unjust oblivion; such works need not be completely sacrificed to the "divinités du jour" (Beethoven).

At first glance, it might seem surprising that Beethoven, in 1842, fifteen years after his death, would be a "divinity" in a contemporary sense in Brussels. His Second Symphony had been composed in 1802, forty years before its January performance at the conservatoire; the Seventh Symphony had been composed in 1812, thirty years before its performance in April. But Beethoven's symphonies had caught on in France and Belgium much later than in Austria or Germany. In France it was not until 1828 that Habeneck had initiated the performances at the Paris Conservatoire of the Beethoven symphonies that were to have such a transforming effect upon Berlioz, among others. François-Joseph Fétis had been an influential professor at the Paris Conservatoire from 1828 to 1833, when Habeneck's performances of Beethoven were first making their mark. In 1833 he had moved to Brussels to become director of the conservatoire, conductor of its orchestra, and champion of Beethoven. By 1842 the success of his efforts was acknowledged in Paris itself. On March 18 L'Indépendant reprinted a February 12 review from Le France musicale in Paris in which Theodore Lebarre gave exceedingly high marks to the orchestra of the Conservatoire Royal for its performances of Beethoven's Second Symphony and Egmont Overture at the January 30 concert.

Reviewing the April 24 concert, the critic of L'Indépendant notes that in earlier years the student orchestra, "in spite of its fine intentions and energy," had lacked the "mass" necessary for Beethoven's "colossal" Seventh Symphony. But "today this orchestra is not less numerous than that of the Conservatoire of Paris, and we have the conviction that neither in Paris nor in Germany could one encounter anything superior in execution to what was heard by the auditors at Sunday's concert." As for the Seventh Symphony itself, "everything is beautiful, majestic, sublime, in this work of genius." The slow movement, with its "melancholy inspiration and expressive profundity that defy all comparison, brought tears to the eyes" (April 30).

Reviewing the January 30 concert, the same critic faulted only the placement of the Second Symphony at the head of the program. After listening "for nearly an hour to conceptions in which are deployed the inexhaustible genius of Beethoven," it was nearly impossible to concentrate on "works of proportions infinitely less" (February 10). Pleased that the Eroica was reserved "for the end" of the March 12 program, he noted that the student orchestra, "each year, displays more color, more richness of nuance." But most of this review is devoted to the first work on the program, the Leonore Overture. The critic uses its relation to

Beethoven's *Fidelio* as the basis for a sophisticated discussion of the extent to which instrumental music can (or should) be programmatic. "It is not indispensable to know the work for which Beethoven has written the overture of *Leonore* that was given its debut Sunday at the concert of the conservatoire in order to judge the merits of this work in terms of its conception and the development of its ideas, but when one knows the succession of incidents by which the musician has been inspired, one can know better the entirety and the details of the composition" (March 20). His review of the April 24 concert, which featured the Seventh Symphony, refers to the conservatoire as a "unique refuge," a "grand historic edifice" which is at our disposal "for the love of Beethoven."

Although the April concert ended the series of symphonic programs at the conservatoire for the first half of the year, neither the conservatoire nor Beethoven remained out of the news for the rest of Emily Brontë's stay. In late July, four days of concerts at the Hotel de Ville were given over to winners of the student competitions at the conservatoire for the term then ending. The winners of the piano competition were featured on July 28, two days before Emily's twenty-fourth birthday. On August 10 the results were reported at great length in *L'Indépendant*. Not only the student winners (M. J. Lemmons, Mlle C. Bondeul) but their teachers (M. Michelot, Mme Lambert) were discussed, with attention given to the works required for the competition and the instruments used. Lemmons, who won first place, was soloist in the Mozart concerto at the conservatoire concert in November, after Emily Brontë left town. If Emily actually did study with "the best professor in Belgium" during the second half-year, one wonders whether her teacher was M. Michelot or Mme Lambert, both of whom were conspicuous in the discussion of conservatoire affairs in the press throughout the year.[25]

An even more prominent event involving the conservatoire had occurred the previous Sunday. On July 24, in the Temple of the Augustins, a musical festival was held to celebrate the tenth anniversary of the independence of Belgium and of the accession of King Leopold to the throne. In the words of *L'Indépendant*, this festival was "the most beautiful musical celebration Brussels had ever known": never had the city seen a concert so well organized or performed by such great artists. One of the artists was Franz Liszt. Another was Laure Damoreau, the celebrated soprano whose stage name was Cinti. A third soloist was Alexandre Artot, the famed violinist who had just returned from a tour of Russia and who in 1843–44 would embark upon what was to become a legendary American tour with Mme Damoreau. A fourth soloist was M. Géraldy, professor of voice at the Conservatoire Royal. A three-hundred-member chorus included students from the conservatoire, choral society members from

Brussels, and singers from cities throughout Belgium. The conservatoire's orchestra was conducted by Fétis.

The program for the festival, divided into two large parts, began with Beethoven's Seventh Symphony. Other works in the first half included "Invocation of the Night" for choir, a violin concerto played by Artot, a grand scene from *Sémiramide* for M. Géraldy and chorus, a septet from *Huguenots*, and the introduction to the oratorio *Last Judgement* by Frederic Schneiger, with the choir of three hundred. The second half began with a fantasie by Hanssens and concluded with Mendelssohn's oratorio *The Conversion of Saint Paul*. In between, Mme Damoreau sang alone and with M. Géraldy, their duet being accompanied by pianist Franz Liszt, who also played his own *Don Juan Fantasy*.

The reviews of this extraordinary musical event emphasized above all else the Beethoven symphony and Franz Liszt. On July 26 *L'Indépendant* noted that "the Symphony in A of Beethoven opened the celebration, and transported the listeners by the perfection with which it was played. The performance was by the orchestra of the Conservatoire Royal, which had played Beethoven's Seventh also at the third conservatoire concert of the spring, in April." A more elaborate account of the symphony appeared the following day.

> The opening work which for all the world dignified the inauguration of this beautiful event was the Symphony in A by Beethoven, a marvelous production in which the master has generously displayed all the treasures of his genius. The performance was imposing in the ensemble, perfect in the details. Scarcely ever have such great numbers of musicians, needed for the explosions of energy, shown such finesse in passages where this quality is indispensable. What was heard in the concert on Sunday broke all the rules. It is impossible that the most delicate nuances could be better expressed; it is impossible to recall in a mass of players such a grand unity of intention, or to speak better of such complete obedience to the spirit of the master. We are not afraid to say that Beethoven never heard his work rendered with such perfection. . . . Salvos of applause burst out after each movement of this admirable symphony."

The review of Liszt's performance of his *Don Juan Fantasy* was equally rhapsodic. The legendary pianist is compared with Napoleon. He is called an angel and a devil. He does the impossible with his technique. One must hear him to believe him. "Les dames" showered him with flowers. The orchestra carried him in triumph. After this breathless performance, the critic asks, is the artist going to rest for a while at the Hotel de Belle Vue? No. Liszt, who, before coming to Brussels from Liège, had gone on to Paris from St. Petersburg, was now to leave immediately for Paris, and from Paris go to Cologne and, eight days later, Constantinople.

One wonders whether Emily Brontë attended this grand festival concert on July 24, this concert of such importance to anyone involved in any aspect of musical life in Brussels. If so, one can easily imagine the strong impression that would have been made on her musical imagination by Beethoven's Seventh Symphony, given such a transcendent performance, or by the pianism and personality of Franz Liszt in his prime. July was the end of a long term in which she had "worked like a horse" since February. It was the month in which she and Charlotte had decided to stay on another half-year in Brussels and at the pensionnat. Sunday, throughout the year, had been the one day on which she had been free to do what she wished; Sunday, throughout the year, had been the day for the symphonic concerts at the conservatory, as well as for most other major musical events in the city. (In March, for example, L'Indépendant had written that "last Sunday Brussels was satiated with music.") No wonder she, with her shy nature and her intense love of music, occasionally demurred when Charlotte wanted to spend their Sundays in parlor conversation with the Wheelwrights and others. If she did not spend Sunday, July 24, at "the most beautiful musical celebration Brussels had ever known," she is certain to have read about it avidly in the next week's press.

The same may also be said for the next out-of-the-ordinary event of the musical year, the arrival of Hector Berlioz in Brussels to conduct a pair of gala concerts, mostly of his own music, in September and October. Berlioz and his music were making their Brussels debut, and a special orchestra of two hundred musicians was assembled in order to give voice to his muse. On September 26, in the Salle of the Société de la Grand Harmonie, the two major symphonic works were the prologue to *Romeo and Juliet* and the *Grande Symphonie funèbre et triomphale* for two orchestras and chorus. On October 9, in the Temple of the Augustins, Berlioz began the program with his overture to *Francs-Juges* and closed it with the *Symphonie fantastique*. Other symphonic selections included a portion of *Harold in Italy* and Berlioz's orchestration of Weber's *Invitation to the Dance*. His music received a mixed response. The critic of L'Indépendant praised the selection from *Harold in Italy* but found the prologue to *Romeo and Juliet* too vague, saying that the melody lacked definition. In the *Grande Symphonie funèbre* he found "the monotony intolerable, with the same phrases repeated to satiety." As for the *Symphonie fantastique*, the program was too explicit. The critic enjoyed the music of the March to the Scaffold, but felt that one does not need "les enfantillages du program" to enjoy it.[26]

Imagine Emily Brontë in the Temple des Augustins watching Berlioz conduct the Brussels premiere of the *Symphonie fantastique!* Her love of Shakespeare and Byron would certainly have made her curious about compositions entitled

Romeo and Juliet and *Harold in Italy*. But again, whether she attended the Berlioz concerts or not, she is certain to have read about his compositions and assimilated them into her understanding of what is musically possible. The discussion of Berlioz's music in October continued the running analysis of the function of program music that had graced the pages of *L'Indépendant* throughout the year. In the discussion of Beethoven's *Leonore* Overture and its relation to *Fidelio* in March the music and theories of Berlioz had been used as a foil. In the same month *L'Indépendant* had reprinted Berlioz's tribute to Cherubini, originally published in Paris.

Liszt and Berlioz made one-time splashes in Brussels that year, but the music of Beethoven was pervasive. We have already noted its prominence in the symphonic concerts at the conservatoire, the center of the city's serious musical life. In the more popular concerts sponsored by the Société Philharmonique and the Société de la Grand Harmonie Beethoven's overtures were often played; a concert in March included the second and third movements of his First Symphony. When the critic of *L'Indépendant* praised the inauguration of the chamber music series in March, the concert he reviewed was all Beethoven: two trios and a sonata played immaculately by Litolff, piano, Bériot, violin, and Demunck, cello.

Given the stimulating musical atmosphere that surrounded Emily Brontë in Brussels in 1842, it is not at all surprising that she acquired an anthology of the quality of *The Musical Library* upon returning to England. Nor is it surprising that she showed a marked preference in its pages for Beethoven symphonies. It is likely that she would have directly encountered Beethoven's music both in her own studies and in whatever concerts she managed to attend. In addition she would have encountered a powerful image of Beethoven simply from reading a daily newspaper such as *L'Indépendant* (which she would have done in any case to improve her French). The Beethoven she encountered in Brussels in 1842 was not simply the composer whose overture and waltzes she had played in Haworth in the 1830s; he was, rather, a compelling artist of extraordinary power and vision who dominated the musical present of life in Brussels, yet who was linked in the strongest way to the music of his predecessors.

Students of the imaginative growth of the Brontë sisters have given considerable attention to the *devoirs* Emily and Charlotte wrote while studying French under the supervision of M. Heger in Brussels. Students of Charlotte have studied the influence of the paintings of the Brussels Salon of 1842 on her novels, even though Charlotte was not nearly the student of painting that Emily was of music. (*L'Indépendant* carried seven separate reviews of the Salon, running from August through mid-October.) Charlotte pointed out that Emily had to "work like a horse" to learn French upon her arrival in Brussels. But music for Emily was a universal language in which she was already well versed the first day she stepped on Belgian soil. Unlike her study of French or her sister's study of that language or of painting, Emily's study of music continued "heart and soul" upon her return to Haworth. Her exposure to great music through her studies in Brussels—augmented by whatever concerts she may have attended and whatever musical knowledge she acquired by reading the daily press— undoubtedly intensified her experience of great art and the better prepared her to produce it herself. In "whatever she got from Brussels" the experience of music must figure highly.

Enid Duthie, considering the influence that Charlotte Brontë's study of French language and literature in Brussels had upon her creative imagination, finds its greatest value to have been in the organic links that Charlotte discovered between French Romanticism and the classical tradition from which it grew. "The teaching of Brussels did more than confirm Charlotte Brontë in her belief in the power of genius; it pointed to the way in which genius could be controlled. . . . She returned to England a Romantic still, but her Romanticism had been enriched by the contact with European authors. Paradoxically it was the contact with Classicism in its most uncompromising aspect, the cult of reason, that first bore fruit in her writings."[27] Emily's Romantic impulses too were tempered with classical discipline. Her own music books of the 1840s, in which the "debased" Romanticism of the music she played in her teens is supplanted by Clementi sonatas and by Haydn and Beethoven symphonies, indicate such a tempering of her artistic taste. So, of course, does *Wuthering Heights,* a literary work whose remarkable blending of Romantic genius and classical control far outstrips the literary use to which even her sister Charlotte was to put the contrasting stylistic tendencies. It is now time to consider to what extent Beethoven's music may actually have acted as a catalyst in the creation of *Wuthering Heights.*

Beethoven's Music and Brontë's Novel

Philip Barford writes that Emily Brontë, according to her sister Charlotte, "used to practise Beethoven's earlier sonatas with fire and spirit." Unfortunately, Barford has lost track of his source for Charlotte's statement and I have been unable to verify it. In her biography of Anne Brontë, Gérin asserts that Anne and Emily possessed "Beethoven's piano sonatas and a keyboard scoring of his overtures." But this undocumented assertion, too, has been impossible to ver-ify.[28] It would be most interesting to know whether Emily played entire sonatas or only isolated movements of the kind that appear in *The Musical Library*. Certainly in Brussels she may well have studied complete sonatas. Until records are found of what she did study there, or of specific sonatas she may have studied at Haworth, we will have to rely upon the music books now at Haworth for our knowledge of Beethoven works she is *certain* to have played. These books indicate that her experience of Beethoven before living in Brussels was restricted to the overture to *Men of Prometheus* and to waltzes from the Sykes collection. After Brussels we can be certain that she played the symphony se-lections and variations that she marked for special attention in *The Musical Library*.

Emily's proclivity for Beethoven symphonies takes on added interest in view of their prominence in the concert life of Brussels during her studies there. The Allegretto of the Seventh Symphony, which she played in volume 2 of *The Musi-cal Library*, is the movement which, according to the critic of *L'Indépendant*, brought tears to the eyes of Belgians at the third conservatoire concert of the season, two months after Emily's arrival in the city. The same Seventh Sym-phony, of course, inaugurated the extraordinary festival concert on July 24. By today's standards it may seem unusual that *The Musical Library* contained only the second movement. But emphasis upon selected movements of a work was common in even the highest musical circles in the 1840s. In *Voyage musical*, published in 1844, Berlioz writes that Beethoven's Seventh Symphony is "cele-brated" for its slow movement. He goes on to say that "in speaking of Beethoven in France, one speaks of 'The Storm' of the *Pastoral* Symphony, the Finale of the Symphony in C minor, the Andante of the Symphony in A, etc." The slow movement of the Seventh Symphony is so popular in France, he notes, that it is sometimes incorporated into the Second Symphony, in place of the Larghetto.[29]

When the Second Symphony was performed at the Conservatoire Royal on 30 January 1842, presumably its own second movement was used. Emily Brontë played that movement, Larghetto, and the third movement, Scherzo-Trio, out of volume 4 of *The Musical Library*. The Larghetto, for Berlioz, is a "ravishing portrait of innocent happiness, scarcely touched with a few rare accents of mel-ancholy."[30] The Scherzo, for Grove, writing fifty years later, is one of the first symphonic examples of Beethoven's unfettered individualism. Its abrupt changes of "key and tone" had caused him to launch into the tirade against Haydn and Mozart, whose "thoughts and feelings" were suppressed by "the perpetual curb and restraint of their social position." Beethoven, by contrast, was "free and unrestrained."

Beethoven's Sixth Symphony, whose first and third movements Emily played in volume 3 of *The Musical Library*, does not seem to have been performed during her residence in Brussels, though it was mentioned in discussions of program music in the press. As early as 1830 *Blackwood's Magazine*, religiously read at the Haworth parsonage, had referred to "the celebrated *Sinfonia Pastorale* of Beethoven" as "an exquisite specimen of descriptive music."[31] As we have seen, the editors of *The Musical Library* did not affix the composer's programmatic labels to the two movements that Emily played. But they did list the work as Beethoven's *Pastoral* Symphony in the table of contents, where she put her mark by it.

The one Beethoven symphony she did not mark in the table of contents, the *Eroica*, was played by the conservatoire orchestra when she was in Brussels. The fact that she did not mark its Funeral March may indicate a conscious decision not to play it. On the other hand, she may have played it without having marked it—as appears to have been the case with the overture to *Fidelio* and the slow movement, Largo appassionato, from the Sonata, Opus 2, No. 2. However that may be, the three symphonies that she did mark provide a sufficient basis in themselves upon which to speculate concerning the influence that Beethoven's music may have had on her creative imagination.

The putative influence of Beethoven's music upon the composition of *Wuthering Heights*, I suggest, is on altogether different an imaginative plane from the kind of musical influence that is found in Charlotte Brontë's *Villette*. There the influence is found in the description of musical events and sensations, the two primary examples occurring in the chapters entitled "The Concert" and "Clouds." In *Wuthering Heights* music does not play any significant role in the plot itself. In fact, music or musical instruments appear only twice. In chapter 4 we learn that Hindley Earnshaw, when his father had left for Liverpool, had requested "a fiddle" for his present. But the fiddle, it turns out, having shared the trip home with young Heathcliff, "had been crushed to morsels in the great coat" (p. 39). In chapter 7 there is music on Christmas day, after Heathcliff has been expelled from the festivities. In the evening, after dancing, "our pleasure," Nelly tells us, "was increased by the arrival of the Gimmerton band, mustering fifteen strong: a trumpet, a trombone, clarionets, bassoons, French horns, and a bass viol, besides singers. They go the rounds of all the respectable houses, and receive contributions every Christmas, and we esteemed it a first-rate treat to hear them. . . . Mrs. Earnshaw loved the music, and so they gave us plenty" (pp. 56–57).

Taken alone, these two allusions to music are little more than one might expect from any novelist (though the list of instruments in the Gimmerton band certainly is precise). In terms of musical knowledge, the teenager who played "debased" variations in the 1830s did not have to study music in Brussels in order to be able to write them. It is not, then, on the level of plot that Emily Brontë's encounter with Beethoven manifests itself. Rather, the influence is felt on the level of inspiration and aspiration. In this sense it is comparable to the influence of her encounter with Shakespeare.

It has long been recognized that the experience of reading Shakespeare's tragedies helped Emily Brontë to conceive of *Wuthering Heights*—even though she has left no explicit biographical testimony of her debt to his example. The surface of the novel alludes to Shakespeare no more than it does to music. The only direct reference comes in chapter 2, when Lockwood tells us that the vociferous dogs drew from him "several incoherent threats of retaliation that, in their infinite depth of virulency, smacked of King Lear" (p. 24). Lockwood's humorously inappropriate allusion does indicate that he is to some degree familiar with Shakespeare's play. But it does not in itself suggest anything about the degree to which *Wuthering Heights* itself was influenced by *King Lear* or any other Shakespearean work. The evidence for this influence is found, not in the one allusion, but in the vision of the book, the texture of it, the conception of it. On this level of inspiration and aspiration the novel has so much more resonance with Shakespeare's tragedies than it does with previous English fiction that one would feel certain of the influence even without knowing that Shakespeare was much read and loved by the Brontë family at Haworth.[32] The influence of Beethoven's music on *Wuthering Heights*, I suggest, is similar in kind.

The central argument of this book has presented Emily Brontë and Beethoven as artists whose works are deeply comparable in style, emotion, and spirit. We have seen the two artists explore comparable imaginative planes— the one in her single novelistic masterpiece, the other in representative piano sonatas from his three "periods." Stylistically, we have seen each artist embody a tense and powerful Romantic equilibrium that contains vehement, chaotic emotion within a powerful classical frame. Emotionally, we have seen each artist express a passionate ferocity that alternates with a transcendent calm, forging in the process an organic form that seems to have been shaped out of a powerful, emotion-laden response to nature. Spiritually, we have seen each artist, in the end, reach a heightened state of consciousness that finally breaks free of "this shattered prison" and attains a mystical vision of unworldly bliss.

The uniqueness of this stylistic, emotional, and spiritual achievement within the context of each artist's separate artistic tradition prompted the comparison of the art works themselves that has formed the core of this study. But the fact that

Emily Brontë was familiar with Beethoven's music, both as a pianist at home and as a student of music in Brussels, now puts us in a position to address the extent to which his artistic achievement may actually have contributed to her own. Although her knowledge of Beethoven probably extended to several of the piano sonatas and to the *Eroica* Symphony, we shall purposely consider only the three symphonies she is certain to have played on her own piano.

In her introduction to *The Foreign Vision of Charlotte Brontë* Enid Duthie summarizes "the value of the Brussels experience to Charlotte Brontë as a creative artist" in these words: "It provided material peculiarly suitable for her creative powers to work on; it enlarged the scope of her vision, giving a new dimension to her delineation of character and milieu; it influenced her style; . . . and it strengthened the ties that linked her art with European culture, making her not only a great English novelist but one of the most eloquent representatives in nineteenth century literature of the undying heritage of the Romantic movement" (p. xiii). The body of Duthie's book relates the fiction Charlotte wrote to such aspects of her Brussels experience as her study of French language and literature, her attendance at concerts, her visits to the Salon of 1842, and her personal relations with M. and Mme Heger, with M. Chapelle, and with students. Duthie's summary of the "value" of the Brussels experience for Charlotte as an influence on her fiction offers a useful framework in which to measure the "value" and influence of Beethoven on the art of Emily Brontë.

1. Beethoven provided material peculiarly suitable for her creative powers to work on.

The music books before and after Brussels, the testimony of Ellen Nussey before and after Brussels, her father's response to her playing, all indicate that musical performance was intrinsically a valuable experience for Brontë, no matter who the composer. For this woman who eschewed the spoken word, even with those she loved, music was obviously a powerful language. When this intrinsic value of music for her is augmented by the emotional, psychic, spiritual, and descriptive power of Beethoven's artistic expression, the "material" upon which her creative powers could operate becomes all the more significant.

More lyrically and more powerfully than any of her predecessors in the English novel, Brontë expressed a "response to nature" in the Beethovenian sense. To have played the graceful opening movement and the robust third movement of Beethoven's *Pastoral* Symphony was to have come into contact with artistic and spiritual "materials" that were certain to have resonated strongly within her own heart and soul.

More profoundly and more movingly than any of her predecessors in the English novel, Brontë expressed spiritually transcendent states of "hymnic" calm comparable to those Beethoven had expressed in music. For her to have played and internalized the soulful calm of the second movement of Beethoven's Seventh Symphony was again to encounter "materials" in musical form comparable to those she would so tellingly express in fiction.

As much as any previous English novelist, Emily Brontë revealed a sense of humor comparable to that which Beethoven had introduced to Viennese music in his powerful scherzos. For her to have played the rustically abrupt Scherzo and Trio of Beethoven's Second Symphony was again to come into contact with "materials" in music comparable to those to which she would give expression in fiction (especially when introducing Mr. Lockwood to the Heights).

Such examples in themselves do not prove that Beethoven's music influenced Brontë's novel. But they do illustrate "material peculiarly suitable for her creative powers to work on," material certain to have been of "value" to her artistic growth. Playing such musical material was certainly neither a sufficient nor a necessary cause for her creation of *Wuthering Heights;* she might well have created what she did without having had Beethoven's "material" to "work on." But since she did have it, and did work on it, this material is certainly likely to have contributed to the artistic growth that led to the creation of her novel.

2. Beethoven enlarged the scope of her vision.

This value of Beethoven's music for Brontë relates to the one described above. If his music provided material suitable for her creative powers to work on, it undoubtedly contributed to her vision as well. Specifically, I would suggest that it contributed to her vision of the compelling realities it was possible for the creative artist to address. It contributed to the vision of an art that could explore humanity's place in the world of nature and spirit with full freedom, the vision of an artistic exploration that could be as compelling in its internal logic as it was vehement in its presentation of materials of maximum emotional intensity.

I would not want to suggest that Beethoven's music was the only artistic material that contributed in this sense to Brontë's vision: Shakespeare's tragedies contributed too. Nor would I want to suggest that the encounter with Beethoven's music was a necessary condition for Brontë's acquiring a vision of her own. Her celebrated independence of character and even some of her early poems attest that she had begun to shape and define her own peculiar vision at Haworth, well before she arrived in Brussels at age twenty-three. But I do believe that her encounter with Beethoven in Brussels and her assimilation of music from at least three of his greatest symphonies after her return to Haworth helped to broaden her field of vision, to see more clearly into the human condition.

3. Beethoven influenced her style.

The style of an artist is a product of the material he or she works on as well as the vision by which he or she shapes those materials. Stylistically, we have argued throughout this book that Brontë and Beethoven represent a very special brand of Romantic equilibrium in their separate artistic traditions, each being notable for the power of their ability to combine equilibrium with tension, vehemence with restraint, clarity with ambiguity, sanity with madness, the classical with the Romantic. As we have seen, each artist manages to fuse such stylistic qualities into an organic form which, though seeming to respond to the very rhythms of nature, somehow manages to preserve the classical symmetries at the same time that it violates them. Each manages to express the most vehement and violent of Romantic emotions within the framework, though muscularized, of traditional form: the domestic novel, the classical sonata or symphony. The result is a tense Romantic equilibrium rarely achieved, in these large-scale forms, by fellow artists in either field.

It is certainly conceivable that Emily Brontë could have created her own brand of Romantic equilibrium without having been exposed to Beethoven's brand. But having been exposed to it, it certainly seems likely that his style served as a catalyst in the creation of her own.

4. Beethoven strengthened the ties that linked her art with European culture, making her not only a great English novelist but one of the most eloquent representatives in nineteenth-century literature of the undying heritage of the Romantic movement.

Here I believe that Beethoven's value for and influence upon Emily Brontë is strongest and most certain. Music in general, and Beethoven in particular (though Handel, Mozart, Haydn, Clementi, Gluck, and others also played a role), did undoubtedly strengthen Brontë's link with European culture. Of the composers whose music she played, Beethoven certainly represented the "undying heritage of the Romantic movement" most strongly, not only in the selections she is certain to have played from his symphonies in the last years of her life but also in the role his music played in Brussels during her residence in that city.

Beethoven had done for European music what *Wuthering Heights* would do for the English novel—unleashed a boldness and vehemence of expression that transformed the genteel domain of the comedy of manners into a world of elemental strife unsanctioned by conventional morality. The emancipating power of a work such as the Seventh Symphony was bound to appeal to the woman who created Heathcliff. The rustic power of the Scherzo of the Second Symphony was certain to appeal to the writer who would explode Mr. Lockwood's genteel pretensions. One wonders whether Brontë encountered such powerful sonatas as the *Pathétique* or the *Appassionata*. Whether she did or not, she was soon to introduce a comparable boldness and vehemence into English fiction.

As we have seen, these two artists are unique in their separate artistic traditions not only for their expression of vehement and passionate strife but also for their expression of a cosmic calm which alternates with that strife. Beethoven introduced such calm into Viennese music in such symphony movements as the Larghetto of the Second, the Allegretto of the Seventh, and the opening movement of the Sixth, all marked for special attention in Brontë's *Musical Library*. She introduced comparable states of cosmic calm into English fiction in Nelly's meditation after Catherine's death in chapter 16 and in the contrasting visions of peace expressed by young Cathy and Linton in chapter 24.

For Beethoven's vision of a cosmic calm that not only alternates with passionate strife but transcends it, as the final visions of Catherine and Heathcliff transcend the strife of their lives, one must turn to the late sonatas and quartets. One wonders whether Brontë, in Brussels, was directly exposed to music of Beethoven's late period, music whose mystical visions correspond not only to those of Catherine and Heathcliff but to the most ecstatic passages of her own poetry.[33] Whether or not she actually encountered Beethoven's late style in Brussels, she would have been acquainted—through reading—with the motions of its spirit by the time she wrote her novel, as we shall see in the chapters to come. Certain of her late poems, in particular, may actually have been influenced by such reading.

The latest Beethoven work that we know she knew is the slow movement of the Seventh Symphony, Opus 92. This movement, with its studied repetition and soulful "decoration" of the opening theme, is a "theme and variations" as far removed as possible from the "debased" variations Brontë had played in her teens. Its A-minor tonality gives it an emotional coloring far different from the variation movements of the *Appassionata* (in D-flat major) or Opus 111 (in C major). For Berlioz, writing in the 1840s, this movement embodies motions of the spirit comparable to those found in two English poets, neither of whom he names. From the one he quotes, in English, two lines: "One fatal remembrance, one sorrow that throws / Its black shade alike o'er our joys and our woes." From the other he translates, into French, four words: "Le reste est silence."[34] If the slow movement of the *Appassionata* expresses, in Tovey's words, "the ultimate faith underlying the tragic emotion," this movement may be said to express the ultimate tragedy underlying the emotional faith. It is my candidate for the music Brontë is most likely to have played for her father during the last years of her life, the years during which his eyesight was deteriorating, the years during which she wrote her fictional masterpiece and her greatest poems, the years immediately before her own swift, terminal illness at age thirty.

The external evidence of Emily Brontë's affinity for Beethoven's music after returning from Brussels, combined with the preeminent position of his music in the concert life of that city during her musical studies there, augmented by the evidence presented throughout this book of the stylistic, emotional, and spiritual affinities between his music and her novel, suggests that her encounter with his music and her assimilation of that music may have provided not only a creative inspiration but perhaps even an artistic model for the vehement, passionate, and transcendent vision she expressed in *Wuthering Heights*. Such evidence suggests that Beethoven may well have influenced Brontë's artistic development as much as any artist who wrote with words. Earlier, we considered Gérin's assertion that Brontë's imagination remained fired not by "the Victorian age of her maturity, but the Romantic age of her adolescence; the era of Byron, Beethoven, and Blake. The influences of that era were lasting, and made her the rebel and visionary she remained to the end." Brontë's heartfelt assimilation of Beethoven in the 1840s, I suggest, revalidated that earlier influence and allowed her to take into her own heart and soul a fellow rebel and visionary as dear to her as any. That not only Beethoven's music but also his by-then legendary life may have helped to inspire the creation of *Wuthering Heights* is the subject of the chapter to come.

One final word on the influence of Beethoven's music, as posited above. Emily Brontë left no memoirs, no biographical commentary about the influences on her art. For that reason, the argument of this chapter has had to extrapolate from the evidence in her music books, to the musical life in Brussels, to her art itself. But I should like to offer some comments by an artist who *has* put into his own words the kind of artistic inspiration Brontë is likely to have received from Beethoven. Chapter 20 of Hector Berlioz's *Memoirs* begins with these words: "In an artist's life one thunderclap sometimes follows swiftly on another. . . . I had just had the successive revelations of Shakespeare and Weber. Now at another point on the horizon I saw the giant form of Beethoven rear up. The shock was almost as great as that of Shakespeare had been. Beethoven opened before me a new world of music, as Shakespeare had revealed a new universe of poetry." For Berlioz, the Beethoven thunderclap sounded in 1828, emanating from Habeneck's performances of the symphonies at the Paris Conservatoire. For Emily Brontë, I suggest, it came in 1842, emanating from Fétis's performances of the symphonies at the Conservatoire Royal.

One might expect a composer to have been strongly influenced by another composer. But can this kind of influence cross from one medium to another, so that a writer can be influenced by a composer, or a composer by a writer? For Berlioz the answer is obvious. Chapter 18 of his *Memoirs* relates his first exposure to Shakespeare. The occasion was the 1827 Paris production of *Hamlet*, in which Harriet Smithson played Ophelia. "Shakespeare, coming upon me unawares, struck me like a thunderbolt. The lightning flash of that discovery revealed to me at a stroke the whole heaven of art, illuminating it to its remotest corners. I recognized the meaning of grandeur, beauty, dramatic truth."[35] Berlioz was twenty-four at the time. Three years later he had composed the *Symphonie fantastique*, the work that had its Brussels debut in 1842, when Emily Brontë was herself twenty-four.

In 1847, five years after leaving Brussels, Brontë published *Wuthering Heights*. If she, like Berlioz, had written her memoirs and traced her artistic development, I think it likely that she too would have attributed much of her inspiration to a writer named Shakespeare and to a composer named Beethoven. She, no less than Berlioz, I suggest, received from at least one artist in the other art a thundering revelation that helped her to "recognize the meaning of grandeur, beauty, dramatic truth"—and to re-create, shape, and express that recognition in her own terms.

182

Chapter Five

Brontë's Heathcliff
and Schindler's Beethoven

Generally speaking, the literary world is in no need of additional possible sources for Heathcliff. The Shakespearean villain, Milton's Satan, the gothic villain, the Napoleonic figure, the Byronic hero, the dark archetypal Romantic outsider, the fictional protagonists of E. T. A. Hoffmann and other German Romantics, even Emily Brontë's own dark-skinned adopted ancestor from Ireland—all have been offered as possible sources for Heathcliff.[1] So little is known about Brontë's reading and use of sources, however, that the actual extent of any of these influences has been impossible to fix. Moreover, none of these possible sources can *explain* Heathcliff, who remains one of literature's most original creations. For Brontë to have imagined and created him is an extraordinary literary feat. Any evidence that can help us understand how she did it—whether literary, biographical, or historical—is certainly welcome.

Some of Heathcliff's power and originality undoubtedly stem from the "dark" side of his creator's own personality. Yet none of the overt details of Brontë's own life prepare us for the extreme harshness and scorn of Heathcliff's personality. These qualities are, however, somewhat anticipated in a series of poems, apparently autobiographical, that Brontë wrote between 1837 and 1841. In May of 1837 she wrote of being "as friendless after eighteen years, / As lone as on my natal day" (H 11). A more assertive poem in November declares,

> Strong I stand, though I have borne
> Anger, hate, and bitter scorn;
> Strong I stand, and laugh to see
> How mankind have fought with me. (H 35)

A poem of two years later speaks of "a time when my cheek burned / To give such scornful friends the lie" and asserts,

> My soul still chafes at every tone
> Of selfish and self-blinded error;

My breast still braves the world alone
Steeled as it ever was to terror. (H 119)

Two years later the speaker, still isolated from society, rejects its claims by asserting her own free spirit: "Through life and death, a chainless soul / With courage to endure!" (H 146). The latter poem ("Riches I hold in light esteem") is dated 1 March 1841, a year before her studies in Brussels.

These poems, whatever their source in her actual life, combine inner courage and outer scorn. But still it is a mighty leap from such works to the creation of Heathcliff. All available evidence suggests that the primary source for her creation of his personality must have been her spirited imaginative life (to be enriched, soon after the last poem above, by "whatever she got from Brussels"). It has long been recognized that Brontë's imagination was vividly peopled with the literary figures alluded to above—with the creations of Shakespeare, Milton, Byron, and Hoffmann traditionally viewed as possible sources for Heathcliff. In Chapter 4 I demonstrated that the music of Beethoven, too, occupied considerable space in her imaginative life. Given her attraction to his music (especially after residing in Brussels) and given certain striking similarities between Beethoven's and Heathcliff's personalities (to be developed in some detail below), I think it likely that her own awareness of Beethoven's by-then legendary life aided in the creation of her powerful fictional protagonist.

The personalities of Beethoven and Heathcliff do have some striking similarities. Goethe's celebrated reference to Beethoven as an "utterly untamed personality" certainly fits Heathcliff.[2] So does the extended analysis Rolland gives of Beethoven's "scorn of all men, terrible of itself," but no less terrible than Heathcliff's scorn. Rolland cites Beethoven's 1801 comment on Zmeskall, "I rate him and those of his species only according to what they bring me; I regard them purely and simply as instruments upon which I play when I please." He cites the 1825 declaration that "our epoch has need of powerful spirits to lash these wretched, small-minded scoundrels of humanity." Summarizing Beethoven's lifelong propensity for scorn, Rolland allows that "imputations of this kind are belied, at every period of his life, by the torrent of his warm humanity. But we must recognize that the two currents, vast love, vast scorn, often seem to clash in him" (pp. 8–9).

In 1971 Philip Barford described Beethoven's personality in words that apply as well to Heathcliff: "rough, powerful, emotional, overreactive, gross, uninhibited, and crude—all these aspects being joined together in a matching physical body which evidently took great satisfaction in physical nature."[3] Similarly applicable is Paul Henry Lang's 1971 portrayal: "Life's flame burned in Beethoven so vehemently, his mental travails were so intense and strenuous, that the passions of a decade in anyone else's life seemed compressed more nearly into one year of his life. He was never calm or objective, for he reacted violently to everything, both embracing and hating life, and he could not remain indifferent to anyone, nor forbear expressing his strong feelings."[4] Maynard Solomon, writing in 1977, pointed out that such strenuous intensity continued throughout Beethoven's life. "Signs of neurotic eccentricity—sudden rages, uncontrolled emotional states, an increasing obsession with money, feelings of persecution, ungrounded suspicions, persisted until Beethoven's death."[5] Exactly such a pattern of "neurotic eccentricity" persisted in Heathcliff's life.

It is relatively easy to compile a series of quotes from the 1970s that describe Beethoven's personality in words applicable to Heathcliff's personality as created by Brontë in the 1840s. The ease of doing so does indicate some strong similarities between the two personalities, but these could be entirely accidental. The only way in which to measure whether one personality could have influenced the other is to investigate what Brontë would have known—or could have known—about Beethoven's life during the decade in which she wrote and published *Wuthering Heights*.

As we have seen, she began to play some of Beethoven's music (overture to *Men of Prometheus*, selected waltzes) in the 1830s. This activity may not have been supplemented by any knowledge of the composer's life. But in 1842, when she studied music in Brussels, Beethoven was the presiding "divinity" of the city's musical life. There she is certain to have been introduced, even in public newspapers such as *L'Indépendant*, to the broad outlines not only of his musical achievement but of his personal legend. She would doubtless have continued to inform herself about him after her return to Haworth, where she had access to English-language sources about his life.

Biographical accounts of Emily at Haworth in the 1840s picture her as a selectively voracious reader. Gaskell's image of her in the parsonage kitchen, "studying German out of an open book, propped up before her, as she kneaded the dough," has been taken by most students of her life as a fair representation of her hunger for ingesting pages she wanted to read. One source of books was the Keighley Mechanics' Institute, a lending library at which the Brontë family had borrowing privileges. Gaskell reports that both Charlotte and Emily made good use of that library in the winter of 1842, as soon as they returned from Brussels. "Winter though it was, the sisters took their accustomed walks on the snow-covered moors; or went often down the long road to Keighley, for such books as had been added to the library there during their long absence from England."[6] Emily also had access to the Ponden Hall library of the Heatons, a family of "gifted musicians" whose sons "formed their own family orchestra."[7]

It is not difficult to imagine which parts of the Beethoven legend would have been available to a curious reader either in Brussels in 1842 or in England in the years immediately following. For 1840 was the year of publication, in German, of the first edition of Anton Schindler's *Life of Beethoven*. This book made available both to scholars and to the general public a wealth of biographical material previously unavailable, including the Heiligenstadt Testament and the letters to the "Immortal Beloved." The original German-language edition would certainly have been available in Brussels in 1842, had Emily sought it out. But whether she read it there or not, she would have had access to Ignace Moscheles's 1841 English-language translation after returning home.[8] Emily already knew Moscheles as a composer; his Fantasia on "Napoleon's Midnight Review and the Sea" was in her early music books.

Published in London, Moscheles's two-volume edition of Schindler included not only the entire *Life of Beethoven* but a great deal of valuable supplementary material as well. It was to remain the standard English-language biography of Beethoven throughout the decade.[9] One would expect Emily to have read this work as soon as it was available to her, whether at the Keighley library, Ponden Hall, or elsewhere.[10] But even in the unlikely event that she did not read it, Schindler's account of Beethoven's life would clearly have shaped whatever she did assimilate of the Beethoven legend in the 1840s, so strongly did it influence other accounts during the decade. We are now in a position to examine the Beethoven who was made available to English readers through Moscheles's 1841 translation of Schindler's *Life*—and to compare him with the fictional protagonist Brontë created later in the same decade.

Beethoven's Life and Heathcliff's Life

Schindler divides Beethoven's life into three periods. His account of the First Period, and especially of Beethoven's childhood in Bonn, is relatively short.[11] Even so, it does suggest certain similarities with Heathcliff's childhood as presented in chapters 4–8 of *Wuthering Heights*.

Beethoven and Heathcliff were of the same generation. Beethoven was born in 1770 (*SM*, 1:25). Heathcliff's birthdate is not indicated in the novel, but he is brought to the Heights as a very young boy in the summer of 1771.[12]

Neither Beethoven nor Heathcliff was certain as to the exact year of his birth.

Beethoven was at pains to clarify the matter in a letter to Wegeler in 1810: "Alas! I have lived some time without knowing my own age" (*SM*, 2:220). Heathcliff, so far as we can tell from the novel, never did know his exact age, having been discovered as a young castaway on the streets of Liverpool.

Beethoven and Heathcliff both had their parentage called into question. Schindler's account of Beethoven's First Period begins with these two subheadings: "Beethoven's Parentage—Contradiction of a Report on that subject." Schindler immediately addresses the persistent rumor that Beethoven was "a natural son of Frederick William II, King of Prussia"; he reports that Beethoven, as late as 1826, dictated a letter to Wegeler in order to dispel the rumor and "make known to the world the unblemished character of his parents, and especially of his mother" (*SM*, 1:26–27). Heathcliff's parentage being unknown, he is often called a "gipsy" by his detractors. But Nelly suggests, in chapter 7, that he might be "a prince in disguise. Who knows but your father was Emperor of China, and your mother an Indian queen, each of them able to buy up, with one week's income, Wuthering Heights and Thrushcross Grange together" (*WH*, p. 54).

Beethoven and Heathcliff were each named after a child whose death had preceded his own arrival into the family. Requesting a copy of his birth certificate in 1810, Beethoven wrote to Wegeler that "I had a brother born before me, likewise named Ludwig, with the second name of Maria, but who died young. . . . Try to find out the birth of the Ludwig Maria, as well as that of the Ludwig who came after him. The sooner you send me the register, the greater my obligation" (*SM*, 2:220). Heathcliff arrived at Wuthering Heights an unnamed "it." But soon the Earnshaws "christened him 'Heathcliff'; it was the name of a son who had died in childhood, and it has served him ever since, both for Christian and surname" (*WH*, p. 39).

Young Beethoven and Heathcliff are both introduced through an episode involving a smashed violin. Schindler immediately tells the story of Ludwig and the spider. Whenever the young boy was playing on the violin, the spider would "let itself down from the ceiling and alight upon the instrument." When his mother, upon discovering the spider, killed it, "little Ludwig dashed his violin to shatters" (*SM*, 1:28). When young Heathcliff is brought to the Heights by Mr. Earnshaw, Hindley searches the pockets of his father's great coat for the violin he has been promised. He draws out "what had been a fiddle, crushed to morsels" (*WH*, p. 39).

As children, Beethoven and Heathcliff both experienced severe conflict with the head of the household. Beethoven's primary conflict was with his father, who "drove" the "stubborn" boy to practice the piano (*SM*, 1:28). Schindler adds that Beethoven's childhood, though it was the "happiest portion of his life," was "frequently embittered by disagreeable circumstances, originating chiefly in his father's irregular course of life" (*SM*, 1:36–37). Young Heathcliff's primary conflict was with Hindley Earnshaw, who became head of the household after Mr. Earnshaw, Heathcliff's protector, died in chapter 5.

Although temperamental and suffering from persecution, Beethoven and Heathcliff were often quite passive in responding to attacks. Schindler says of Beethoven that "he never defended himself against criticism or attacks so long as they were not addressed against his honor" (*SM*, 1:46). Nelly says of young Heathcliff that "he seemed a sullen, patient child, hardened, perhaps, to ill-treatment: he would stand Hindley's blows without winking or shedding a tear, and my pinches moved him only to draw in a breath, and open his eyes as if he had hurt himself by accident, and nobody was to blame" (*WH*, p. 40).

Beethoven and Heathcliff were both "adopted" into an upper-class society in which they found themselves to be relatively lowborn and uncultivated. Beethoven, after arriving in Vienna in 1792, was taken in by Prince and Princess Lichnowsky, who were nothing less to him than a "paternal friend" and "a second mother" (*SM*, 1:41). The Earnshaws were hardly the English equivalent of the Viennese Lichnowskys, but along with the Lintons they were the landed gentry of the region, with indications of a pedigree going back to "1500" (*WH*, p. 14).

Beethoven and Heathcliff both openly challenged the values of the society that took them in. Schindler points out that "rank and wealth were to [Beethoven] matters of absolute indifference—accidents for which he had no particular respect." As a result, his "manners were sometimes deficient in polish." "His energetic nature . . . broke through all barriers, and, spurning the etiquette of high life, would not submit to any shackles" (*SM*, 1: 47, 44). Heathcliff was similarly indifferent to rank and wealth in his youth, demonstrating an unpolished, energetic, unshackled nature that spurned "the etiquette of high life" in much the same way.

Although Beethoven and Heathcliff were often boorish and offensive according to the standards of the society that adopted them, both were indulgently treated by those who cared for them. Schindler speaks of the "extreme indulgence" the Lichnowskys allowed the young Beethoven, treating him like an "adopted son" in spite of behavior that was "frequently obstinate." For "the princess in particular," anything that "the often ill-tempered and sullen young man chose to do or to let alone" was "right, clever, original, amiable" (*SM*, 1:42). Mr. Earnshaw treats his adopted Heathcliff with equal indulgence: he "took to [him] strangely, believing all he said," being "painfully jealous lest a word should be spoken amiss to him" (*WH*, pp. 40–42). After Mr. Earnshaw's death, Catherine Earnshaw and Isabella Linton indulge Heathcliff's ill-tempered outbreaks and sullen withdrawals.

Beethoven and Heathcliff had great difficulty accepting affection from those who did lavish it upon them. Beethoven showed considerable ambivalence toward the Lichnowskys. Schindler provides this "characteristic" complaint from the adult Beethoven: "They would have brought me up there with grandmotherly fondness, which was carried to such a length that very often the princess was on the point of having a glass shade put over me" (*SM*, 1:42–43). The "ill-tempered and sullen" behavior Schindler reports seems to have been a way for Beethoven to keep his distance. Nelly often wondered what Mr. Earnshaw "saw to admire so much in the sullen boy who never, to my recollection, repaid his indulgence by any sign of gratitude. [Heathcliff] was not insolent to his benefactor; he was simply insensible, though knowing perfectly the hold he had on his heart, and conscious he had only to speak and all the house would be obliged to bend to his wishes" (*WH*, p. 40).

Blocked from full social acceptance by accidents of birth, temperament, and education, both sought fulfillment in the love of higher-born women from the society that had adopted them. But, as Schindler points out, Beethoven's intended "attachments" to women of "higher rank" did not result in "permanent happiness," the difference in social status being, "in regard to love," not "advantageous" (*SM*, 1:55–56). In an 1801 letter to Wegeler included in Moscheles's supplement to Schindler, Beethoven writes of "a dear and charming girl" who has helped him "to mix in society again," to cease being a "misanthrope." "She loves me as I do her" but "she is not, unfortunately, of my station in life" (*SM*, 2:213–14). By the time of chapter 8 in *Wuthering Heights* Heathcliff and Catherine are "constant companions still," but her interest in the higher-born Edgar Linton has already begun to cloud their relationship. Heathcliff "had ceased to express his fondness for her in words, and recoiled with angry suspicion from her girlish caresses, as if there could be no gratification in lavishing such marks of affection on him" (*WH*, p. 63).

Beethoven's Second Period, in Schindler's account, is presided over by "the evil principle." This principle "incessantly besets him in the shape of his two brothers, Carl and Johann" (*SM*, 1:72). But two other manifestations of the "evil principle" are given more attention by Schindler. At the beginning of the Second Period, Beethoven recognizes the permanence of his loss of hearing. After he has been forced to assimilate this blow, he loses his "Immortal Beloved." Schindler's account of this unfortunate period in Beethoven's personal life suggests certain similarities with Heathcliff's personal life as presented in chapters 9–15 of *Wuthering Heights*.

Beethoven and Heathcliff both lose, seemingly irremediably, that which is most important to their happiness. When Beethoven discovers that there is no cure for his loss of hearing, he loses access to music. In Schindler's words, "fate deprives him of his hearing, and thus bars the access to word or tone" (*SM*, 1:72). Heathcliff, of course, is deprived of his access to Catherine. This happens in chapter 9, when he overhears her tell Nelly that "it would degrade me to marry Heathcliff." He had already heard her tell Nelly that she plans to marry Edgar Linton because he is "handsome, and pleasant to be with," and because "he will be rich, and I shall like to be the greatest woman of the neighborhood" (*WH*, pp. 72, 70).

Beethoven's loss of hearing and Heathcliff's loss of Catherine are both so devastating that each voluntarily withdraws from society itself. Beethoven's misfortune is so "mortifying" to him, he writes in the Heiligenstadt Testament, that "I dare not venture into society more than absolute necessity requires. I am obliged to live as in exile" (*SM*, 1:81). Heathcliff, after the loss of Catherine, also goes into exile. He leaves the Heights and is not seen or heard of for three years.

Beethoven's loss of hearing and Heathcliff's loss of Catherine are both so devastating that each contemplates suicide. In the Heiligenstadt Testament, written in October 1802, Beethoven admits that "such circumstances brought me to the very brink of despair, and had well nigh made me put an end to my life." After going on to say how he has overcome that temptation, he adds, "I go to meet death with joy" (*SM*, 1:80–85). Heathcliff, returning from exile in chapter 10, tells Catherine that he had planned to take his own life soon after hearing that she had actually married Edgar. "I heard of your marriage, Cathy, not long since; and, while waiting in the yard below, I meditated this plan: just to have one glimpse of your face; . . . afterwards settle my score with Hindley; and then prevent the law by doing execution on myself." Only her "welcome has put these ideas" out of his mind (*WH*, p. 85).

After deciding to continue to live, each becomes even more willful and self-centered than before. Schindler speaks of Beethoven as a man "whose will in everything becomes absolute law, even for the purpose of trying and condemning himself" (*SM*, 1:78). Heathcliff's plan to "prevent the law by doing execution on myself" certainly represents a similar outlook. It is at this point in his life that Beethoven wrote, "Now, no more friendship for me" (*SM*, 2:217). Heathcliff too, by chapter 10 of the novel, is beyond friendship.

Yet each remains capable of vehement, powerful, wholehearted love.

Schindler's account of Beethoven's love life in the first edition of his biography emphasizes the passionate letters to the "Immortal Beloved."[13] The feelings Beethoven expresses in these letters rival the extremes of love expressed by Heathcliff and Catherine in *Wuthering Heights*. Beethoven equates the loved one with the self when he writes, "My angel, my all, my other self!" Catherine does the same when she says "I *am* Heathcliff" and when she speaks of "my all in all, as Heathcliff was at the time." Heathcliff equates her self with his during their last reunion, when he cries out "Oh, Cathy! Oh, my life!" (*WH*, pp. 74, 107, 132).

Beethoven writes of a love both unworldly and eternal: "Is not our love a truly heavenly structure, but firm as the vault of heaven!" Catherine expresses a comparable feeling when she tells Nelly, "If all else perished, and *he* remained, I should continue to be; and if all else remained, and he were annihilated, the Universe would turn to a mighty stranger." Their love was so strong, Heathcliff tells Catherine, that "misery, and degradation, and death, and nothing that God or Satan could inflict would have parted us," had she herself not separated them (*WH*, pp. 74, 135).

In the paragraph in which he uses the phrase "my immortal beloved," Beethoven writes, "I cannot live unless entirely with thee, or not at all." This was Heathcliff's condition in chapter 10 when he planned to take his own life. Beethoven's epistle continues, "Nay, I have resolved to wander about at a distance, till I can fly into thine arms, call myself quite at home with thee, and send my soul wrapped up in thee into the realm of the spirits." Heathcliff wanders about at a distance from Catherine in chapters 10–14; in chapter 15 he flies into her arms. Not until chapter 34, eighteen years after her death, does he send his soul wrapped up in her into the realm of the spirits. In the meantime he is the living embodiment of another concept in Beethoven's letter: "Never can another possess my heart—never!—never!"

"Oh God!" Beethoven writes, "why must one flee from what one so fondly loves!" Heathcliff fled from Catherine in chapter 9, when he heard her say it would "degrade" her to marry him. In chapter 15, in their final encounter, he asks why she had fled him. "You loved me—then what *right* had you to leave me?" (*WH*, p. 135). It remains his great unanswered question.

Schindler, concluding his account of Beethoven's "Immortal Beloved," cites "another paper, likewise in [Beethoven's] own hand-writing, of a rather later period, attesting his ardent longing for domestic happiness." In the Moscheles translation it reads: "Love, and love alone, is capable of giving thee a happier life. O God, let me at length find her" (*SM*, 1:108). For Beethoven this quest was, on this earth, as fruitless as Heathcliff's was to be. Moscheles includes as a

191

supplement to Schindler the 1816 letter to Ries in which Beethoven writes, "My best wishes for your wife; alas, I have none; and *one* only have I met, but shall never possess her" (*SM*, 2:234).

Schindler devotes by far the largest part of his biography of Beethoven to the Third Period, running from November 1813 until the composer's death in 1827. His account of this period, in which Schindler came to know Beethoven personally, suggests certain similarities with Heathcliff's life in chapters 17–34 of *Wuthering Heights*.

For both Beethoven and Heathcliff the loss of the "Immortal Beloved" seems to have led to a perverse need, whether conscious or not, to adopt, dominate, and shape the life of a child previously in the hands of a near relation. After pointing out that one of the first reviewers of the Seventh Symphony thought the composer "ripe for the mad-house" (*SM*, 1:163), Schindler goes on to describe Beethoven's terrible battle with his sister-in-law over the custody of his nephew Carl following the death of Beethoven's elder brother (also Carl) in November of 1815. This protracted episode, Schindler argues, brings Beethoven "for the first time . . . into closer contact with civil life" (*SM*, 1:168). It reveals a side of Beethoven's nature that Schindler claims he would have preferred to ignore. Whatever his conscious motives, Beethoven shows a need to dominate Carl and persecute the boy's mother that, for the reader of *Wuthering Heights*, calls to mind the sadistic side of Heathcliff's nature.

Schindler reports that Beethoven's nephew Carl was about eight years old when his father died. Beethoven, in justifying to a Viennese court his desire to have custody of the boy, wrote, "The shoot is still flexible; but, if more time be wasted, it will grow crooked for want of the training hand of the gardener" (*SM*, 1:179). Hareton Earnshaw is about six years old when his father Hindley, Heathcliff's longtime nemesis, dies at the end of chapter 17. Heathcliff says to the boy, "Now, my bonny lad, you are *mine!* And we'll see if one tree won't grow as crooked as another, with the same wind to twist it!" (*WH*, p. 154). Heathcliff asserts his dominion over Hareton, as Beethoven does over Carl, throughout the boy's youth and adolescence. Schindler's account of Carl's attempted suicide in August of 1826 is prefaced by a long series of letters Beethoven wrote to his nephew in the summer of 1825, accusing Carl, among other things, of "hateful ingratitude" (*SM*, 2:47).

During this long period of personal loneliness and civil conflict, Beethoven and Heathcliff both become even more morbidly suspicious than before of the motives of others. Schindler writes that certain events increased Beethoven's "mistrust of those about him to the degree that . . . it was impossible to hold intercourse with him" (*SM*, 1:154). Such was often the case with Heathcliff, from the time he "adopts" Hareton through to the time he "welcomes" his son Linton to the Heights and on to his "welcoming" of Mr. Lockwood to the Heights at the beginning of the book.

In each case the uncompromising manner is matched by a forbidding physical appearance. Schindler says this about Beethoven's "personal appearance" during the Third Period: "His figure was compact, strong, and muscular. His head, which was unusually large, was covered with long bushy grey hair, which, being always in a state of disorder, gave a certain wildness to his appearance. This wildness was not a little heightened when he suffered his beard to grow to a great length, as he frequently did" (*SM*, 2:191–92). The adult Heathcliff that Mr. Lockwood encounters on the first page of the novel is "a dark-skinned gypsy in aspect . . . rather slovenly perhaps . . . and rather morose." Such qualities are intensified by "black eyes" that "withdraw suspiciously under the brows" and fingers that "shelter themselves, with a jealous resolution," in his waistcoat (*WH*, pp. 15, 13).

After years of obsession with cruelty and suspicion, Beethoven and Heathcliff both find themselves suddenly abstracted from daily life and yearning toward a new, unspeakable contentment in the world of the spirit. Schindler reports that Beethoven's experience of a state of *raptus* became particularly intense in 1819, the year after he composed the *Hammerklavier* Sonata, Opus 106 (and the year before he began composing Opus 111). Suddenly, Schindler writes, "he seemed to be quite a different man. The change was more particularly noticed by his earlier friends; I must confess that, never, before or since that time, have I seen Beethoven in such a state of absolute abstraction from the world" (*SM*, 1:187) Heathcliff's "strange change" begins in chapter 33, when he tells Nelly that "I'm in its shadow at present. I take so little interest in my daily life, that I hardly remember to eat, and drink." Rather than planning further retaliation upon young Hareton and Cathy, he begins to see his Cathy's eyes in their eyes and, indeed, in "the entire world"—which has now become "a dreadful collection of memoranda that she did exist" (*WH*, p. 255).

These states of abstraction become so intense that (in the words of Brontë's "Prisoner") the "outward sense is gone," while the "inward essence feels." Schindler, reporting on Beethoven's improvisations at the piano in the last years of his life, observes that all too often "the inward mind alone was active; but the outward sense no longer co-operated with it." As a result, "the outpourings of his fancy became scarcely intelligible. Sometimes he would lay his left hand flat upon the key-board, and thus drown, in discordant noise, the music to which his right was feelingly giving utterance" (*SM*, 2:175). A similar dichotomy between

Heathcliff's inner and outer selves opens up in chapter 34 when "his frame shivers, not as one shivers with chill or weakness, but as a tight-stretched cord vibrates." Soon thereafter Nelly notes "the anguished, yet raptured expression of his countenance." And he says to her, "I'm too happy, and yet I'm not happy enough. My soul's bliss kills my body, but does not satisfy itself" (*WH*, pp. 258, 261, 262).

Beethoven and Heathcliff both die in the face of a springtime storm. Schindler reports that Beethoven died on 26 March 1827 "during a tremendous hailstorm" (*SM*, 2:77). On a May morning, Nelly encounters Heathcliff's dead body, its face and throat "washed with rain" (*WH*, p. 264).

In both cases, attention is given to the closing of the eyes. Schindler regrets that "I am not so fortunate as to be able to say that it was I who closed the eyes of the artist." As he was away from Beethoven's residence at the time of death, and was "prevented from returning by the violence of the storm," someone else fulfilled "this sacred duty" (*SM*, 2:77). Nelly herself tried to close Heathcliff's eyes but "they would not shut" (*WH*, p. 264).

Both men are buried under somewhat unusual conditions. Schindler reports that "M. von Breuning had the grave watched every night for some time." This precaution was thought necessary because "the wife of the sexton" had reported that her husband had been offered "a considerable sum" if he would agree to deliver "the head of Beethoven to a place specified in Vienna" (*SM*, 2:79). Heathcliff, of course, "bribed the sexton" himself (*WH*, p. 228) so that when he was buried his coffin *would* be disturbed, allowing his "outward essence" a head start toward its merger with the mortal remains of his immortal beloved.

All three periods of Schindler's *Life of Beethoven* offer similarities with the life of the fictional protagonist Emily Brontë introduced to the world in 1847. A brief summary of the long arcs of Beethoven's and Heathcliff's lives will help us determine whether those similarities resulted from accident or influence.

In the realm of parental history, we have seen that Beethoven and Heathcliff were both of the same generation; that both were uncertain about the year of their birth; that the nature of the parentage of each was in some doubt; and that both were named after children who had died before their own arrival in the family.

In the realm of family and social history, we have seen that both were very temperamental from an early age, a tendency exacerbated by severe conflict with the head of the household; that both, though suffering from persecution, were often quite passive in responding to attacks; that both were "adopted" into an upper-class society in which they stood out as relatively low-born and uncultivated; that both openly challenged the assumptions of the society that took them in, yet were nevertheless indulged by leading members of that society; that each, though indulged, had great difficulty accepting affection from those who lavished it upon them; and that both sought affection through "attachments" to women of "higher rank" than themselves.

In the realm of psychological trauma, we have seen that each suffered the shocking loss of that which was most important to his happiness; that each responded to the devastation by voluntarily withdrawing from society and by considering suicide; that each became even more willful toward the self and others after resisting that temptation; and that each found solace in an "Immortal Beloved" even though that love offered no earthly possibility of fulfillment. Both "Immortal Loves" involved a perceived identity between the loved one and the self; an unworldly, eternal definition of the nature of the relation; a need to flee from what one dearly loves; a permanent separation in life, with souls eventually to merge in death; an injunction never to let "another possess my heart—never!— never!"; and an assumption that "love, and love alone" is capable of providing happiness.

We have seen both men turn, after the loss of the loved one, to personal domination over the young son of a near relative. These periods of protracted conflict are heightened by each man's forbidding appearance and morbid suspicion of people in general. But each gives way, eventually, to a rapt spiritual abstraction from everyday life so intense that the "inward essence" becomes entirely detached from the "outward sense." This final drama eventually leads to death in the midst of a springtime storm, eyes unclosed. The security of the coffins becomes, for the survivors, a cause for concern.

Perhaps none of these separate arcs, by themselves, would be worthy of great notice. But together and in succession, as they are found in each narrative, they suggest that Schindler's portrayal of Beethoven enriched Brontë's portrayal of Heathcliff. This is not to argue that Heathcliff, in any sense, is Beethoven. Heathcliff was not an artist, he was not deaf; all the similarities between the two men can be matched with manifold differences. It *is* to argue that there are enough resemblances in the familial, social, psychological, romantic, and spiritual histories of the two men that Heathcliff's life pattern, seen in the context of Beethoven's, does not seem as absolutely idiosyncratic as it might otherwise appear. Of all the literary characters who have been proposed as possible sources for Heathcliff, it would be difficult to find a single one whose life patterns match his to the extent of Schindler's Beethoven. Whether Brontë consciously planned any of the larger similarities (or any of the smaller ones involving earlier namesakes, shattered violins, and crooked shoots) is, I believe, impossible to say. But that they are all entirely accidental seems unlikely. Between the legend of Beethoven and the life of Heathcliff some transaction occurred, with Moscheles's translation of Schindler as the likely intermediary.

Beyond Schindler

The comparisons enumerated above were purposely restricted to material available in Schindler, the book most likely to have provided Emily Brontë with the basis for whatever she knew about Beethoven's by-then legendary life. Today's reader, of course, applies perspectives other than those of the 1840s to personalities such as Beethoven or Heathcliff. I shall close this chapter by viewing several of the aforementioned similarities from the perspectives of our own century.

As one contemplates Beethoven and Heathcliff from the vantage point of the late twentieth century, each stands out as a striking manifestation (the one in life, the other in fiction) of what has come to be known as the archetype of the nineteenth-century rebellious Romantic protagonist. In both figures we find the doubtful parentage, the temperamental response to social abuse, and the difficulties of integrating oneself into the larger society that have come to characterize the archetypal Romantic rebel. In each figure we find the energetic spurning of etiquette, the distinctive and often unkempt appearance, the frustration in love owing to social background, and yet the turning to love for personal redemption that commonly mark the "coming of age" of the Romantic protagonist. This leads, in each case, to the irremediable loss of the loved one, who then becomes the "Immortal Beloved," followed by the desperate persecution of those who come under one's dominion, until the exhausted soul somehow turns away from worldly cares into the realm of the pure spirit, preparing the way for an unworldly death in the face of the elements.

The archetypal nineteenth-century Romantic protagonist often has one additional trait not mentioned in the above summary: dark skin color. Although Schindler does not emphasize this trait in Beethoven, Brontë does emphasize it in Heathcliff, particularly in his youth and early maturity. When the young boy first arrives at the Heights in chapter 4, Mr. Earnshaw introduces him by saying, "It's as dark almost as if it came from the devil" (WH, p. 38). When Catherine and Heathcliff first arrive at Thrushcross Grange in chapter 6, Mrs. Linton accuses Catherine of "scouring the country with a gipsy!" (WH, p. 49). And when Mr. Lockwood first encounters the adult Heathcliff in chapter 1, he refers to him as "a dark-skinned gypsy in aspect" (WH, p. 15).

Although Schindler does not call special attention to Beethoven's dark skin, many of the composer's other (and earlier) contemporaries do. The Fischer family, among whom Beethoven passed a good deal of his childhood in Bonn, gave this picture of the boy: "Short of stature, broad shoulders, short neck, large head, round nose, dark brown complexion. . . . In the house he was called *der Spagnol* (the Spaniard)."[14] According to Czerny, Beethoven gave the appearance of "Satan himself" when Prince Lichnowsky introduced him into the world of Vienna's fashionable soirées. He stood out, with his "black hair, black beard, and dark-complexioned form."[15] Beethoven, no less than Heathcliff, was notable for his dark skin—dark not in the absolute sense but in relation to the lighter-skinned society by which he was surrounded, and into which he was adopted.

A second twentieth-century perspective would treat Beethoven and Heathcliff as psychological case studies, their "neurotic eccentricities" providing subjects for analysis. Maynard Solomon, for example, elevates into elaborate theory items that to a Schindler were only fact—or even fiction. When Schindler begins his biography with a discussion of Beethoven's parentage, he tries to present the rumored illegitimacy merely as an inaccurate blot on the composer's memory. To Solomon the same rumor is a key to the composer's character. After speculating upon Beethoven's concern over this matter as late as a year before his death, he determines that the composer was suffering from the common fantasy of the "Family Romance."

Drawing upon Freud and Otto Rank, Solomon explains that in this fantasy "the child replaces one or both of his parents with elevated surrogates, heroes, celebrities, kings, or nobles." Usually this fantasy "arises during childhood or adolescence and thereafter recedes into amnesia, from which it can be recovered only by analysis. With Beethoven it if anything gained in strength and tenacity as he grew to maturity" (p. 21). Speculative with regard to the adult Beethoven, this diagnosis would seem most appropriate for the young Heathcliff, orphaned as a child and, in adolescence, imaginatively endowed by Nelly with two royal parents (the emperor of China and the Indian queen). Solomon states that Freud found the fantasy of the "Family Romance" particularly intense and enduring among the creative and the talented. This concept would certainly embrace those imaginary creations of Emily Brontë's own adolescence, the royal personages who populated her poetic land of Gondol.

Weaving together Beethoven's presumed doubts about the legitimacy of his birth with the fact that he was given the name of the earlier Ludwig who had died, Solomon asserts that "Beethoven's Family Romance signified his belief that he was the 'false' son, who would never take the place of his dead brother.

. . . All of his fantasies then, may have a single, transparent source: they may be the expression, denial, and symbolic transcendence of the feeling that he was unloved and unwanted. They are the rectification of a presumed illegitimacy. They are the heartfelt—and unanswered—cry of a child for his parents' love" (p. 24). Whatever the exact source, such a heartfelt, unanswered cry for love does sound again and again from the passionate, scornful lives of both Beethoven and Heathcliff.

Analyzing Beethoven's early life in Bonn, Solomon repeats an anecdote from Cäcilia Fischer, of the family alluded to above. She says to young Ludwig, "How dirty you are again—you ought to keep yourself clean." To which he replies, "What's the difference—when I become a Lord no one will pay that any mind." Solomon speculates: "It is possible that Beethoven's unclean and uncared-for appearance was a mute cry for help, an expression of an anguish which he could not express in words" (pp. 20–21). He could as well be commenting on Heathcliff's actions in chapters 7 and 8, beginning with Cathy's return to the Heights, when she says, "You are so dirty!" and he replies, "I shall be as dirty as I please, and I like to be dirty, and I will be dirty."

In Solomon's analysis, Beethoven's ambivalence toward the Lichnowskys reveals that he was "unable freely to accept" the "favor and affection" of his benefactors (p. 63). The "affair with the Immortal Beloved" therefore exacerbated a lifelong conflict in Beethoven "between a defensive narcissism and a wild, thrusting desire to break out of a painful isolation" (p. 157). At this point there is no need to belabor the extent to which this analysis applies to Heathcliff's psyche too, especially as he relates to Catherine in chapters 8 through 15.

For many twentieth-century minds not caught up in the quest for Romantic archetypes or drawn into psychological speculation, Beethoven and Heathcliff each live as embodiments of existential endurance in the face of monumental despair.

Much earlier in this study I referred to John Hagan's vision of Heathcliff as a man who has been "stripped of his humanity through intolerable suffering and loss." I also referred to Mary Visick's vision of a man who, in spite of all he has suffered, manages in the end to love more than he hates, to approach "an end which is free of meanness." In chapter 29 we caught our first glimpse of the spiritual solitude Heathcliff had endured since Catherine's death. We began to see the extent to which the psychological terror he has inflicted on others has been accompanied by the existential anguish of a man who has nothing living to live for. During the "strange change" in chapter 33 Nelly asks, "You are not afraid of death?" He replies, "Afraid? No! I have neither a fear, nor a presentiment, nor a hope of death. Why should I? With my hard constitution, and temperate mode of living, and unperilous occupations, I ought to, and probably *shall* remain above ground, till there is scarcely a black hair on my head. And yet I cannot continue in this condition! I have to remind myself to breathe—almost to remind my heart to beat!" (p. 256).

Heathcliff is here in transition from the eighteen years of solitary endurance to the attainment of the "single wish" which his "whole being and faculties" have all that time been "yearning to attain." His psychological state compares to the one J. W. N. Sullivan finds in Beethoven's *Hammerklavier* Sonata, Opus 106—the sonata composed one year before "the change" that Schindler noted in Beethoven ("Never, before or since that time, have I seen Beethoven in such a state of absolute abstraction from the world"). For Sullivan the *Hammerklavier* "does not, in its spiritual content, belong to what is called Beethoven's third period. Neither does it belong to its second. It stands alone, a great and grim memorial to the long and painful journey between the two worlds." This sonata records Beethoven's realization that "his essential loneliness was terrible and complete." It is "the expression of a man of infinite suffering, of infinite courage and will, but without God and without hope." Sullivan's movement-by-movement account of its spiritual content closely parallels the process by which Heathcliff is prepared for his saving vision. Beethoven's greatness, he concludes, "is shown in the fact that having passed through an experience that left him little to express he yet expressed so much."[16]

Beethoven's reward for this existential endurance is the sublime state of spiritual concord he was to experience one year later, which lifted him out of his spiritual prison into the vision that would irradiate the last sonatas and quartets (including the Arietta of Opus 111). Heathcliff's reward for a comparable endurance is the rapturous vision that shatters his prison, carrying him from "my body" to "my soul's bliss."

Chapter Six

Emily Brontë
and Beethoven the Creator

Schindler's biography, after its detailed discussion of the three periods in the composer's life, concludes with sections entitled "Musical Observations" and "Characteristic Traits and Peculiarities of Beethoven." Both sections would have been of considerable interest to Emily Brontë, not only as a student of Beethoven, but as one who aspired to be, herself, a creative artist. After considering the importance these sections of Schindler's *Life* may have had for her as a creator, we shall take a brief look at the Beethoven who would have been presented to her reading eye in the pages of *Blackwood's Magazine*. This will allow us to locate her personal experience of Beethoven within the larger intellectual climate of England in the 1840s.

Schindler's Composer

A number of Schindler's "musical observations" refer to music Emily Brontë had marked for special attention in the table of contents of *The Musical Library*. He discusses the proper pace at which to play the Allegretto of the Seventh Symphony as well as the circumstances that led Beethoven to change its label to Andante quasi allegretto (2:101–2). Later, discussing proper phrasing in the symphonies, Schindler gives an extended example from the Larghetto of the Second Symphony, making a number of recommendations that Moscheles supports in an editorial note (2:140–46). Further performing instructions are given for the Allegretto of the Seventh Symphony and the Funeral March of the *Eroica*. Discussing the *Eroica* as a whole, Schindler writes of "the firm resolution of the hero to overcome his fate." In the Fifth Symphony, he writes, "Fate knocks at the door" (2:148, 150).

Schindler constantly emphasizes Beethoven's belief that his compositions express specific "poetic" ideas. He begins the "Musical Observations" by telling of the composer's intention in 1816 of preparing an edition of his piano sonatas. Such an edition would have allowed Beethoven to "indicate the poetic ideas, which form the groundwork of many of those Sonatas; thereby facilitating the comprehension of the music, and determining the style of its performance" (2:80–81). It is in this connection that Schindler first introduces the idea that Beethoven's two sonatas, Opus 14, were designed to illustrate "the conflict of two principles, or a dialogue between two persons." (He claims that this intention was "immediately recognized" by "everyone, at the time when they were composed.") He later becomes even more specific, claiming that the dialogue is between "a husband and a wife, or a lover and his mistress" and that the composer designated the two principles as "the *entreating* and the *resisting*." Schindler quotes a number of passages from the sonatas themselves to show how the "two principles" are actually embodied (2:85–86, 123, 131–40). He concludes his discussion by asserting that the Opus 14 sonatas and a number of others (including the *Pathétique*, Opus 13, and Opus 27, No. 2, now known as the *Moonlight*) are "all pictures of feeling" (2:140). [1]

Emily Brontë might have been particularly interested in the "poetic idea" which, according to Schindler, Beethoven provided for his piano sonatas in F minor, Opus 57, and in D minor, Opus 31, No. 2. Schindler writes that when he asked Beethoven to furnish him with "the keys" to these works, the answer was, "Read Shakespeare's 'Tempest'" (2:86). Commentators today still argue as to whether this report should be taken seriously; some dismiss it out of hand, others have erected portentous structures upon it. [2] But for Brontë, reading in the 1840s, the interest would have been in seeing Shakespeare as a potential source for the realities Beethoven expressed in music. In his discussion of the composer's "characteristic traits and peculiarities," Schindler asserts that Beethoven had "as intimate a knowledge" of Shakespeare (and of certain Greek writers in translation) as he had "of his own scores" (2:187). Schindler objects to comparisons between Beethoven and the German writer Jean Paul Richter, arguing that "a comparison with Shakespeare or Michael Angelo might be more correct. Shakespeare was Beethoven's favorite poet" (2:179–80).

In chapter 4 I argued that Brontë's own experience with Beethoven's music had brought her into contact with artistic materials, with a vision and a style, that were to be of use to her in her own artistic work. If this was so, the fact that Schindler attributed to Beethoven a conscious attempt to embody in music such concepts as "fate," a conflict between "two principles," and even the dynamics of Shakespearean drama would certainly have legitimated for her any intuitive connection she may have felt between Beethoven's music and her own artistic impulses.

Brontë would have discovered from the discussion of his "characteristic traits" that Beethoven, like herself, received artistic inspiration not only from Shakespeare but directly from nature itself. In Schindler's words, "as the bee gathers honey from the flowers of the meadows, so Beethoven often collected his most sublime ideas while roaming about in the open fields. The habit of going abroad suddenly and as unexpectedly returning, just as the whim happened to strike him, was practised by Beethoven alike at all seasons of the year: cold or heat, rain or sun-shine, were all alike to him" (2:176). One of Beethoven's summer excursions with Ferdinand Ries is offered by Moscheles as a supplement. According to Ries (known to Brontë as the composer of Grand Triumphal March), Beethoven "had been humming to himself the whole way, and keeping up a kind of howling up and down, without articulating any distinct sounds. Upon asking him what he meant by this, he said, 'I have just thought of a subject for the last movement of the Sonata'" (2:295). It was the Sonata in F minor, the *Appassionata*.

Beethoven's intimate involvement with nature as a source for creative inspiration would surely have struck a harmonious chord in Brontë herself. The same can be said of his "natural religion," as Schindler terms it. Schindler was the first to point out the importance for Beethoven of the passage from Schiller on Oriental religion that he kept framed on his desk. The entire passage reads as follows: "I am all that is, that was, and that will be. No mortal man hath my veil uplifted! He is One, self-existent, and to that One all things owe their existence" (2:162–63). In these words Brontë would have encountered thoughts very similar to her own; she was to express them in "No coward soul is mine," dated 2 January 1846.

The possibility that her reading of Schindler may have actually influenced her poetic activity is raised by a passage a few pages later in the discussion of the composer's "characteristic traits." Here Schindler presents Beethoven improvising at the piano in his later years, the painful scene in which "the inner mind alone was active; but the outward sense no longer co-operated with it" (2:175). We have already speculated that this picture of Beethoven's later life may have contributed to Brontë's portrayal of the dichotomy that opens up in Heathcliff shortly before his death. But perhaps its distinction between the "outward sense" and the "inner mind" contributed in a more direct way to the phrasing of her 1845 poem "The Prisoner," which distinguishes between the "outward sense" and the "inward essence."

One final section of the *Life of Beethoven* may have been of particular interest to Brontë. It is a letter from Bettine von Arnim to Goethe, dated 28 May 1810, and included by Moscheles as a supplement. In it von Arnim reports to Goethe conversations she claims to have had with Beethoven about his artistic beliefs. A number of modern commentators doubt that Beethoven actually spoke the words she attributes to him.[3] But here as elsewhere in Schindler, Brontë would have encountered the image of an artist whose views toward nature, humanity, spirit, and art tally with her own, perhaps even to the point of helping her to shape a vision of the artist she would become.

Beethoven, in the first words von Arnim attributes directly to him, defines his own artistic creed over against the worldly creed to which he sees others submitting. "When I lift up mine eyes I must sigh, for that which I behold is against my creed; and I must despise the world. . . . I have no friend—I must live all to myself; yet I know that God is nearer to me than to my brothers in the art. I hold converse with him, and fear not, for I have always known and understood him. Nor do I fear for my works; no evil can befall them; and whosoever shall understand them, he shall be freed from all such misery as burthens mankind" (1:276–77). Emily Brontë's artistic quest was carried out in a comparably proud isolation.

For Beethoven, in the words Bettine attributes to him, music is the "link between intellectual and sensual life." He describes his creative process while writing his symphonies in these words: "The mind would embrace all thoughts, both high and low, and embody them into one stream of sensations, all sprung from simple melody. . . . This is the unity which lives in my Symphonies— numberless streamlets meandering on, in endless variety of shape, but all diverging into one common bed. Thus it is I feel that there is an indefinite something, an eternal, an infinite, to be attained" (1:280). Doubtless such a passage would have been of interest to the young woman who played piano transcriptions from the Second, Sixth, and Seventh symphonies—and who wrote *Wuthering Heights,* a novel whose implicit artistic goals are closer to the kind of organic aesthetic expressed here than they are to the aesthetic of earlier English novels.

If Emily Brontë drew spiritual nourishment from the music she played "heart and soul" on her own piano in the 1840s, she would have appreciated what Beethoven had to say about the rare mind that can truly be "encompassed" by music, that can "comprehend its mysteries, its divine inspirations, and can alone speak to the senses of its intellectual revelations." Von Arnim maintained that Beethoven told her to tell Goethe this: "Although spirits may feed upon [music] as we do upon air, yet it may not nourish all mortal men; and those privileged few alone, who have drawn from its heavenly source, may aspire to hold spiritual converse with it. How few are these! for, like the thousands who marry for love, and who profess love, whilst Love will single out but one amongst them, so also will thousands court Music, whilst she turns a deaf ear to all, but the chosen few" (1:280–81).

Von Arnim continues her letter with Beethoven's definition of the "true principles" and the "morality" upon which music, "like her sister-arts," is based. For Beethoven, any creator who devotes himself to any of the arts must "bow to their immutable terms, lay all passion and vexation of spirit prostrate at their feet, and approach their divine presence with a mind so calm and so void of littleness as to be ready to receive the dictates of Fantasy and the revelations of Truth. . . . We know not whence our knowledge is derived. The seeds which lie dormant in us require the dew, the warmth, and the electricity of the soil, to spring up, to ripen into thought, and to break forth" (1:281–82).

Charlotte Brontë attributes to Emily similar creative principles. "The writer who possesses the creative gift owns something of which he is not always master—something that at times strangely wills and works for itself." This power "will perhaps for years lie in subjection; and then, haply without any warning or revolt . . . it sets to work on statue-hewing." Her description of the process by which Emily called *Wuthering Heights* into being is a celebrated description of "organic form." It is also Beethovenesque. The creator "found a granite block on a solitary moor; gazing thereon, he saw how from the crag might be elicited a head, savage, swart, sinister; a form moulded with at least one element of grandeur—power. He wrought with a rude chisel, and from no model but the vision of his meditations. With time and labour, the crag took human shape; and there it stands colossal, dark, and frowning, half statue, half rock."[4] One wonders whether Charlotte's prose, here descriptive of Emily's, was itself inspired by such Beethoven material as the letter from von Arnim to Goethe.

Beethoven, in von Arnim's words, goes on to say that "the mind can scarcely call its own that, which it produces through inspiration"; even so, "it feasts upon these productions, and feels that in them alone lies its independence, its power, its approximation to the Deity, its intercourse with man, and that these, more than all, bear witness of a beneficent Providence." Here again Beethoven's natural religion anticipates Brontë's creed in "No coward soul is mine," especially in the prayer,

> O God within my breast
> Almighty ever-present Deity
> Life, that in me hast rest
> As I Undying Life, have power in Thee.

Certainly Emily did not need to read the words attributed to Beethoven in

Bettine von Arnim's letter to Goethe in order to be able to write "No coward soul is mine." But if she did read them she would have encountered what certainly would have been rare in her experience: the expression of a "natural religion" whose spirit and habitation tallied closely with her own.

All evidence suggests that Emily Brontë was an extremely strong-willed, independent woman. In Charlotte's words, she "had no thought of filling [her] pitcher at the well-spring of other minds."[5] Even so, her encounter with Beethoven's music in the atmosphere that surrounded it in Brussels in 1842, followed by her playing of that music on her own piano during the years in which she wrote *Wuthering Heights* and her greatest poems, certainly appears to have been an influential element in the history of her creative development. It is the importance of the encounter with the music itself that has led us to consider the further creative possibilities that would have been opened up to her through reading Schindler's biography. One final possibility remains to be briefly suggested.

In the *Life of Beethoven* Brontë would have encountered not only Beethoven but also his biographer and story-teller. One wonders whether Schindler may have helped her to imagine Lockwood, for Lockwood too is a biographer of sorts. Like Schindler, he is a story-teller of inhibited habits whose decorous mind tries to understand and record the mysteriously inspiring life of a protean Romantic figure he has recently come to know. As a nineteenth-century novel, the structure of *Wuthering Heights* is strange and idiosyncratic. But as a nineteenth-century biography of an incisive Romantic individualist, encountered late in his life by a more conventional observer, Lockwood's story has much in common with Schindler's.[6] It has long been an unexamined truism that *Wuthering Heights* somehow sprung up *ex nihilo*, without any relation to the intellectual currents of Brontë's own day. Our extended consideration of its author's relation to Beethoven's music, to his legend, and to his published biography is a modest attempt to expand the context in which her work is viewed.

Beethoven in Blackwood's

While Emily Brontë was in Brussels in 1842, Anton Schindler was in Paris. He went there to hear Beethoven's music, which he could no longer hear to his own satisfaction either in Germany (where he had recently been living) or in Vienna. In Vienna, Schindler complains, very little of Beethoven's music is heard any more: "The banners of the present day are no longer inscribed with his immortal name" (1:185). In Paris, as in Brussels, they *were* so inscribed, particularly at the symphony concerts of the conservatoire. In his section "Musical Observations," Schindler notes that at the Conservatoire of Paris the orchestra under Habeneck "assiduously" practiced Beethoven's symphonies "from twelve to sixteen months" before performing them, whereas in Vienna, even during Beethoven's lifetime, the premiere of the Ninth Symphony received only two rehearsals in 1824. Schindler asserts that Beethoven's symphonies can receive the kind of performance they need only "with the well-organized orchestra of a chapel or a musical *Conservatoire*" (2:152–53). He therefore visited Paris in 1841 and 1842 specifically to hear conservatoire performances of the Beethoven symphonies, performances of the same order as those offered by the Conservatoire Royal in 1842.[7] Had Emily Brontë studied in Vienna rather than Brussels, she would not have had such strong exposure to Beethoven's music.

When he bewails the decline of Beethoven's popularity in Vienna Schindler sounds very much like the editor of *The Musical Library*, who excoriated the pianistic fluff of the 1830s that his anthology was designed to supplant. Schindler writes that "the sensual music of the day, and the overstretched mechanical dexterity of modern pianoforte playing, bid fair to thrust the intellectual compositions of Beethoven into the shade, if not consign them entirely to oblivion" (2:96–97). But in a footnote to this passage Moscheles points out that such, fortunately, is not the case in London, where Beethoven's music "is now deeply studied by the profession and eagerly sought after by the public." Moscheles himself had done much to advance Beethoven's popularity in London, one early effort being the ambitious commemorative concert he and Cramer had helped to organize in 1837 (2:365–72). One measure of Beethoven's growing popularity in England was his prominence in the instrumental volumes of *The Musical Library* itself. Its publisher, Charles Knight, produced another multivolume work for the general public in 1844. His six-volume *London* uses a performance of Beethoven's *Eroica* by the London Philharmonic to represent (in highly charged prose) the city's music.[8] Even *Blackwood's Magazine*, required reading in the Brontë home, reflects the growing appreciation of Beethoven's music in the 1840s.

In 1830 *Blackwood's* published an exceedingly judicious essay entitled "Musical Literature." Emily Brontë, only eleven at the time, had not yet begun studying the piano, but the essay does represent something of the intellectual approach to music that she would soon imbibe at the Parsonage. This is the essay that refers to "the celebrated *Sinfonia Pastorale* of Beethoven" as "an exquisite specimen of descriptive music." Unsigned, it was written by the music critic George Hogarth. Showing a clear awareness of historical and stylistic change, Hogarth states that "the laws of harmony are far from being fixed . . . the works of Beethoven and Weber contain sounds that would have made every hair of Handel's wig stand upright with horror." He lists Handel, Haydn, Mozart, and Beethoven as the greatest composers of instrumental music—anticipating the later preferences of *The Musical Library* and of Emily Brontë herself.[9]

Blackwood's was primarily a literary magazine, and there is very little further mention of music in its pages throughout the decade of the 1830s. But music does begin to receive more attention—and attention of a new kind—in the 1840s. A passage in the April 1842 issue (when Emily was abroad in Brussels) singles out the same four composers that Hogarth had mentioned in 1830. But here the context is performance, not academic analysis: "We wish to have Beethoven, Mozart, Haydn, and Handel simply and elegantly treated. This is the course adopted by the professors of the quartett concerts, and we trust we may have many more of them."[10]

In 1843, the year after Emily studied in Brussels, *Blackwood's* carried two major essays on music. The first, "Taste and Music in England," attempts to explain why England lacks in the fine arts the supremacy it displays in industry. The second, "English Music and Musicians," suggests that the situation might be changing, at least as regards music. "Music is the fashion now," it declares, "and no one would dare to avow that he had no music in his soul." And the "fashion" is spreading beyond London. The essay suggests that serious music is reaching into the lower classes and into the provinces in exactly the way that the editor of *The Musical Library* would have hoped. "In the densely populated manufacturing districts of Yorkshire, Lancashire, and Derbyshire, music is cultivated among the working classes to an extent unparalleled in any other part of the kingdom."[11] The Keighley Mechanics' Institute, at which the Brontës borrowed books, seems to have represented this trend. By the 1840s there was apparently "a powerful group devoted to music" and concerts were given on the premises. In January 1845, nine-year-old J. Tiplady Carrodus, later a famous violinist, "made his first public appearance at an orchestral concert given in the Mechanics', when he played a violin solo by De Beriot and his father led the orchestra."[12]

In the year of the young violinist's debut *Blackwood's* printed an unsigned review of Edward Holmes's *Life of Mozart* by Charles Neaves, a Scottish judge and publisher. He too names Handel, Haydn, Mozart, and Beethoven as the greatest of all composers. But the most interesting aspect of his review for our purposes is the impassioned plea he makes for composers as the creative equals of painters and poets—in relation to whom, he argues, they have for too long been accorded an inferior status.

> The mighty magic that lies in the highest manifestation of musical composition, must command the wonder and reverence of all who understand, or even observe, its operation. The power of giving birth to innumerable forms of exquisite melody, delighting the ear and stirring every emotion of the soul, agitating us with fear or horror, animating us with ardour and enthusiasm, filling us with joy, melting us with grief, now lulling us to repose amidst the luxurious calm of earthly contentment, now borrowing wings more ethereal than the lark's, and wafting us to the gate of heaven, where its notes seem to blend indistinguishably with the songs of superior beings—this is a faculty that bears no unequivocal mark of a divine descent, and that nothing but prejudice or pride can deem of trivial or inferior rank.[13]

The rapturous tone in which Neaves praises the powers of music is much closer to the tone of *L'Indépendant* in Brussels than it is to anything that had previously appeared in *Blackwood's* in the 1830s or 1840s. Emily Brontë is one regular reader who would not have been surprised, owing to her personal experience of music's power.

Blackwood's does not appear to have reviewed Moscheles's 1841 edition of Schindler's *Life of Beethoven*, Neaves's review of the Mozart biography being the only review of a book on music that I have found in its pages in the decade. But the figure of Beethoven does play a major role in "The Vision of Cagliostro," an unsigned prose meditation by Charles Kent that appeared in *Blackwood's* in October of 1847. Cagliostro, ranging through time, envisions five individuals who embody extremes of the human condition: Tiberius, Agrippa, Milton, Mirabeau, and Beethoven. His vision of the late Beethoven, whom he sees improvising on his piano in the house near Währing, is the climax of this ambitious prose piece. Kent, its author, was twenty-four at the time. His prose gives explicit testimony to the impact that Beethoven (via Schindler) made on sensitive minds of Emily Brontë's generation. Brontë was then twenty-nine, awaiting the imminent publication of *Wuthering Heights*.

The central paragraph of Kent's "Beethoven" section is much too long to reproduce in full here. But excerpts from its first half indicate the skill with which he uses the device of Beethoven at the keyboard to summarize the main stages of the composer's musical development.

> At first, the fingers of the player seemed to frolic over the keys, as though they toyed with the vibrations of the strings. . . . Then they merged into a sweet and

warbling cadence—a cadence of inimitable tenderness, the very suavity of which was rendered the more piquant by its lavish variations. The measure changed, with an abrupt fling of the treble-hand: it gushed into an air quaint and sprightly as the dance of Puck. . . . Gradually, however, the humorous movement resolved itself into a strain of preternatural wildness—a strain that made the blood curdle, and the flesh creep, and the nerves shudder. . . . And through the very fury of those passages there would start tones of ravishing and gentle beauty. . . . Again the musician changed the purpose of his improvisation; it was no longer dismal and appalling, it was pathetic. The instrument became, as it were, the organ of sadness, it became eloquent with an inarticulate woe. . . . Then the variable harmonies rose from pensiveness into frenzy, from frenzy into the noise and the shocks of a great battle.

All this time "Cagliostro was listening in an ecstasy of admiration." But now "he was startled by a sudden clangour among the bass-notes—the music seemed to be jumbled into confusion, and the ear was stunned by a painful and intolerable dissonance. On looking more intently, he perceived that the composer had let one hand fall abstractedly upon the key-board, while the other executed, by itself, a passage of extraordinary difficulty and involution." A footnote at this point refers to the "touching sentence" in Schindler in which "the outward sense no longer co-operated with the inward mind of the great composer." Cagliostro wonders whether "the musician was deaf." The narrator verifies that indeed "Beethoven was cursed with the loss of his most precious faculty." And Kent launches into this heartfelt tribute:

Those who appreciate the full splendour of his gigantic genius, those who conceive, with a distinguished composer now living, that "Beethoven began where Haydn and Mozart left off;" those who coincide with an eminent critic, in saying that "the discords of Beethoven are better than the harmonies of all other musicians;" those, in fine, who worship his memory with the devotion inspired by his compositions, can sympathize in that terrible deprivation of the powers of hearing, by which his art was rendered a blank, and the latter years of his life were imbittered. They will remember with gratitude the joys they have derived from the effusions of his fruitful intellect. . . . And, bearing these wonders in their memory, their hearts will ache for the doom of Ludwig van Beethoven. [14]

Among those Kent was writing to, and perhaps speaking for, were Emily and Patrick Brontë at Haworth Parsonage.

Charlotte Brontë's *Jane Eyre* was published in October of 1847, the month of Kent's "Cagliostro." Emily's *Wuthering Heights* followed in December. During the last year of Emily's life the Brontës, in search of reviews, would have consulted more journals than *Blackwood's*. In more than one they would have encountered fresh tributes to Beethoven's genius. Early in 1848 *Bentley's Miscellany* published Thomasina Ross's "Memoir of Beethoven." Following the chronology (and often the phrasing) of Schindler, this four-page essay celebrates Beethoven as the Romantic redeemer who "daringly [broke] through pre-established rules" and who "was happily endowed with an independence of mind which enabled him to pursue his course heedless of critical reproof." Ross's sympathetic summary of his life includes the spider story, the "grandmotherly fondness" of the Lichnowskys, Beethoven's "ardent and romantic attachment" to the Immortal Beloved, von Arnim's "interviews with the composer in her letters to Goethe," and the "dreary end" of the great Beethoven, "dead, even before death, to the glory which was expanding around his name."[15] Even stronger as a measure of the penetration of Beethoven's music (and legend) into early Victorian culture is a review essay that appeared in the September 1848 issue of *Quarterly Review*, the magisterial counterpart and curmudgeonly companion of *Blackwood's*. This thirty-five-page unsigned essay, entitled "Music," was written by Elizabeth Rigby. It did for the *Quarterly Review* what the unsigned pieces by Neaves and Kent had done for *Blackwood's*—elevated music to an artistic and spiritual level fully equal to that of painting and literature.

Rigby's sustained appreciation of the powers of music is eloquent and impassioned. Showing a hearty acquaintance with descriptive and programmatic music from many eras, she reserves her strongest enthusiasm for pure instrumental music, for "that delicious *German ocean* of the symphony and the sonata" which Beethoven, following Haydn and Mozart, had brought to its full power of expression. Like Ross and Kent, Rigby incorporates details from Schindler into her extended discussion of Beethoven ("Fate knocking at the door" in the Fifth Symphony, the alleged quarrel of the lovers in the Opus 14 sonatas). Unlike them, she also incorporates her own experience of playing Beethoven's music at the keyboard—an experience that appears to have had much in common with Emily Brontë's own. Rigby suggests that "the most really enviable" musician, "the one in whom the pleasure is most pure for himself and least selfish for others," is the person who plays music in the home for the enrichment of self and family. Such a person "sits at overture, symphony, or chorus with closed eyes and swimming senses—brightens at major keys, saddens at minors— smiles at modulations, he knows not why,—and then goes forth to his work next morning with steady hand and placid brow, while ever and anon the irrepressible echoes of past sounds break forth over desk or counter." Rigby writes of the pleasure of playing particular movements from Beethoven sonatas and symphonies. For her, the "Storm" in the *Pastoral* Symphony is the "grandest and most fearful" of all musical tempests. And the "sweet enchantment" of the modulations that lead out of that storm—"when the thunder is heard retreating in the distance, and timid sounds of inquiry rise up from leaf and flower, and birds answer"—is so refreshing that "we grin to ourselves at our lonely piano."

Rigby's heartfelt love of Beethoven's music, curiously, does not extend to the man himself. "This grand genius and crabbed eccentric man never loved or trusted. He shut himself up with his music to be out of the way of his fellow-creatures. His deafness only gave him the excuse of being more morose." Elizabeth Rigby, it turns out, was equally impatient with the morose eccentricities of Heathcliff. She was the author of another unsigned review essay in the *Quarterly Review*, "Vanity Fair and Jane Eyre," published in December of 1848, the month of Emily Brontë's death. This essay could not have brought much joy to anyone at Haworth Parsonage. It is the essay, cited in the early pages of this book, which condemns *Wuthering Heights* for its "repulsive vulgarity." Its thirty-three pages are primarily devoted to demonstrating that Thackeray's *Vanity Fair* is far superior to *Jane Eyre*. *Wuthering Heights* merits two sentences—to demonstrate its own inferiority to *Jane Eyre*. Rigby does find a family resemblance between the two books: Catherine and Heathfield (sic) are the "Jane and Rochester animals in their native state," "too odiously and abominably pagan to be palatable even to the most vitiated class of English readers."[16] Forty years earlier, of course, many of Beethoven's greatest works had aroused exactly this kind of brutal censure. In time, Emily Brontë's own passionate utterance was to be embraced with the same kind of imaginative rapture that the leading English journals had newly bestowed, late in the 1840s, on Beethoven's.

Notes

Introduction

1. Jacques Barzun, "The Meaning of Meaning in Music: Berlioz Once More," *Musical Quarterly* 66 (1980): 20. This assertion is not accepted by all—or even most—twentieth-century literary or music critics, even when writing about such artists as Beethoven, Schumann, or Berlioz, for whom the concept was undeniably true. Those critics who *have* tried to compare the meaning of Beethoven's music with the meaning of literary works have often overstated the case, the most notorious example being Arnold Schering, especially in *Beethoven und die Dichtung* (Berlin: Junker and Dünnhaupt, 1936). For a brief summary of Schering's undertaking see William S. Newman's *Sonata in the Classic Era*, 2d ed. (New York: W. W. Norton, 1972), pp. 504–5.

2. For a discussion of some of the problems inherent in comparing prose fiction with instrumental music, see the introduction to my *Jane Austen and Mozart: Classical Equilibrium in Fiction and Music* (Athens: University of Georgia Press, 1983).

3. *Thayer's Life of Beethoven*, ed. Elliot Forbes (Princeton: Princeton University Press, 1967), 2:851–52. This passage is drawn from Louis Schlösser's written account of his "conversations" with Beethoven in the early 1820s.

4. David Cecil, "Emily Brontë and *Wuthering Heights*," reprinted in the Revised Norton Critical Edition of *Wuthering Heights*, ed. William M. Sale, Jr. (New York: W. W. Norton, 1972), p. 303.

5. Romain Rolland, *Beethoven the Creator*, trans. Ernest Newman (1929; New York: Dover, 1964), p. 9.

6. A recent essay by Maynard Solomon calls into question the paragraph in Schlösser (note 3 above) from which this quotation is taken. Solomon claims that Schlösser was passing off as Beethoven's account of his own creative process a second-hand version of Mozart's creative process. But Solomon omits from his analysis the sentence quoted here, in which Beethoven speaks of receiving his inspiration when "out in Nature's open." Neither in concept or in tone could that sentence have been derived from Mozart. See "On Beethoven's Creative Process: A Two-Part Invention," *Music and Letters* 61 (July–October, 1980): 272–83.

7. Philip Barford, "The Piano Music II," in *The Beethoven Companion*, ed. Denis Arnold and Nigel Fortune (London: Faber and Faber, 1971), pp. 174n–75n. An American version of this volume was published in 1971 by W. W. Norton as *The Beethoven Reader*.

8. Philip Henderson, introduction to Emily Brontë, *Poems* (London: Lawson and Dunn, 1947), p. xxviii.

9. The working definition in *Jane Austen and Mozart* of *classical equilibrium* is both intrinsic and relative: it refers to qualities inherent in individual works of art as they are perceived in the context of the history of styles.

10. Jacques Barzun, *Berlioz and the Romantic Century*, 3d ed. (New York: Columbia University Press, 1969), 1:383.

11. Charles Rosen, *The Classical Style: Haydn, Mozart, and Beethoven* (New York: W. W. Norton, 1972). Rosen's book is the obvious starting point for anyone concerned with present-day views of Beethoven's style and its relation to that of Haydn and Mozart.

12. I presented a preliminary version of these findings in "Emily Brontë and Music: Haworth, Brussels, and Beethoven," *Brontë Society Transactions* 18 (December 1982): 136–42.

13. Winifred Gérin, *Emily Brontë: A Biography* (Oxford: Clarendon Press, 1971), p. 94.

14. See the *Quarterly Review* 84 (December 1848), and the *American Review* 7 (June 1848). The latter also includes this comment about Brontë (under her pseudonym of Ellis Bell) of the sort that was often made about Beethoven: "But the taint of vulgarity with our author extends deeper than mere snobbishness; he is rude, because he prefers to be so."

15. These English translations appear in George Grove's *Beethoven and His Nine Symphonies*, 3d ed. (New York: Dover, 1962), pp. 15, 44.

16. *Britannia*, 15 January 1848.

17. Grove, *Beethoven*, p. 89.

18. For Moscheles's account of his early encounters with Beethoven's music see the editor's preface to his translation of Schindler's *Life of Beethoven* (London: Henry Colburn, 1841). The Prague reaction to the *Eroica* is reported in Grove, *Beethoven*, p. 90.

19. Grove, *Beethoven*, p. 35.

20. Paul Henry Lang, introduction to *The Creative World of Beethoven* (New York: W. W. Norton, 1971), pp. 3–5.

21. Rosen, *The Classical Style*, pp. 380–81.

22. Lang, *Creative World*, p. 9.

23. Donald Grout, *A History of Western Music*, rev. shorter ed. (New York: W. W. Norton, 1973), p. 347.

24. Sanger's essay is reprinted in the Revised Norton Critical Edition of *Wuthering Heights*, pp. 286–98.

25. See the chapter on *Wuthering Heights* in Dorothy Van Ghent, *The English Novel: Form and Function* (New York: Harper and Row, 1953).

26. Inga-Stina Ewbank, *Their Proper Sphere: A Study of the Brontë Sisters as Early Victorian Female Novelists* (Cambridge: Harvard University Press, 1966), p. 128.

27. Northrop Frye, *Anatomy of Criticism* (New York: Athenaeum, 1966), p. 304.

28. Maynard Solomon, *Beethoven* (New York: Schirmer Books, 1977), p. 184.

Part One

1. Newman, *The Sonata in the Classic Era*, p. 507.

2. Two excellent British publications indicate in their allocation of space the relative importance of piano sonatas and concertos in Mozart and Beethoven. *The Mozart Companion* (Faber and Faber, 1956) contains two essays on the keyboard concertos (82 pages), one on the sonatas (33 pages). *The Beethoven Companion* contains two essays on the sonatas (130 pages), one on the concertos (13 pages).

3. Of Beethoven's thirty-two piano sonatas, only nine are in a minor key. But these have had an influence disproportionate to their numbers, as evidenced by the *Pathétique*, the *Moonlight*, the *Tempest*, the *Appassionata*, and Opus 111. Comparably influential major-key sonatas include Opus 10, No. 3, the *Waldstein*, *Les Adieux*, and the *Hammerklavier*.

4. Because it was generally assumed that a sonata would have at least three movements, many early commentators thought that Beethoven's Opus 111 was unfinished. Newman tabulates the movement forms used by Haydn, Mozart, and Beethoven in *The Sonata in the Classic Era*, pp. 133–34.

5. I refer here to readers encountered during a decade of teaching *Wuthering Heights*. They are not professional critics but rather "naive" readers—in a sense analogous to Tovey's naive listener.

6. Donald Francis Tovey, *A Companion to Beethoven's Pianoforte Sonatas* (London: The Associated Board of the R.A.M. and the R.M.C., 1931), p. 74.

Chapter One

1. Emily Brontë, *Wuthering Heights*, Revised Norton Critical Edition, p. 15. All subsequent citations from the novel are from this edition and are indicated parenthetically in the text.

2. See Newman's excellent account, "Style and Form," in *The Sonata in the Classic Era*, especially pp. 112–32.

3. Ibid., p. 514. For a more detailed account of the affinities with Mozart's C-minor Sonata, see Newman's "K. 457 and Op. 13: Two Related Masterpieces in C minor," *Music Review* 28 (1967): 38–44.

4. Tovey, *Companion*, p. 68.

5. Eric Blom, *Beethoven's Pianoforte Sonatas Discussed* (New York: Da Capo Press, 1968), p. 58.

6. Jane Austen, *Pride and Prejudice* (New York: New American Library, 1961), pp. 6, 7.

7. Many of the most dramatic verbal exchanges in Austen have no exclamations at all. The exchange between Emma and Miss Bates at Box Hill in volume 3 of *Emma* is as painful as the one between Heathcliff and Mr. Lockwood at the beginning of *Wuthering Heights*, but its drama is so restrained in presentation that it would have meant little had it appeared on the opening page of the novel. Full appreciation of the exchange requires prior knowledge of the speech patterns as well as the character of both Emma and Miss Bates. Only in the context of such knowledge can we realize that something intensely dramatic is happening when Emma says, in a seemingly polite consequent to Miss Bates's antecedent, "Pardon me—but you will be limited as to number—only three at a time."

8. Rosen, *The Classical Style*, p. 60. See chapter 4 of my *Jane Austen and Mozart* for an extended comparison of *Pride and Prejudice* and K. 271.

9. Paul Henry Lang, *Music in Western Civilization* (New York: W. W. Norton, 1941), p. 740.

10. In *Pride and Prejudice*, for example, the action begins in August and the marriages occur late the following summer. In *Emma* the action begins in the fall and the marriages occur the next fall. In *Persuasion*, which opens in the summer of 1814, Anne's marriage to Wentworth takes place the next summer.

11. Structurally, the two intrusions of the Grave material into the Allegro per se correspond to the occasional intrusion of the Lockwood material into Nelly's narrative. Such a complex integration of introductory and narrative material did not occur in the more linear progressions of Mozart's piano sonatas and Austen's novels. Mozart's Sonata in C minor, K. 457, does have an introduction, the C-minor Fantasy, K. 475. But the Fantasy was composed after the sonata itself and it functions as a self-contained entity, not as an integral part of the sonata's structure. In fictional and musical structures of the Romantic age, introductions were to become increasingly important, and exceedingly varied. They were to range from the extremely short introductions found in Poe's short stories (one paragraph in "The Masque of the Red Death") and in Chopin's short works (one bar in the B-flat-minor Prelude, Opus 28, No. 16) to the massive introductions found in such works as Melville's *Moby-Dick* (1851) and Liszt's B-minor Sonata (1854). In the latter works, the introductory material is so organically integrated into the larger structure that critics argue vehemently as to where the one ends and the other begins. The concept of "organic form" is addressed in Chapter 2 of this study.

12. Kenneth Drake, *The Sonatas of Beethoven as He Played and Taught Them* (Bloomington: Indiana University Press, 1981), p. 120.

13. Newman, *The Sonata in the Classic Era*, pp. 513–14.

14. Mathis Lussy, *La Sonate Pathétique de L. van Beethoven, Op. 13* (Paris: Costallat, 1912). Lussy's analysis of the sonata, published after his death, gives particular attention to the Grave introduction and the following Allegro. He finds the drama

between the composer and fate in the music itself, more than in extramusical evidence. See pp. 81–105.

15. Arnold Schmitz, *Beethovens "zwei Prinzipe," ihre Bedeutung für Themen- und Satzbau* (Berlin: Ferdinand Dümmler, 1923). Schmitz carefully distinguishes the "two principles" that he finds central to Beethoven's musical expression from the more general principle of musical contrast as expressed by Beethoven's classical predecessors, especially Mozart.

16. Ernest Newman, "Beethoven: The Last Phase," in *Testament of Music* (London: Putnam, 1962), pp. 246–47.

17. *Thayer's Life of Beethoven*, 1:185.

18. Arthur Hutchings, *A Companion to Mozart's Piano Concertos*, 2d ed. (London: Oxford University Press, 1948), p. 112.

Chapter Two

1. Cecil, "Emily Brontë and *Wuthering Heights*," p. 301.

2. Later in the Romantic era Chopin would create numerous short works whose "whole created cosmos" consists of sharp contrast between two such principles. The "Octave" Étude is an excellent example, its furious outer sections and passive inner one presenting a miniaturized version of the strife in Opus 57. In the three-movement sonata form, however, the expression of so stark a contrast is nearly as rare after Beethoven as it was before him.

3. Newman, *The Sonata in the Classic Era*, p. 519.

4. Rolland, *Beethoven the Creator*, p. 133. Further citations will be incorporated within the text.

5. Anton Schindler, *Beethoven as I Knew Him*, trans. Donald W. MacArdle (New York: W. W. Norton, 1966), pp. 162–63.

6. Tovey, *A Companion to Beethoven's Pianoforte Sonatas*, p. 177. Further citations will be incorporated within the text.

7. Rosen, *The Classical Style*, p. 400. Further citations will be incorporated within the text.

8. John Hagan, "Control of Sympathy in *Wuthering Heights*," *Nineteenth-Century Fiction* 21 (1967): 323.

9. Rudolph Réti argues that much of the thematic material of the first movement of Opus 13 is "an intentional repetition of the shapes and phrases of the 'Grave' introduction," but if this is so, the derivation is not nearly so evident on the surface of the music as is the case with the first and second themes of the *Appassionata*. See Réti's *Thematic Patterns in the Sonatas of Beethoven* (New York: MacMillan, 1967).

10. Charles Rosen, *Sonata Forms* (New York: W. W. Norton, 1980), pp. 191–94. See also idem, *The Classical Style*, p. 89.

11. Blom, *Beethoven's Pianoforte Sonatas Discussed*, p. 167.

12. Harold Truscott, "The Piano Music I," in *The Beethoven Companion*, ed. Arnold and Fortune, p. 122.

13. Beethoven's fusion of separate movements that Mozart by temperament and by convention kept inviolate is an early example of "organic" form in music, as is his elimination of the traditional repeat of the exposition in many of his later sonata-allegro movements. Liszt's B-minor Sonata (1854), which fuses principles of the multimovement sonata form into a one-movement conception, is a much later example in the history of the sonata. By the time Emily Brontë wrote *Wuthering Heights* (1847) the idea of "organic form" had long been alive in literary circles; new manifestations of the principle soon after her novel occur in Melville's *Moby-Dick* (1851), Thoreau's *Walden* (1854), and Whitman's *Leaves of Grass* (1855).

14. Solomon, *Beethoven*, p. 196.

15. Barzun, *Berlioz and the Romantic Century*, 1:383.

16. Van Ghent, *The English Novel: Form and Function*, pp. 156–58.

17. See *Jane Austen and Mozart*, pp. 134–35.

18. Schindler, *Beethoven as I Knew Him*, p. 406.

19. For a particularly arrogant example of ostensibly "objective" analysis, see Hans Keller's study of Mozart's Piano Concerto in C major, K. 503, in the Norton Critical Score, ed. Joseph Kerman (New York: W. W. Norton, 1970). A critic who totally dismisses Tovey's analytical method needs to offer something valuable in its place. But one must ask of Keller, even more than of Schenker, whether the questions he so meticulously pursues are the most important ones for understanding the music. His quest for hidden unity ignores many of the most important moments in the temporal and emotional unfolding of the music. Even the nineteenth-century effusion quoted by Newman responds in a recognizable way to the temporal and emotional unfolding of the first movement of the *Appassionata*. To call the second theme of the movement "consoling" is certainly no sin, though Keller would no doubt ask, "Consoling to whom?"

20. Barzun puts this point nicely in "The Meaning of Meaning in Music": "So we might as well cease to be troubled by verbal programs, explanations, or the loose poeticizing of amateurs and reviewers. They are all wrong and all right at one and the same time, the wrongness being really in those who take the words literally" (p. 17).

21. Beethoven's comments are efficiently summarized in the preface to the Dover edition of the *Sixth and Seventh Symphonies* (New York: Dover, 1976), p. i.

22. Beethoven's *Tempest* Sonata, Opus 31, No. 2, if we can believe Schindler, was inspired not by the tempests of nature but by Shakespeare's *Tempest*, which Beethoven allegedly told Schindler to read if he wanted to understand the meaning of either this sonata or the *Appassionata*. In *Beethoven the Creator* Rolland, addressing this question, speaks not of direct influence but of *Stimmung*, finding that what Shakespeare's play has in common with the two Beethoven sonatas is "the unchaining of elementary forces, passions, madnesses of man and of the Elements; also the domi-

nation of the Spirit—the magician who at his will can assemble and dissipate illusion. . . . The torrent of a wild, implacable Force; the sovereignty of thought, that soars above it all" (p. 164).

23. Robert Simpson, "The Chamber Music for Strings," *The Beethoven Companion*, ed. Arnold and Fortune, p. 266.

24. Margaret Homans notes many examples of this anomaly in "Repression and Sublimation of Nature in *Wuthering Heights*," *PMLA* 93 (January 1978): 9–19. She, however, contends that Brontë presents nature indirectly because she is psychologically incapable of presenting it directly.

25. Alfred Brendel, *Musical Thoughts and Afterthoughts* (Princeton: Princeton University Press, 1976), p. 30.

26. In the first event that has contributed to the legend, Ries describes how Beethoven, during a long walk, "had been all the time humming and sometimes howling, always up and down, without singing any definite notes." Returning home, "he ran to the pianoforte without taking off his hat" and "stormed for at least an hour with the beautiful finale" of the *Appassionata*. The storm in this part of the story is at the piano. The water damage to the score occurred some time later, during Beethoven's return to Vienna in 1806, when a trunk containing the manuscript was "penetrated" by "pouring rain." For both events, see *Thayer's Life of Beethoven*, pp. 356, 407.

27. Basil Deane, "The Concertos," *The Beethoven Companion*, ed. Arnold and Fortune, pp. 326–27.

28. Simpson, "The Chamber Music for Strings," pp. 252–54.

29. J. W. N. Sullivan, *Beethoven: His Spiritual Development* (New York: New American Library, 1927), pp. 90–91.

30. Joseph Kerman, *The Beethoven Quartets* (New York: W. W. Norton, 1966), p. 148.

31. Simpson, "The Chamber Music for Strings," pp. 258–60.

Chapter Three

1. Barford, "The Piano Music II," p. 179. Further references to this essay will be made parenthetically in the text.

2. Ernest Newman, "Beethoven: The Last Phase," pp. 246–47.

3. Henderson, introduction to *Poems*, p. xxvii.

4. Cecil, "Emily Brontë and *Wuthering Heights*," p. 301.

5. Mary Visick, *The Genesis of Wuthering Heights*, 2d ed. (Hong Kong: Hong Kong University Press, 1965), pp. 70, 77.

6. Sullivan, *Beethoven: His Spiritual Development*, pp. 132–33.

7. Martin Cooper, *Beethoven: The Last Decade, 1817–1827* (London: Oxford University Press, 1970), p. 197.

8. Tovey gives a more technical account of the accelerations in pace in *A Companion to*

Beethoven's Pianoforte Sonatas, p. 293. I have followed Tovey's lead in assigning bar numbers for Opus 111; in the first movement he renumbers at the start of the Allegro.

9. This curious review, printed in Berlin, was entitled "The Death of a Great Man— Namely Beethoven." According to Schindler, it "greatly disturbed" the composer. See the Norton edition of *Beethoven as I Knew Him*, p. 232.

10. Kerman, *The Beethoven Quartets*, pp. 265–66. Kerman suggests, parenthetically, that "in this matter of extramusical 'meaning' lack of purity may be less damaging to the critic than lack of imagination."

11. Writing of Beethoven's E-minor Piano Sonata, Opus 90, Tovey argues that Beethoven's treatment of theme and harmony during his "third manner" often expresses "the dramatic discovery that the questions 'When and where' are to be answered by 'Already here and now' " (p. 211). Nowhere is such a process more dramatic than in the motivic exchange across the trilling abyss in the Arietta of Opus 111.

12. Philip Barford, "Beethoven's Last Sonata," *Music and Letters* 35 (1954): 331. Unless otherwise noted, subsequent references to Barford will be to "The Piano Music II."

13. Heathcliff's confession to Nelly that he feels a "change approaching" is provoked by his last deep look into the eyes of young Cathy and Hareton. When he sees only Catherine's eyes in their eyes, his vengeance is "disarmed" (p. 254).

14. One wonders whether Emily Brontë may have intended the word *trilling* rather than *thrilling*. As I show in Chapter 4, she was intimately familiar with the *trilling* vibrations made by the tight-stretched strings of the piano. The existence of numerous printer's errors in the first and all subsequent editions of *Wuthering Heights* is a notorious problem. Unfortunately, the manuscript of the novel does not survive, nor does it seem currently possible to locate Brontë's personal copy of the first edition, in which she had corrected a number of printer's errors. See William M. Sale, Jr., "Textual Commentary," Revised Norton Critical Edition, pp. 267–74.

15. Thomas Mann, *Doctor Faustus*, trans. H. T. Lowe-Porter (New York: Modern Library, 1948), p. 55. Kretschmar, a music theorist, lectures on Opus 111 in chapter 8 of the novel. He feels that in the aesthetic forms of Beethoven's late period "the subjective and the conventional assumed a new relationship, conditioned by death." That new relationship is expressed in the Arietta of Opus 111 by the transformations undergone by the opening theme and its three-note motif, the "added C-sharp" being its final embodiment.

16. The interval of descent in this anticipation of motif z is a half-step wider than was its counterpart in the Maestoso introduction. As we have seen, however, the interval of motif z itself changes constantly during its successive manifestations in the Arietta, beginning with the widening of the interval during the restatement of the motif in the opening bars. Because the rhythmic outline of the motif and the melodic shape of its descent are always constant (the second note is always repeated as the third note),

this motif, no matter what the exact interval of descent, is consistently recogniz-able—as is motif x in the first movement, whose intervals also vary.

17. Alfred Brendel notes a similar anticipation of a later solution in "the first movement of the *Hammerklavier* Sonata in B-flat major, Op. 106," where a "modulation to B minor in the recapitulation" introduces "formal and psychological problems that it takes all the remaining movements to solve." In Beethoven's Sonata, Opus 110, Brendel finds that the celebrated *Ermattete Klage* ("exhausted lament") section leads us "to the brink of death," allows us to witness "the gradual resurgence of the heartbeat," and expresses, in the process, an "exertion of the will to banish suffer-ing." As for Opus 111, Brendel finds that the last chord "does not close something off; rather it opens up the silence that follows, a silence we now perceive to be more important than the sound that preceded it." See "Form and Psychology in Beetho-ven's Piano Sonatas," in *Musical Thoughts and Afterthoughts*, pp. 44, 51–53.

18. Two of Mozart's late piano concertos, No. 24 in C minor (K. 491) and No. 25 in C major (K. 503), illustrate this difference. K. 491 resembles Beethoven's last piano sonata in having a C-minor first movement, a contrasting second movement, and theme-and-variation form for its last movement. It differs from Opus 111 in having three movements rather than two, and in achieving its unity by returning in the third movement to the C-minor strife of the first movement. Although not as tempestuous as Beethoven's *Appassionata*, or even the *Pathétique*, this concerto is like them in that it achieves its long-range minor-key equilibrium with balancing minor-key outer movements. K. 503 resembles Beethoven's last piano sonata in having a C-major finale, in reaching its ultimate C-major harmony through complex emotional dynam-ics, and in achieving expressive unity within both its outer movements through the use of contrasting motifs (a four-note descending motif in the first movement, a three-note descending motif in the third; see chapter 5 of *Jane Austen and Mozart*). This concerto differs from Opus 111 in having three movements rather than two; more important, *its* C-major finale answers, and is balanced by, a C-major opening movement. The finale resolves its energies on an imaginative plane that is emo-tionally richer but psychically unchanged from the plane on which the concerto began.

19. Barford, "Beethoven's Last Sonata," p. 331.

Part Two

1. René Wellek, "German and English Romanticism: A Confrontation," in *Confronta-tions* (Princeton: Princeton University Press, 1965), p. 33. For a more extended discussion of this position see *Jane Austen and Mozart*, esp. pp. 7–9.
2. Paul Henry Lang, introduction to *The Creative World of Mozart* (New York: W. W. Norton, 1963), p. 11.

3. Gérin, *Emily Brontë*, p. 127.
4. Basil Deane, "The Symphonies and Overtures," *The Beethoven Companion*, ed. Arnold and Fortune, p. 300.
5. Currer Bell (Charlotte Brontë), "Editor's Preface to the New Edition of *Wuthering Heights* (1850)," reprinted in the Revised Norton Critical Edition, p. 10.
6. Reprinted in H. C. Robbins Landon, *Beethoven: A Documentary Study* (New York: Macmillan, 1975), p. 129.
7. "Extract from the Prefatory Note to 'Selections from Poems by Ellis Bell,'" reprinted in *Wuthering Heights*, ed. Hilda Marsden and Ian Jack (Oxford: Clarendon Press, 1976), pp. 445–46.
8. Henderson, introduction to *Poems*, p. xxvii–xxviii.
9. *The Complete Poems of Emily Jane Brontë*, ed. C. W. Hatfield (New York: Columbia University Press, 1941), H. 191. Further quotations from the poems will be from this edition, with each poem identified by the number Hatfield assigned.
10. Currer Bell, "Editor's Preface," p. 10.

Chapter Four

1. Gérin, *Emily Brontë*, p. 40. Further citations will be incorporated parenthetically in the text.
2. These bound volumes also include music Emily and Anne played together (piano duets, selections by Handel) and music presumably played by Branwell (arrangements for organ of "Masses" by Mozart, Beethoven, and Haydn). In these volumes such of Emily's music as is dated at all has a date in the 1830s, though in many cases the last number of a particular year is impossible to decipher. The only later dates appear on some short pieces inscribed by Anne and dated 1844 that are found at the back of one volume.
3. Rey M. Longyear, *Nineteenth-Century Romanticism in Music* (Englewood Cliffs, N.J.: Prentice Hall, 1972), p. 52.
4. Richard Hoffman Andrews (1803–1891) was a teacher, composer, and publisher (Ward and Andrews) in Manchester. An American edition of his "Introduction and Brilliant Variations to the Much Admired Air 'The Swiss Boy'" (Philadelphia: G. Willig, ca. 1840) is preserved at the Library of Congress.
5. Two fantasias on literary works are also included in the early music books: Henri Rosellen's "Fantaisie sur *La Favorite*," Opus 36, and F. Burgmüller's "Fantaisie sur la romance favorite *Mère & soeur* d' Ed. Bruguière," Opus 20. One would not expect these French editions (one of them published in Brussels) to have been available in the music stores of Haworth or Keighley in the 1830s; I expect they were acquired in Brussels in 1842 and bound up with the other sheet music in 1844.
6. For performances of piano works that each novelist played, consult my audiocassette

entitled "A Musical Evening with Jane Austen and Emily Brontë." (New York: Jeffrey Norton Publishers, 1982).

7. *The Musical Library*, 8 vols. (London: Charles Knight and Company, 1844). The edition owned by the Brontë family, currently at the Parsonage Museum, is in the form of four double volumes. Although some single volumes appear to have been issued as early as 1837 (the date of the prefaces cited in note 9), the collected edition acquired by the Brontës is dated 1844 for both the vocal and instrumental volumes.

8. The circular, now in the Parsonage Museum, reads: "The Misses Brontës' Establishment for the Board and Education of a limited number of Young Ladies, the Parsonage, Haworth, near Bradford." Subjects to be studied included Writing, Arithmetic, History, Grammar, Geography, and Needle Work, with options in French, German, Latin, Music, and Painting.

9. These comments by the editor ("W. A.") are from the "Preface to the Fourth Volume of Vocal Music" and the "Preface to the Fourth Volume of Instrumental Music."

10. The marks in the table of contents take three forms: plus marks, circles, and dashes. It is possible that a few of these marks were made by someone other than Emily (Anne, for example) but this seems unlikely. Emily was the serious pianist in the house, even before her study in Brussels. All of the markings are found in the instrumental (i.e., piano) volumes. There are no marks in the table of contents of the vocal volumes, for which Anne would have had the primary interest.

11. One notable mistake was made by the editors of *The Musical Library:* they labeled the Second Symphony as the Fourth, though they did list the opus number (36) correctly. The misidentification occurs both in the table of contents to volume 4 of the instrumental music (in which this symphony is the first work) and on the first page of the score.

12. Pleyel's Sonatina in C major, a set of variations on an Andante theme, is performed on the cassette cited in note 6 above.

13. The editors label this sonata Beethoven's Third Sonata, Opus 2. It is known today as Opus 2, No. 2.

14. Curiously, Emily Brontë's music books of the 1840s show more congruence with Jane Austen's music books of the 1790s and 1810s than do her books of the 1830s. Pleyel, Haydn, Steibelt, Krumpholz, Schobert, Clementi—all these names are found not only in Brontë's *Musical Library* but in Jane Austen's music books. Significantly, however, the one composer most conspicuous by his absence in Austen's music books by the 1810s—Beethoven—is the one most prominent in Emily Brontë's markings in the 1840s. For more on the absence of Beethoven in Austen's music books, see "Jane Austen at the Keyboard" in *Jane Austen and Mozart*.

15. John Lock and Canon W. T. Dixon, *A Man of Sorrow: The Life, Letters and Times of the Rev. Patrick Brontë 1777–1861* (London: Thomas Nelson and Sons, 1965), pp. 448–49, 370.

16. Currer Bell, "Biographical Notice of Ellis and Acton Bell," reprinted in Revised

Norton Critical Edition of *Wuthering Heights*, pp. 3–5. Charlotte claims that she and her sisters did not begin their novels until after their first collection of poems, itself not begun until autumn 1845, was published.

17. This translation from the French of M. Heger's letter is from *The Brontës: Their Lives, Friendships and Correspondence in Four Volumes* (Oxford: Shakespeare Head Press, 1932), 1:281. The date for the letter is given as 5 November 1842.

18. Charlotte's brief comments on the difficulties her sister faced in Brussels are found in "Extract from the Prefatory Note to 'Selections from Poems by Ellis Bell.'" See also J. J. Green, "The Brontë-Wheelwright Friendship," *Friends' Quarterly Examiner*, 1916.

19. Romer Wilson, *The Life and Private History of E. J. Brontë* (New York: Albert and Charles Boni, 1928), pp. 200–201.

20. For this information I am grateful to P. Raspe of the Bibliothèque du Conservatoire Royal de Musique in Brussels and to A. Smolar-Meynart of the Archives of the Ville de Bruxelles. In *Charlotte Brontë: The Evolution of a Genius* (London: Oxford, 1967), Gérin writes that M. Chapelle was "a pianist, a man of fine and sensitive feelings" (p. 224). This may well be true, but I have so far been unable to document so much about him as his first name.

21. If Emily took the music she studied in Brussels home to Haworth, most of it must have been destroyed along with other papers and belongings after her death. A few undated piano works bound up in the volumes of scores dating primarily from the 1830s (such as the Burgmüller *Fantaisie*, published in Brussels) might have been acquired in Brussels. But such stray works, even if she did acquire them there, could not have represented the core of her studies in Brussels. Nor could the 1844 edition of *The Musical Library* have been acquired there. Perhaps in Brussels she borrowed musical scores from the library of the Pensionnat or from her professors, in which case she might have been obliged to leave them behind when she returned to England.

22. This concert program is discussed in the major works on Charlotte Brontë's life and art. It is also discussed by Gustave Charlier in "Brussels Life in *Villette*," tr. Phyllis Bentley, *Brontë Society Transactions* 12 (1955): 386–90. Charlier's original essay appears in *Passages: Essais* (Brussels: La Renaissance du Livre, 1947), pp. 75–102.

23. See Charlier, "Brussels Life," and Enid L. Duthie, *The Foreign Vision of Charlotte Brontë* (New York: Harper and Row, 1975). Charlotte's musical experience in Brussels figures strongly in *Villette*, especially in chapters 20 ("The Concert") and 38 ("Cloud").

24. A leading Belgian newspaper of the day in its coverage of cultural events, *L'Indépendant* featured a column entitled "Chronique Musique" written by one "X.X." The excerpts presented in this chapter give some idea of the high quality of its commentary.

25. An earlier concert for student winners from the conservatory had been held on

March 1, two weeks after Emily's arrival in Brussels. (The program included Beethoven's *Egmont* Overture, from the January 30 symphonic concert.) One might
expect that Emily's professor would have taken her to such events, especially in
July, when she and Charlotte decided to continue their studies for another term.
Chapter 20 of Charlotte's *Villette* describes such a concert, in which student winners
from the piano competition at the conservatoire are the featured soloists. M. Paul
and M. Emanuel (both clearly modeled to some degree on M. Heger and M. Chapelle, who taught Charlotte and Emily) are prominent in organizing the concert.
Charlier points to actual concerts in 1843 (when Emily was home in Haworth) as the
likely inspiration for this chapter and for the outdoor musical celebration in chapter
38 of *Villette*. But surely Emily was as closely acquainted as Charlotte with the world
of the conservatoire and of student competition winners.

26. Berlioz describes this visit to Brussels in chapter 51 of *The Memoirs of Hector
Berlioz*, ed. David Cairns (New York: W. W. Norton, 1975). He gives a less acerbic
account in chapter 1 of *Voyage musical en Allemagne et en Italie. Études sur Beethoven, Gluck et Weber. Mélanges et nouvelles*, 2 vol. (Paris: Jules Labitte, 1844). Fétis,
director of the conservatoire and conductor of its orchestra, had been Berlioz's
nemesis ever since his student days at the Paris Conservatoire. An 1835 review by
Fétis of the *Symphonie fantastique* had prompted Robert Schumann's celebrated
rebuttal in "A Symphony by Berlioz." Both reviews are printed in *Hector Berlioz,
Fantastic Symphony*, Norton Critical Score, ed. Edward Cone (New York: 1971).

27. Duthie, *Foreign Vision*, pp. 209–10.

28. Barford, "The Piano Music II," p. 175n; Winifred Gérin, *Anne Brontë* (London:
Allen Lane, 1976), p. 74. Both statements are tantalizing, but the extensive music
collection at the Parsonage offers no corroborative evidence for either one. To evalu-
ate the impact upon Emily Brontë one would need to know which sonatas she played
and when she played them.

29. See Berlioz, *Voyage musical*, 1:321–22, 265–66.

30. Ibid., 1:274.

31. *Blackwood's Magazine* 27 (March 1830): 479. See Chapter 6 for more on Beethoven
in *Blackwood's*.

32. Shakespeare's influence on Herman Melville's *Moby-Dick* (1851) is comparable.
One can infer it from the text itself, even without the copious secondary evidence
that, in Melville's case, "proves" the influence.

33. Romer Wilson lists "Beethoven's late sonatas and quartets" among her references for
The Life and Private History of E. J. Brontë. She does not, however, provide evidence that Brontë was familiar with any of these works.

34. Berlioz, *Voyage musical*, 1:326–27. Grove, who draws considerably upon Berlioz's
Voyage in *Beethoven and His Nine Symphonies*, attributes the two-line quote to
Thomas Moore (p. 254). The four-word passage in French is Berlioz's literal transla-
tion of "The rest is silence" from Shakespeare's *Hamlet*. This allusion to Shake-

speare is missed in Edwin Evans's translation of the passage in his volume entitled *A Critical Study of Beethoven's Nine Symphonies* (London: Reeves, 1913). He renders the French back into English as "and *all is silence*" (p. 89).

35. Berlioz, *Memoirs*, pp. 104, 95.

Chapter Five

1. The various comparisons with the Byronic hero, the Shakespearean villain, the Napoleonic figure, Milton's Satan, and the Gothic villain are so familiar as not to require documentation. Clement Shorter was one of the first to suggest that the "German fiction which she had devoured during the Brussels period" helped to "inspire" Emily Brontë to create *Wuthering Heights*. See *The Brontës and Their Circle* (1917; rpt. New York: Kraus, 1970), p. 143. The dark-skinned adopted boy is described in William Wright, *The Brontës in Ireland* (London: Hodder and Stoughton, 1893).

2. Goethe's comment was made in a letter to Zelter after meeting Beethoven in Teplitz in the summer of 1812 (*Thayer's Life of Beethoven*, 1:537).

3. Philip Barford, "Beethoven as Man and Artist," in *The Beethoven Companion*, ed. Arnold and Fortune, p. 29.

4. Lang, introduction to *The Creative World of Beethoven*, p. 5.

5. Solomon, *Beethoven*, p. 257.

6. Gérin discusses Gaskell's kitchen image in *Emily Brontë*, p. 144. The winter trek to the library is found in Elizabeth Gaskell, *The Life of Charlotte Brontë* (1900; rpt. New York: AMS, 1973), p. 257. The Brontës' use of that library is discussed in Clifford Whone, "Where the Brontës Borrowed Books: The Keighley Mechanics' Institute," *Brontë Society Transactions* 11 (1950): 344–58. Additional background is provided by Ian Dewhirst in "The Rev. Patrick Brontë and the Keighley Mechanics' Institute," *Brontë Society Transactions* 14 (1965): 35–37. Dewhirst doubts that the Mechanics' Institute played as large a role in the Brontës' reading as Whone (or Gaskell before him) supposes; certainly the family had a number of other sources for reading material.

7. Emily's access to the Heatons' library at Ponden Hall is well established. The family's musical gifts are discussed in Gérin, *Emily Brontë*, p. 41.

8. Ignace Moscheles, ed. and trans., *The Life of Beethoven, Including His Correspondence with His Friends, Numerous Characteristic Traits, and Remarks on His Musical Works*, 2 vols. (London: Henry Colburn, 1841). As early as 1842 an American printing of Moscheles's edition of Schindler (with the further addition of Dr. Heinrich Doring's "The Life and Characteristics of Beethoven") was published by Oliver Ditson in Boston.

9. In the 1980s any conscientious reader of Schindler must be aware of the doubtful authenticity of a number of the details in his work. Schindler himself became unhappy with the first edition of the *Life* as he gathered material for the third edition

(1860), which is what is generally read today. In his notes Moscheles quibbles with Schindler here and there. But a reader in Emily Brontë's day would have had no reason to doubt Schindler's authenticity.

10. Although the Keighley and Ponden Hall libraries are the most obvious sources from which Emily Brontë might have borrowed Moscheles's edition of Schindler, I have not yet been able to authenticate its presence in either one. Given the musical cultivation of the Heaton family, one would expect their library at Ponden Hall to have included a major biography such as Schindler's. But Charles Lemon of the Brontë Society informs me that the records that remain today of books that would have been held in Emily's lifetime, unfortunately incomplete, do not show it. Whone publishes a list of the contents of the library at the Keighley Mechanics' Institute, but it is drawn from the Annual Report of 1841, the year in which the Moscheles edition was published. Whone writes of "a powerful group devoted to music" at the Institute, but the list of books he prints includes only one musical title, "Lectures on Music." It is possible that the Brontës, who purchased the eight-volume *Musical Library*, themselves purchased Moscheles's two-volume edition of Schindler. But this is another possibility that cannot be fully investigated on the basis of information available today. Juliet Barker, the Parsonage librarian, informs me that there is no mention of the work in the various sale catalogues of family effects.

11. Schindler reports that Beethoven was extremely vague about details from his childhood. He points to Wegeler and Ries for accurate information about this period, which he sees no need to reproduce himself. Moscheles includes considerable material from Wegeler and Ries in his supplements to Schindler.

12. All page numbers from Schindler incorporated into the text are from the Moscheles edition and are indicated by the initials *SM*. The 1771 date for Heathcliff's arrival at the Heights is taken from Sanger's "Structure of *Wuthering Heights*."

13. *SM*, 1:101–6. Schindler identifies the recipient as Julia (Giulietta Guicciardi) and specifies the year as 1806 (it is now thought by most scholars to have been 1812). These errors of Schindler's, if errors they are (the identity of the "Immortal Beloved" remains a matter of scholarly dispute), would not in any appreciable way have detracted from the power the letters themselves might have had on a mind such as Emily Brontë's in the 1840s.

14. *Thayer's Life of Beethoven*, 1:72.

15. Reprinted in Robbins Landon, *Beethoven: A Documentary Study*, pp. 69–70.

16. Sullivan, *Beethoven: His Spiritual Development*, pp. 115–17. Beethoven considered the *Hammerklavier* to be his greatest sonata (*Thayer's Life of Beethoven*, 2:174).

Chapter Six

1. In the first edition of his *Life of Beethoven* Schindler does not extend the concept of the "two principles" beyond the Opus 14 sonatas, as he does elsewhere in the context of the 1823 Conversation Book.

2. Tovey, *Companion* (p. 128), is generally skeptical of such remarks. He is not so dismissive of this comment as it relates to the D-minor Sonata, which has come to be known as the *Tempest*. But *The Tempest* is hardly the most tempestuous of Shakespeare's plays: Beethoven may well have been sporting with Schindler in keying it to this sonata and the *Appassionata*. Rolland, *Beethoven the Creator*, finds the remark valuable in connection with both sonatas. The most ambitious attempt to connect specific Beethoven works with individual works by Shakespeare (and other literary "sources") was made by Arnold Schering in *Beethoven und die Dichtung*. For the sonatas analyzed at length in the present study (opp. 13, 57, and 111) Schering posits the following sources: *Hero and Leander* (in the Musäus, not the Schiller version), Shakespeare's *Macbeth*, and Shakespeare's *Henry the Eighth*(!). These and Schering's other "sources" are listed in Newman's *Sonata in the Classic Era*, pp. 504–5.

3. Schindler, who does not print this entire letter in his text, doubts the accuracy of its style, observing that Beethoven's own expression of these concepts would not be so "flowery." He does not question the accuracy of the concepts themselves, which he claims to have heard Beethoven express, though in terser form (1:132–33). Moscheles, justifying his printing of the entire letter, takes issue with Schindler on the question of style. He points to extant letters from Beethoven to von Arnim as evidence that he did use such a style—at least when addressing her.

4. Currer Bell, "Editor's Preface to the New Edition of *Wuthering Heights* (1850)," p. 12.

5. Currer Bell, "Biographical Notice of Ellis and Acton Bell," p. 8.

6. Lockwood, in order to understand and re-create Heathcliff's childhood, youth, and early maturity, is forced to depend upon Nelly Dean's account in much the same way that Schindler was forced to depend on sources such as Wegeler and Ries. In both biographies the youth of the subject remains shrouded in relative obscurity, the most detail being given to the subject's later years, in which the biographer knew him personally. Lockwood only knew Heathcliff for one year (1801–2) but this year receives as much attention in the book (chapters 1–3, 30–34) as do the first sixteen years of Heathcliff's life (chapters 4–9). The relative proportions in Schindler's biography of Beethoven are comparable.

7. Donald W. MacArdle notes that "in January and February 1841 and again in the following spring Schindler spent some months in Paris, and excerpts from the journal that he kept on those two visits formed the appendix 'Beethoven in Paris' in the second (1845) edition of his *Biographie*" ("Anton Schindler: A Biographical Sketch," *Beethoven as I Knew Him*, p. 23). MacArdle's edition of Schindler's biography of Beethoven is based on the third edition (1860).

8. J. Saunders, "Music," in *London* (London: Charles Knight, 1844), 6:191–92.

9. *Blackwood's Magazine* 27 (March 1830): 472, 479. The Wellesley Index to Victorian Periodicals makes the attribution to Hogarth (and to the other *Blackwood's* authors discussed below).

10. *Blackwood's Magazine* 51 (April 1842): 429. One other mention of music was made in the magazine that year, in the May issue under the heading "Things of the Day." Its dismissive tone toward music (and Franz Liszt) contrasts sharply with what Brontë would have read in July of the same year in Brussels. "The kind of public homage paid in foreign countries to musicians, dancers, singers, and all that race, exhibits an extravagance which would be amusing, if it were not preposterous. Listz [*sic*], a mere piano player, which is a mere artizan of music, a mechanical affair, very little above a weaver at stocking a loom, wholly a thing of practice, and capable of being equalled by an automaton figure at a travelling show, has been received, fêted, and followed with almost royal honours in Berlin" (p. 621).

11. *Blackwood's Magazine* 53 (January 1843): 127–40; and 54 (July 1843): 33, 36.

12. Whone, "Where the Brontës Borrowed Books," p. 345.

13. *Blackwood's Magazine* 58 (November 1845): 572.

14. *Blackwood's Magazine* 62 (October 1847): 419–22. The material omitted from the long quoted paragraph includes a detailed description of Beethoven's physiognomy drawn directly from Schindler. The Wellesley index lists Kent (1823–1902) as author and editor.

15. Thomasina Ross, "Memoir of Beethoven," *Bentley's Miscellany* 23 (1848): 115–20.

16. "Music," *Quarterly Review* 83 (September 1848): 481–515; "Vanity Fair and Jane Eyre," *Quarterly Review* 84 (December 1848): 153–185. The Wellesley Index identifies the author of both reviews as Elizabeth Eastlake. But Elizabeth Rigby, nine years older than Emily Brontë, did not marry Charles Eastlake, the eminent painter, until April of 1849.

Index